MASTER •THE Basics

Third Edition

SPANISH

by
Christopher Kendris
B.S., M.S., Columbia University
in the City of New York
M.A., Ph.D., Northwestern University
in Evanston, Illinois

Diplômé, Faculté des Lettres, Université
de Paris et Institut de Phonétique,
Paris (en Sorbonne)

Former Assistant Professor
Department of French and Spanish
State University of New York
Albany, New York

D0927616

BARRON'S

Central Islip Public Library
33 Hawthorne Avenue
Central Islip, NY 11722

3 1800 00246 7153

For Saint Sophia Greek Orthodox Christian Church
of Albany, New York, our parish,

and

To the eternal memory of my sweet beloved wife

Yolanda (Ariadne) Fenyo Kendris

who is always by my side wherever I go,
with all my love and devotion.
My time will come when God will call me, too,
and our souls will live together forever.

Excerpt from *The New York Times* on p. 342 taken from "In Spanish, Two Fewer Letters in the Alphabet." Used with permission of The Associated Press Copyright © 2007. All rights reserved.

© Copyright 2007, 1995, 1987 by Barron's Educational Series, Inc.

All rights reserved.
No part of this book may be reproduced
in any form, by photostat, microfilm, xerography,
or any other means, or incorporated into any
information retrieval system, electronic or
mechanical, without the written permission
of the copyright owner.

All inquiries should be addressed to:
Barron's Educational Series, Inc.
250 Wireless Boulevard
Hauppauge, NY 11788

Library of Congress Catalog Card No. 2007923835

ISBN-13: 978-0-7641-3746-4
ISBN-10: 0-7641-3746-8

Printed in Canada
9 8 7 6 5 4 3 2 1

Contents

Preface to the Third Edition

This third edition contains two new parts. In the new part, you will have a chance to put into practice what you studied in Part One and improve your reading comprehension in a variety of short paragraphs as well as long selections. Many exercises have been added with answers.

Another new feature in this edition is the use of drawings with questions based on them. Your ability to understand what you read is tested in multiple-choice questions. You will also have considerable practice in writing Spanish; for example, short lists of words on everyday topics to communicate your thoughts, simple guided composition for conversational expression, and word games to increase your vocabulary. All the essential vocabularies and phrases you need to know when doing the exercises and tests throughout this book are given in the lessons where the exercises and tests are presented. If there are any new words and phrases you want to use that are not in the vocabulary lists, please consult a standard English-Spanish, Spanish-English dictionary.

The basic vocabularies beginning on page 349 are also new. The Spanish-English and English-Spanish vocabularies have been extensively revised and expanded.

These new features are offered for your enjoyment and to help you improve your knowledge of Spanish. Answers to practice questions in Part Two appear on pages 258 and 267. To achieve your best, consult Part One, the end vocabularies, and the index. The verb tables and the section on definitions of basic grammatical terms with examples, beginning on pages 270 and 316, are useful references.

This is one of a series of language grammar reviews with many new exercises for speaking and writing skills in Spanish. This book is intended to help you review your Spanish grammar for instant communication and comprehension because the original numerical arrangement gives you fast and easy access to what you need to know or verify.

Two other new features are in §27., which is about the Spanish alphabet and the new system of alphabetizing. The other new feature is in §28., which is a special vocabulary of telecommunications in today's world of the 21st century.

Beginning on page 3 there is a diagnostic test that you ought to take immediately. It consists of 60 questions. Three questions are taken from each of the first 20 chapters, which are listed in the table of contents as **§1.** through **§20**. Take the test to find out what you know, what you don't know, and what your strengths and weaknesses are. An answer key and explained answers are at the end of the diagnostic test. There, you will also find an analysis of the question numbers and the **§** numbers. In this way, you can refer to particular **§** numbers where your answers were not correct and brush up where needed. The complete Review section consists mainly of the Basics, the Parts of Speech, and Special Topics, all of which are outlined in detail in the table of contents.

Occasionally I offer some mnemonic tips (memory aids) to help you remember certain aspects of Spanish grammar and vocabulary. For example, if you cannot remember that the Spanish word for twenty *(veinte)* is spelled with *ei* or *ie,* remember it this way:

Mnemonic tip	T W	E	N T Y
	V	E	I N T E

Mnemonic devices are very useful in learning and remembering. Students learn and remember in different ways. What works for you may not work for someone else. You must think of ways to help yourself remember. If you think of a way that seems foolish, don't tell anyone. Just let it work for you. One of my students told me that she finally figured out a way to remember the meaning of *buscar* / to look for. She said, "I'm looking for a *bus* or a *car.*" How many can you make up? Here are a few more mnemonic tips. Some students confuse **hoy** and **hay.** See these pictures in your mind:

Mnemonic tip	H	O	Y		H	A Y	
	T	O	D A Y		T H	E R E	I S
					T H	E R E	A R E

The pronunciation of *hay* is like the English word eye. You don't remember the Spanish word for eyes / *los ojos?!*

Watch this:

And this:

Mnemonic tip	A	Y	E R
		Y	E S T E R D A Y

If I have omitted anything you think is important, if you spot any misprints, or if you have any suggestions for the improvement of the next edition, please contact the publisher.

Christopher Kendris, B.S., M.S., M.A., Ph.D.

How to Use This Book

So that you can get the most out of *Master the Basics: Spanish*, follow these steps.

Step 1 The first thing to do is to become familiar with this book. Turn the pages and look at each page for a few seconds. When you reach the Contents, examine it carefully. If you find something that strikes your interest, turn to that section to see exactly what is there. Do you want to know when the subjunctive should be used? Fan the pages until you come to **§7.5—18** or go straight to the page given in the Contents. I'm sure you will find **§12.2** of special interest and value. Do not begin to do any studying until you have reviewed every page. It won't take more than about ten minutes.

Step 2 Take the diagnostic test, beginning on page 3. At the end of the preliminary test, you will find the explained answers and a diagnostic analysis. Check the question numbers that you had right or wrong and, if wrong, turn to the appropriate section and study it, making certain you understand the explanations, so that you can learn more about that particular element of Spanish. And if you happen to have many answers right, do not assume that you know that particular element of Spanish thoroughly. Asking only three questions from each of the first 20 chapters is just to give you an idea of your strengths and weaknesses.

Step 3 The next step is to go through the entire Grammar Review, reviewing some portions and studying others in depth. The final section of Part One is Let's Review. You can do the more than two hundred items in the exercises and activities in this section either after having done the Grammar Review or as you work through the book. The questions are keyed to the numerical reference system in the Review and the Answers sections. Another possibility is to do both: try the questions corresponding to each chapter after you have studied the chapter, and then do them again for a final review after you have worked through the Review sections.

Step 4 Now you are ready to tackle Part Two of the book. It contains a variety of exercises for self-testing to help you improve your skills in grammar, reading comprehension, and writing by using paragraphs, long selections, simple guided composition, pictures, and word games. Answers to exercises in this part appear at the end of each section. To do your best, you must review Part One of the book and use the bilingual vocabulary list beginning on page 349. The index provides an easy reference to any basic grammatical point that you may want to check.

If you cannot find a Spanish or English word in the vocabularies, please consult a standard Spanish-English, English-Spanish dictionary.

Now begin with Step 1!

Abbreviations in This Book

adj.	adjective
adv.	adverb
ant.	anterior **(anterior)**
art.	article
cond.	conditional **(potencial simple)**
cond.p.	conditional perfect **(potencial compuesto)**
conj.	conjunction
def.	definite
dem.	demonstrative
dir.	direct
e.g.	for example
f.	feminine
fam.	familiar use
fut.	future **(futuro)**
ger.	gerund **(gerundio)**
imp.	imperative **(imperativo)**
impf.	imperfect **(imperfecto)**
ind.	indicative **(indicativo)**
indef.	indefinite
indir.	indirect
inf.	infinitive
int.	interjection
m.	masculine
n.	noun
nfpl.	plural feminine noun
nmpl.	plural masculine noun
num.	numeral
obj.	object
part.	participle
perf.	perfect **(perfecto)**
pers.	person
pl.	plural
plup.	pluperfect or past perfect **(pluscuamperfecto)**
poss.	possessive
pp.	past participle **(participio de pasado)**
pr.	present **(presente)**
prep.	preposition
pret.	preterit **(pretérito)**
pron.	pronoun
rel.	relative
rv.	reflexive verb, pronominal verb
s.	singular
sbj.	subjunctive **(subjuntivo)**
v.	verb

About the Author

Dr. Christopher Kendris was born in Albany, New York, of immigrant parents from Greece who had about three years of elementary school education in a mountain village in Greece. They emigrated to America in 1910 and were married in Lowell, Massachusetts.

Dr. Kendris has worked as interpreter and translator of French for the U.S. State Department at the American Embassy in Paris. He earned his B.S. and M.S. degrees at Columbia University in the City of New York, where he held a New York State Scholarship, and his M.A. and Ph.D. degrees at Northwestern University in Evanston, Illinois, where he held a Teaching Assistantship and Tutorial Fellowship for four years. He also earned two diplomas with *Mention très Honorable* at the Université de Paris (en Sorbonne), Faculté des Lettres, École Supérieure de Préparation et de Perfectionnement des Professeurs de Français à l'Etranger, and at the Institut de Phonétique, Paris.

In 1986, he was one of 95 teachers in the United States who was awarded a Rockefeller Foundation Fellowship for outstanding Teachers of Foreign Languages in American High Schools.

He has had forty years of teaching experience. He has taught French at the College of The University of Chicago as visiting summer lecturer, at Colby College, Duke University, Rutgers—The State University of New Jersey, the State University of New York at Albany, the Albany Academy of Albany, New York, the Schenectady School District, and the Community College of Schenectady, New York. He was Chairman of the Department of Foreign Languages and Supervisor of 16 foreign language teachers on the secondary level at Farmingdale High School, Farmingdale, New York, where he was also a teacher of all levels of French and Spanish, and prepared students for the New York State French and Spanish Regents exams, SAT exams, and AP tests.

Dr. Kendris is the author of 22 school and college books, workbooks, and other language guides of French and Spanish, some of which are best sellers, and all of which have been published by Barron's Educational Series. He is listed in *Contemporary Authors* and *Directory of American Scholars*. You may see the titles of all his popular books if you enter, on your computer Internet, Barron's Educational Series and enter Kendris, Christopher, author.

FIND OUT WHAT YOU KNOW

This diagnostic test will help put some touching up on your brushing-up. The test covers material presented in the Basics, the Parts of Speech, and Special Topics, all of which are included in **§1.—§20.** in this book. On page xv, where you find the section on how to use this book, read again Step 2. That's what this diagnostic test is all about.

Test Yourself

THE BASICS

Choose the correct answer by circling the letter. Do not refer to the Answer Key and Explained Answers until after you have answered all questions. The answers and explanations start at the end of the last question, which is number 60.

1. In Spanish, the letter *g* in front of the vowels *e* or *i* (as in the Spanish word *general*), is pronounced as the underlined letter in the English word
   A. <u>h</u>elp   B. <u>j</u>et   C. <u>g</u>o   D. ar<u>g</u>ue

2. The double *ll* in a Spanish word, as in *llamo,* is pronounced similarly as in the English word
   A. he<u>ll</u>o   B. <u>l</u>ame   C. <u>y</u>es   D. mi<u>lli</u>on

3. The letter *d* in a Spanish word, as in *cada*, is pronounced similarly as in the English word
   A. <u>d</u>are   B. <u>th</u>in   C. da<u>d</u>   D. <u>th</u>e

4. In pronouncing a Spanish word, if the word ends in a vowel, *n* or *s*, raise your voice on the vowel in the _____ that last vowel, *n* or *s*.
   A. syllable just in front of
   B. syllable at the beginning of the word
   C. syllable right after
   D. middle of

5. Stressing a vowel means _____ your voice on that vowel.
   A. lowering   B. raising   C. modulating
   D. shouting

6. The punctuation mark called *comillas* is
   A. a comma   B. a period
   C. quotation marks   D. a hyphen

PARTS OF SPEECH

On the line in front of each of the following nouns, write *el* if the noun is masculine or *la* if it is feminine.

7. _____ mano   8. _____ día   9. _____ foto

Write the Spanish words for each of the following.

10. the little girl's doll _____

11. John's book _____

12. little Joseph _____

13. a tall, beautiful, and intelligent woman _____

_____

3

14. a tall, handsome man _____

15. This sentence is easier than you think. _____

_____

Each of the following sentences contains a blank. From the four choices given, select the one that can be inserted to form a grammatically correct sentence and circle the letter of your choice.

16. ¿La carta? Juan está _____ .
    A. la escribiendo
    B. escribiéndola
    C. la escribir
    D. escribirla

17. ¿El libro? José quiere _____ .
    A. me lo dar
    B. darmelo
    C. dármelo
    D. démelo

18. Me gustan estos guantes y _____ .
    A. esos   B. estas   C. aquello   D. ésos

Read the following paragraph carefully. Then answer the questions under it.

   Antes de regresar a su asiento, Juanita vio a un hombre. Cuando Juanita vio al hombre, ella le dijo: "Buenos días, señor". Juanita le dio al hombre su programa y su pluma para escribir su autógrafo. El hombre lo escribió en el programa que Juanita tenía en la mano.

19. How many Spanish verb forms are there in the preterit tense in the above paragraph?
    A. 5   B. 7   C. 6   D. 3

20. How many Spanish verb forms are there in the imperfect indicative tense in the above paragraph?
    A. 0   B. 1   C. 2   D. 3

21. How many Spanish verb forms are there in the present indicative tense in the above paragraph?
    A. 0   B. 1   C. 2   D. 3

22. Write ten commonly used adverbs in Spanish which do not end in *mente*.
    A. ___   B. ___   C. ___   D. ___   E. ___
    F. ___   G. ___   H. ___   I. ___   J. ___

In the next two questions, read the Spanish statements given and select the best translation into English.

23. Paula trabaja mejor que Anita e Isabel trabaja peor que Elena.
    A. Paula works worse than Anita but Isabel works better than Helen.
    B. Paula travels more than Anita and Isabel travels less than Helen.
    C. Paula works faster than Anita and Isabel works more poorly than Helen.
    D. Paula works better than Anita and Isabel works worse than Helen.

24. María corre tan rápidamente como Enrique.
    A. Mary runs much more rapidly than Henry.
    B. Mary runs as fast as Henry.
    C. Mary runs less rapidly than Henry.
    D. Mary runs faster than Henry.

Each of the following sentences contains a blank. From the four choices given, select the one that can be inserted to form a grammatically correct sentence and circle the letter of your choice.

25. ¿Conoce Ud. _____ Roberto?
    A. al   B. a   C. el   D. nothing needed

26. ¿Cuánto dinero me da Ud. ____ mi trabajo?
    A. para   B. por   C. para que   D. de

27. Ud. habla español muy bien _____ norteamericano.
    A. por un   B. pro ser un   C. por ser   D. para ser

Read the following paragraph carefully. Then answer the question under it.

Yo no puedo ir a la fiesta en casa de Juanita esta noche porque tengo muchas tareas y, como mi madre está enferma, debo quedarme en casa; pero mañana es posible o en tres días.

28. How many conjunctions can you find in the above paragraph?
    A. 5   B. 4   C. 3   D. 2

Complete the following conjunctions by writing on the blank line the Spanish word that is missing.

29. a fin _____ que / so that, in order that

30. sin _____ / nevertheless, however

SPECIAL TOPICS

Write the Spanish words for each of the following.

31. What a pretty girl! _____

_____

32. How easy it is! _____

_____

33. What an interesting book! _____

_____

Each of the following sentences contains a blank. From the four choices given, select the one that can be inserted in the blank to form a grammatically correct sentence and circle the letter of your choice.

34. Hacía una hora que yo _____ cuando Ud. entró en la sala de clase.
    A. hablo   B. estoy hablando   C. hablé
    D. hablaba

35. Estaremos en México _____ la semana que viene.
    A. a bordo
    B. a tiempo
    C. a fines de
    D. a través de

36. Para hacer este viaje, tengo que comprar un billete __.
    A. de ida y vuelta
    B. de rodillas
    C. de acuerdo
    D. de arriba

37. ¿Cuál es la fecha?—Hoy es el ____ de octubre.
    A. un   B. uno   C. primer   D. primero

38. ¿A cuántos estamos hoy?—Estamos____ cinco de abril.
    A. el   B. a   C. la   D. al

39. Generalmente, en Nueva York hace frío en _____ .
    A. el verano   B. el invierno   C. la primavera
    D. el otoño

Study the clocks and underneath each clock write on the blank line in Spanish words the time that is given.

40.

41.

42.

_____   _____   _____

Read the statement in English and select the correct equivalent in Spanish by drawing a circle around the letter of your choice.

43. Is there much snow here in winter?
   A. ¿Hay mucha nieva aquí en el verano?
   B. ¿Hay mucha lluvia aquí en la primavera?
   C. ¿Hay mucha nieva aquí en el invierno?
   D. ¿Hay mucho lodo aquí en el invierno?

44. It was snowing when I woke up.
   A. Estaba nevando cuando se despertó.
   B. Estaba nevando cuando me desperté.
   C. Estaba lloviendo cuando me desperté.
   D. Estaba lloviendo cuando se despertó.

45. It was very foggy this morning.
   A. Había mucho polvo esta mañana.
   B. Había neblina esta mañana.
   C. Había mucha neblina esta mañana.
   D. Hay mucha neblina esta mañana.

Each of the following sentences contains a blank. From the four choices given, select the one that can be inserted in the blank to form a sensible and grammatically correct sentence and circle the letter of your choice.

46. Veinte _____ diez son dos.
   A. menos   B. por   C. y   D. dividido por

47. Dos _____ tres son cinco.
   A. menos   B. por   C. y   D. dividido por

48. Cinco _____ seis son treinta.
   A. y   B. por   C. dividido por   D. menos

Read the synonyms in English in each of the following and select the correct equivalent in Spanish by drawing a circle around the letter of your choice.

49. jest, joke, fun
    A. camarero, mozo   B. chiste, chanza, broma
    C. aún, todavía   D. anillo, sortija

50. to break
    A. quebrar, romper   B. esperar, aguardar
    C. burlarse de, mofarse de   D. luchar, pelear

51. to shout, to cry out
    A. cruzar, atravesar   B. rogar, suplicar
    C. dar voces, gritar   D. mostrar, enseñar

Read the words in English that are antonyms in each of the following and select the correct equivalent in Spanish by drawing a circle around the letter of your choice.

52. to have a good time / to be bored
    A. apresurarse a / tardar en
    B. olvidarse de / acordarse de
    C. aparecer / desaparecer
    D. aburrirse / divertirse

53. slowly / quickly
    A. arriba / abajo
    B. aprisa / despacio
    C. barato / caro
    D. flaco / gordo

54. inside / outside
    A. éxito / fracaso
    B. dentro / fuera
    C. hembra / macho
    D. ancho / estrecho

55. Write a word in Spanish that ends in *mente* and is a cognate of a word in English that ends in *ly*.

_____

56. Write a word in Spanish that ends in *ario* and is a cognate of a word in English that ends in *ary*.

_____

57. Write a word in Spanish that ends in *oso* and is a cognate of a word in English that ends in *ous*.

_____

For each Spanish word select the English word whose meaning is the same.

58. éxito

    A. success   B. failure   C. exit   D. exciting

59. constipado

    A. constituted   B. constipated

    C. sick with a common cold   D. farmer

60. vaso

    A. pitcher   B. vase

    C. drinking glass   D. cup

Answers

RIGHT   WRONG
(check one)

1. A. Review **§1.**, A Guide to Pronouncing Spanish Sounds, Other Sounds.

2. C. Review **§1.**, where *llave* is given as an example.

3. D. Review **§1.**, Consonant Sounds, where *cada* and *father* are given as examples.

4. A. Review **§2.**

5. B. Review **§2.**

6. C. Review **§2.**

7. *la.* Review **§3.1.**

8. *el.* Review **§3.1.**

9. *la.* Review **§3.1.**

10. *la muñeca de la chiquita.* Review **§4.1–1.**

11. *el libro de Juan.* Review **§4.1–1.**

12. *el pequeño José.* Review **§4.1–1.**

13. *una mujer alta, hermosa e inteligente.* Review **§5.4–1.** To understand the use of **y** and **e** (both meaning *and*), consult **§10.2–4.**

14. *un hombre alto y guapo.* Review **§5.4–1.**

15. *Esta frase es más fácil de lo que Ud. cree.* Review **§5.6–1.**

16. B. Review **§6.1–4.**

17. C. Review **§6.1–5.**

18. D. Review **§6.3.**

19. A. Review the preterit in **§7.5–3.**

20. B. Review the imperfect indicative in **§7.5–2.**

21. A. Review the present indicative in **§7.5–1.**

22. *abajo, arriba, bien, mal, hoy, mañana, siempre, nunca, aquí, allí.* Review **§8.1.**

23. D. Review irregular comparative adverbs in **§8.2.**

24. B. Review regular comparison of adverbs in **§8.2.**

RIGHT   WRONG
(check one)

_____	_____	25.	B. Review the personal *a* in **§9.5–1.**
_____	_____	26.	B. Review the uses of *para* and *por* in **§9.5–3.**
_____	_____	27.	D. Review the uses of *para* and *por* in **§9.5–3.**
_____	_____	28.	A. Review the common conjunctions in **§10.1.**
_____	_____	29.	de. Review the common conjunctions in **§10.1.**
_____	_____	30.	embargo. Review the common conjunctions in **§10.1.**
_____	_____	31.	*¡Qué chica tan bonita!* Review exclamatory sentences in **§11.**
_____	_____	32.	*¡Qué fácil es!* Review exclamatory sentences in **§11.**
_____	_____	33.	*¡Qué libro más interesante!* Review exclamatory sentences in **§11.**
_____	_____	34.	D. Review the use of *Hacía* + length of time + *que* + imperfect indicative tense in **§12.1.**
_____	_____	35.	C. Review common expressions with *a* in **§12.2.**
_____	_____	36.	A. Review common expressions with *de,* as in *billete de ida y vuelta* in **§12.2.**
_____	_____	37.	D. Review asking and stating the date in **§13.1.**
_____	_____	38.	B. Review asking and stating the date in **§13.1.**
_____	_____	39.	B. Review the seasons of the year in **§13.4.**
_____	_____	40.	*Son las cinco y diez.* Review telling time in **§14.**
_____	_____	41.	*Es la una.* Review telling time in **§14.**
_____	_____	42.	*Son las seis menos cuarto.* Review telling time in **§14.**
_____	_____	43.	C. Review weather expression in **§15.**
_____	_____	44.	B. Review weather expressions in **§15.**
_____	_____	45.	C. Review weather expressions **§15.**
_____	_____	46.	D. Review numbers in **§16.** and simple arithmetical expressions in **§16.1.**
_____	_____	47.	C. Review numbers in **§16.1.**
_____	_____	48.	B. Review numbers in **§16.1.**
_____	_____	49.	B. Review synonyms in **§17.**
_____	_____	50.	A. Review synonyms in **§17.**

RIGHT   **WRONG**
  (check one)

_____	_____	51. C. Review synonyms in **§17**.
_____	_____	52. D. Review antonyms in **§18**.
_____	_____	53. B. Review antonyms in **§18**.
_____	_____	54. B. Review antonyms in **§18**.
_____	_____	55. *correctamente, finalmente, naturalmente.* Review cognates **§19**.
_____	_____	56. *necesario, vocabulario.* Review cognates in **§19**.
_____	_____	57. *famoso, generoso.* Review cognates in **§19**.
_____	_____	58. A. Review tricky words in **§20**.
_____	_____	59. C. Review tricky words **§20**.
_____	_____	60. C. Review tricky words in **§20**.

Diagnostic Analysis

Section	Question Numbers	Number of Answers	
		Right	Wrong
THE BASICS			
1. Pronunciation	1, 2, 3		
2. Capitalization, Punctuation, Word Division	4, 5, 6		
THE PARTS OF SPEECH			
3. Nouns	7, 8, 9		
4. Articles	10, 11, 12		
5. Adjectives	13, 14, 15		
6. Pronouns	16, 17, 18		
7. Verbs	19, 20, 21		
8. Adverbs	22, 23, 24		
9. Prepositions	25, 26, 27		
10. Conjunctions	28, 29, 30		
SPECIAL TOPICS			
11. Exclamatory Statements	31, 32, 33		
12. Idioms	34, 35, 36		
13. Dates, Days, Months, Seasons	37, 38, 39		
14. Telling Time	40, 41, 42		
15. Weather Expressions	43, 44, 45		
16. Numbers	46, 47, 48		
17. Synonyms	49, 50, 51		
18. Antonyms	52, 53, 54		
19. Cognates	55, 56, 57		
20. Tricky Words	58, 59, 60		
TOTAL QUESTIONS:	60		

Use the following scale to see how you did.

58 to 60 right:	*Excellent*
. 55 to 57 right:	*Very Good*
52 to 54 right:	*Average*
49 to 51 right:	*Below Average*
Fewer than 49 right:	*Unsatisfactory*

PART ONE

GRAMMAR REVIEW

In the chapters that follow, a numerical decimal system has been used with the symbol § in front of it. This was done so thay you may find quickly and easily the reference to a particular point in Spanish grammar when you use the index. For example, if you look up the entry "adjectives" in the index, you will find the reference given as §5. Sometimes additional § reference numbers are given when the entry you consulted is mentioned in other areas in the chapter §. The index also includes some key Spanish words, for example ser *and* estar, *and § references to them are also given.*

The Basics

§1.

A Guide to Pronouncing Spanish Sounds

English words given here contain sounds that only approximate Spanish sounds.

Letters	Pronounced as in the	
	Spanish Word	English Word
PURE VOWEL SOUNDS		
a	*la*	father
e	*le*	let
i	*ti*	see
o	*yo*	order
u	*tu*	too
DIPHTHONGS (2 vowels together)		
ai	*baile*	
ay	*hay* }	eye
au	*aula*	cow
ei	*reino*	
ey	*ley* }	they
eu	*Europa*	wayward
ya	*enviar*	
	ya }	yard
ye	*tiene*	
	yendo }	yes
yo	*iodo*	
	yodo }	yore
yu	*viuda*	
	yugo }	you
oi	*oigo*	
oy	*estoy* }	toy
wa	*cuando*	want
we	*bueno*	way
wi	*suizo*	week
wo	*cuota*	woke

17

	Pronounced as in the	
Letters	**Spanish Word**	**English Word**

TRIPHTHONGS (3 vowels together)

yai	*enviáis*	yipe
yau	*mi<u>au</u>*	m**eow**
yei	*envi<u>éi</u>s*	**yea**
wai	*g<u>uai</u>na*	
	Urug<u>uay</u>	**wi**se
wau	*g<u>uau</u>*	**wow**
wei	*contin<u>uéi</u>s* ⎫	
	b<u>uey</u> ⎭	**wai**t

The accent mark (') over a vowel sound indicates that you must raise your voice on that vowel sound.

CONSONANT SOUNDS

b	*<u>b</u>ien*	**b**oy
	<u>v</u>a	
d	*ca<u>d</u>a*	fa**th**er
f	*<u>f</u>alda*	**f**an
g	*<u>g</u>ato* ⎫	
	<u>g</u>oma ⎬	**g**ap
	<u>g</u>usto ⎭	
k	*<u>c</u>asa* ⎫	
	<u>c</u>ulpa ⎬	**c**ap
	<u>qu</u>e	
	<u>qu</u>ito ⎭	
l	*<u>l</u>a*	**l**ard
m	*<u>m</u>e*	**m**ay
n	*<u>n</u>o*	**n**o
ñ	*ni<u>ñ</u>o*	can**y**on
p	*<u>p</u>a<u>p</u>á*	**p**a**p**a
r	*pe<u>r</u>o*	Ap**r**il
rr	*pe<u>rr</u>o*	bu**rr**, g**r-r-r**
s	*<u>s</u>opa* ⎫	
	<u>c</u>ero ⎬	**s**oft
	<u>c</u>ita	
	<u>z</u>umo ⎭	
t	*<u>t</u>u*	**s**it
ch	*mu<u>ch</u>o*	**church**

OTHER SOUNDS

h	*<u>j</u>usto* ⎫	
	<u>g</u>eneral ⎬	**h**elp
	<u>g</u>igante ⎭	

	Pronounced as in the	
Letters	**Spanish Word**	**English Word**

OTHER SOUNDS

The letter *h* in a Spanish word is not pronounced.

| y | <u>y</u>o ⎫
<u>ll</u>ave ⎭ | yes |

The pronunciation given in phonetic symbols is that of most Latin American countries and of certain regions in Spain.

Note: The pronunciation guide above contains Spanish and English words as examples to illustrate sounds that are approximately like those in acceptable standard speech. Sometimes there are variations; for example, the pronunciation of the Spanish consonant **d** changes from soft **d**, as in the sound of **th** in the English words "**th**is fa**th**er," to hard **d**, as in the English word **d**id. At other times, it is almost silent when the tip of the tongue scarcely touches the upper teeth. The pronunciation also depends on the position of **d** in the word or in a phrase. It also depends on the speaker in any of the many Spanish-speaking countries in the world as well as in some regions of the United States.

If you want to improve your pronunciation of Spanish, I would recommend Barron's *Pronounce It Perfectly in Spanish,* which includes three audio CDs. You can listen to authentic Spanish pronunciation and imitate during the pauses.

§2.

Capitalization, Punctuation Marks, and Division of Words into Syllables

CAPITALIZA-TION

Generally speaking, do not capitalize days of the week, months of the year, languages, nationalities, and religions.

> *domingo, lunes, martes,* etc.; *enero, febrero, marzo,* etc.; *español, francés, inglés,* etc.; *Roberto es español, María es española, Pierre es francés; Elena es católica.*

PUNCTUATION

Common punctuation marks in Spanish are as follows:

> *apóstrofo* / apostrophe '
> *comillas* / quotation marks " "
> *paréntesis* / parentheses ( )
> *principio de interrogación* / beginning question mark ¿
> *fin de interrogación* / final question mark ?
> *punto* / period .
> *coma* / comma ,
> *punto y coma* / semicolon ;
> *dos puntos* / colon :
> *puntos suspensivos* / ellipses . . .

DIVISION OF WORDS

It is good to know how to divide a word into syllables (not only in Spanish but also in English) because it helps you to pronounce the word correctly and to spell it correctly. The general rules to follow when dividing Spanish words into syllables are:

In General

- A syllable must contain a vowel.
- A syllable may contain only one vowel and no consonant: *e / so (eso).*

Consonants

- If you are dealing with single separate consonants, each consonant remains with the vowel that follows it: *mu / cho (mucho), ca / ba / llo (caballo), pe / ro (pero), pe / rro (perro).* Did you notice that the consonants *ch, ll,* and *rr* are considered as one consonant sound and are not separated?
- If you are dealing with two consonants that come together (other than *ch, ll,* or *rr* as stated above), the two consonants are separated; the first remains with the preceding syllable and the second remains with the following syllable when they are split: *her / ma / no (hermano), at / las (atlas), ter / cer (tercer)*

But if the second of the two consonants that come together is / or *r,* do not separate them: *ha / blo (hablo), a / pren / do (aprendo), li / bro (libro)*

- If you are dealing with three consonants that come together, the first two remain with the preceding vowel and the third consonant remains with the vowel that follows it: *ins / ti / tu / to (instituto)*
  But if the third of the three consonants is / or *r,* do not separate that third consonant from the second; it remains with the second consonant: *com / pren / der (comprender), sas / tre (sastre), sal / dré (saldré)*

Vowels

- Two vowels that are together are generally separated if they are strong vowels. The strong vowels are: *a, e, o: a / e / ro / pla / no (aeroplano), o / a / sis (oasis), re / a / li / dad (realidad)*
  But if you are dealing with a weak vowel *(i, u)* it ordinarily remains in the same syllable with its neighboring vowel, especially if that other vowel is a strong vowel: *trein / ta (treinta), ru / bio (rubio), hue / vo (huevo)*
- If a vowel contains a written accent mark, it becomes strong enough to remain in its own syllable: *Ma / rí / a (María), re / ú / ne (reúne), dí / a (día)*

Other

- The letter *y* is considered a consonant when a vowel follows it. Keep it with the vowel that follows it: *a / yer (ayer), a / yu / dar (ayudar)*

Syllable Emphasis

If a Spanish word ends in a vowel, the letter *n* or *s,* emphasize the second-to-last syllable of the word:

mu / CHA / cho	*re / SU / men*	*mu / CHA / chas*
(boy)	(summary)	(girls)

If a Spanish word ends in a letter other than a vowel, *n* or *s,* emphasize that last syllable:

com / pren / DER	*re / a / li / DAD*	*es / pa / ÑOL*
(to understand)	(reality)	(Spanish)

Sometimes, a written accent (´) is placed over the vowel that must be stressed, indicating an exception to the rule. The accent mark tells the reader which vowel to stress:

LA / piz (lápiz)	*DE / bil (débil)*
(pencil)	(weak)
LA / pi / ces (lápices)	*DE / bi / les (débiles)*
(pencils)	(weak)

| Mnemonic Tip | Most words in Spanish, including verb forms, end in a vowel, *n* or *s*. Therefore, apply the first rule by keeping in mind the following Mnemonic tip: |

El muCHAcho y las muCHAchas CANtan en espaÑOL.
(The boy and the girls are singing in Spanish.)

Note, finally, that *el corazón* (heart) requires an accent mark on the vowel *o* because the pronunciation does not follow the simple rule stated above. Spanish-speaking people pronounce the word as *co / ra / ZON* with an accent mark on *ZÓN* to show this exception. There are hundreds of Spanish words that require an accent mark because their pronunciation does not follow the general rule.

The Parts of Speech

§3.

Nouns

DEFINITION

A noun is a word that refers to a person, a place, a thing, or a quality.

Nouns are either masculine or feminine and normally require an article: *el, la, los, las.* See **§4.** about articles.

The gender of nouns that do not refer to persons or animals, where the gender is apparent, must be learned.

Gender	Noun Endings	Examples
masculine	- *o*	*el libro*
feminine	- *a*	*la casa*
	- *ción*	*la lección*
	- *sión*	*la ilusión*
	- *dad*	*la ciudad*
	- *tad*	*la difficultad*
	- *tud*	*la solicitud*
	- *umbre*	*la costumbre*
masculine or feminine, referring to a specific person	- *nte*	*el estudiante* *la estudiante*
some masculine some feminine	- *e*	*el aire, el coche* *la gente, la leche*

§3.1 IRREGULAR GENDER OF NOUNS

Ending	Gender	Examples
- *o*	feminine	*la mano*/hand *la radio* / radio *la foto* / photo
- *a*	masculine	*el día*/day *el drama* / drama *el clima* / climate
- *ista*	masculine or feminine, referring to a specific person	*el dentista* } dentist *la dentista* } *el novelista* } novelist *la novelista* }

§3.2
PLURAL OF
NOUNS

Noun Ending	Plural	Examples
vowel	add *s*	*el chico* / los chicos
consonant	add *es*	*la flor* / las flores
z	change *z* to *c* and add *es*	*la luz* / las luces

§3.2–1
Other
Exceptions

Sometimes a masculine plural noun refers to both male and female persons:

los padres / the parents, the mother and father

Generally, a noun that ends in *ión* drops the accent mark in the plural:

la lección / *las lecciones; la ilusión* / *las ilusiones*

Generally, a noun that ends in *és* drops the accent mark in the plural:

el francés / the Frenchman; *los franceses* / the Frenchmen

Sometimes the accent mark is kept in the plural in order to keep the stress where it is in the singular: *el país* / *los países*

Some nouns have a plural ending but are regarded as singular because they are compound nouns:

el paraguas / the umbrella; *los paraguas* / the umbrellas

Generally speaking, a noun that ends in *s* in the singular with no stress on that final syllable remains the same in the plural: *el lunes* / *los lunes*

Generally speaking, a noun that ends in *s* in the singular with the stress on that syllable requires the addition of *es* to form the plural: *el mes* / *los meses*

Some nouns that contain no accent mark in the singular require an accent mark in the plural:

el joven / the young man; *los jóvenes* / the young men

§3.3
SPECIAL
CASES

§3.3–1
Nouns Used
as Adjectives

It is common in English to use a noun as an adjective: a history class. When this is done in Spanish, the preposition *de* is usually placed in front of the noun that is used as an adjective and both are placed after the noun that is being described:

> *una clase de historia* / a history class (a class of history)
> *una corbata de seda* / a silk tie (a tie of silk)
> *un reloj de oro* / a gold watch (a watch of gold)

Also note that the preposition *para* (for) is used in order to indicate that something is intended for something:

> *una taza para café* / a coffee cup (a cup for coffee)

However, if the cup is filled with coffee, we say in Spanish:

> *una taza de café* / a cup of coffee

§3.3–2
Nouns in the
Diminutive

Nouns ending in *ito* or *illo*
    Generally speaking, the ending *ito* or *illo* can be added to a noun to form the diminutive form of a noun. This makes the noun take on the meaning of little or small in size:

> *un vaso* / a glass (drinking); *un vasito* / a little drinking glass
> *una casa* / a house; *una casita* / a little house
> *un cigarro* / a cigar; *un cigarrilo* / a cigarette

To form the diminutive in Spanish, ordinarily drop the final vowel of the noun and add *ito (ita)* or *illo (illa): una casa / una casita*. If the final letter of the noun is a consonant, merely add *ito* or *illo*:

> *papel* / paper; *papelito* OR *papelillo* / small bit of paper

At other times, these diminutive endings give a favorable quality to the noun, even a term of endearment:

> *una chica* / a girl; *una chiquita* / a cute little girl

Here, note that before dropping the final vowel *a* to add *ita*, you must change *c* to *qu* in order to preserve the hard sound of *k* in *chica*.

un perro / a dog; *un perrito* / a darling little dog
una abuela / a grandmother; *abuelita* / "dear old granny"

| Mnemonic Tip | In English, we do something similar to this:

drop / droplet; doll / dolly OR dollie; pig / piggy OR piggie OR piglet; bath / bathinette; book / booklet; John / Johnny; Ann / Annie.

§3.3–3 Nouns That Change Meaning According to Gender

Some nouns have one meaning when masculine and another meaning when feminine. Here are two common examples:

Noun	Masculine Gender Meaning	Feminine Gender Meaning
capital	capital (money)	capital (city)
cura	priest	cure

§3.3–4 Campo, País, Patria, Nación

The first three nouns (*el campo, el país, la patria*) all mean country. However, note the following:

- *campo* means country in the sense of countryside:

  en el campo / in the country; *Vamos a pasar el fin de semana en el campo* / We are going to spend the weekend in the country.

- *país* means country in the meaning of nation:

  ¿En qué país nació Ud.? / In what country were you born?

- *patria* means country in the sense of native land:

  El soldado defendió a su patria. / The soldier defended his country.

- *nación* means country in the sense of nation:

  Las Naciones Unidas / the United Nations

EJERCICIOS/EXERCISES

The following exercises are essential to do in order to help you see what your strengths and weaknesses are in your knowledge of Spanish. This is very good practice for review. The answers to these exercises begin right after the last question in each group.

A. Escriba tres oraciones en español. Dé su nombre, su edad, y su nacionalidad/*Write three sentences in Spanish. Give your name, your age, and your nationality.* Example: Mi nombre es Juan (*or* Carmen). *Tengo dieciséis años. Soy norteamericano (or norteamericana).*

_____

_____

_____

B. Escriba un sinónimo/*Write a synonym, in Spanish of course, for each of the following.* Example: divertirse/*pasar un buen rato.*

  1. divertirse _____

  2. regresar _____

  3. quizá _____

  4. célebre _____

  5. cruzar _____

C. Escriba un antónimo/*Write an antonym for each of the following.* Example: ausente/*presente.*

  1. ausente _____

  2. a la derecha _____

  3. ligera _____

  4. arriba _____

  5. agradecido _____

D. Escriba las siguientes palabras en el plural/*Write the following words in the plural.* Example: el mes/*los meses.*

  1. el mes _____

  2. la lección _____

  3. el jardín _____

  4. el joven _____

  5. la luz _____

E. Escriba el participio pasado de cada verbo/*Write the past participle of each verb.* Example: hablar/*hablado.*

   1. hablar _____

   2. aprender _____

   3. vivir _____

   4. abrir _____

   5. hacer _____

F. Escriba tres oraciones en español. Diga que usted no fue al cine anoche con sus amigos, que usted se quedó en casa para leer un libro, y que usted escribió una carta a un amigo (a una amiga) en España/*Write three sentences in Spanish. Say that you did not go to the movies last night with your friends, that you stayed at home in order to read a book, and that you wrote a letter to a friend in Spain.* Example: Use the following words in a correct word order: *al cine, yo no fui, con mis amigos, anoche. Me quedé, leer para un libro, en casa. Una carta, yo escribí, a amigo un (una), España en.*

   _____

   _____

   _____

G. Traduzca al inglés/*Translate into English.*

   1. hacerse médico _____

   2. darse cuenta de _____

   3. un billete de ida y vuelta _____

   4. desempeñar el papel _____

   5. Si yo tuviera dinero, iría a España. _____

H. Match the following. On the blank line write the number of the English word or phrase that matches the Spanish.

1. unfortunately	___	dar un paso
2. to take a step	___	al llegar
3. to take a walk	___	Tengo mucha hambre.
4. upon arriving	___	dar un paseo
5. I am very hungry.	___	por desgracia (desgraciadamente)

I. Traduzca al español/*Translate into Spanish.*

1. Of the four seasons of the year, I prefer summer.

   _____

2. I like this season because there are no classes in July and August. _____

   _____

3. Generally, the weather is very pleasant in summer.

   _____

J. Complete las siguientes oraciones con la forma correcta de *ser* o *estar*, según convenga/*Complete the following sentences with* the correct form of *ser* or *estar,* according to which is needed.

1. Ahora María _____ cansada.

2. Hoy _____ el primero de junio.

3. Nosotros _____ norteamericanos.

4. ¿Qué hora _____ ?

5. _____ las neuve de la mañana.

K. Match the following. On the blank line write the number of the English word or phrase that matches the Spanish.

1. to take a nap ____ el domingo por la noche

2. to make fun of ____ sin despedirse (sin decir adiós)

3. without saying good-bye ____ dormir la siesta

4. tonight ____ burlarse de

5. Sunday night ____ esta noche

Answers to the preceding group of exercises.

A. Mi nombre es _____ Tengo _____ años. Soy norteamericano (*or* norteamericana, or whatever your nationality is).

B. 1. pasar un buen rato
   2. volver
   3. tal vez (*or* acaso)
   4. famoso (*or* ilustre)
   5. atravesar

C. 1. presente
   2. a la izquierda
   3. pesada
   4. bajo
   5. desagradecido (*or* ingrato)

D. 1. los meses
   2. las lecciones
   3. los jardines
   4. los jóvenes
   5. las luces

E. 1. hablado
   2. aprendido
   3. vivido
   4. abierto
   5. hecho

F. Yo no fui al cine anoche con mis amigos. Yo me quedé en casa para leer un libro. Yo escribí una carta a un amigo (a una amiga) en España.

G. 1. to become a doctor
   2. to realize
   3. a round-trip ticket
   4. to play the role (part)
   5. If I had money, I would go to Spain.

H. (Matching the two columns) 2, 4, 5, 3, 1

I. 1. De las cuatro estaciones del año, (yo) prefiero el verano.
   2. Me gusta esta estación porque no hay clases en julio y agosto.
   3. Por lo general, hace muy buen tiempo en el verano.

J. 1. está   2. es   3. somos   4. es   5. Son

K. (Matching the two columns) 5, 3, 1, 2, 4

§3.3–5
Hora, Tiempo, and Vez

These three nouns all mean time; however, note the differences:

La hora refers to the time (the hour) of the day:

¿A qué hora vamos al baile? / At what time are we going to the dance? *Vamos al baile a las neuve.* / We are going to the dance at nine o'clock.
¿Qué hora es? / What time is it? *Es la una.* / It is one o'clock.
Son las dos. /It is two o'clock.

El tiempo refers to a vague or indefinite duration of time:

No puedo ir contigo porque no tengo tiempo. / I cannot go with you because I don't have time.

As you know, *tiempo* is also used to express the weather:

¿Qué tiempo hace hoy? / What's the weather like today?
Hace buen tiempo. / The weather is fine.

La vez means time in the sense of occasions or different times:

the first time / *la primera vez;* this time / *esta vez;*
many times / *muchas veces*

§4.

Articles

There are four forms of the definite article (the) in Spanish. They are:

	Singular	**Plural**
Masculine	*el*	*los*
Feminine	*la*	*las*

EXAMPLES:

el libro (the book) / *los libros* (the books)
la pluma (the pen) / *las plumas* (the pens)

A definite article agrees in gender and number with the noun it modifies.

Noun	**Article**
m. singular	*el*
m. plural	*los*
f. singular	*la*
f. plural	*las*

If a feminine singular noun begins with stressed *a* or *ha,* use *el,* not *la.* For example, *hambre* (hunger) is a feminine noun but in the singular it is stated as *el hambre.* NOTE: *Tengo mucha hambre.* And NOTE:

Mnemonic Tip

> *el agua* / the water; BUT *las aguas* / the waters
> *el hacha* / the axe; BUT *las hachas* / the axes

However, if the definite article is in front of an adjective that precedes the noun, this is not observed:

la alta montaña / the high (tall) mountain
la árida llanura / the arid (dry) prairie

Contraction of the definite article *el*:

When the preposition *a* or *de* is in front of the definite article *el,* it contracts as follows:

| Mnemonic Tip |

> *a + el* changes to *al*
> *de + el* changes to *del*

EXAMPLES:

Voy al parque. / I am going to the park.
Vengo del parque. / I am coming from the park.

But if the definite article *el* is part of a denomination or title of a work, there is no contraction: *Los cuadros de El Greco.*

§4.1–1
The Definite
Article Is Used:

• In front of each noun even if there is more than one noun stated, as in a series, which is not always done in English:

Tengo el libro, el cuaderno, y la pluma. / I have the book, notebook, and pen.

• With a noun when you make a general statement:

Me gusta el café / I like coffee.

• With a noun of weight or measure:

un dólar la libra; un peso la libra / one dollar a pound (per pound)

• In front of a noun indicating a profession, rank, title followed by the name of the person:

El profesor Gómez es inteligente. / Professor Gómez is intelligent.

| Mnemonic Tip |

> But in direct address (when talking directly to the person and you mention the rank, profession, etc.), do not use the definite article:
>
> *Buenas noches, señor Gómez.* / Good evening, Mr. Gómez.

• With the name of a language when subject of a verb:

El español no es difícil. / Spanish is not difficult.

But not normally when the name of a language is direct object of a verb:

Estudio español. / I study Spanish.

See also §4.1—2.

- With the name of a subject matter:

    Estudio la historia / I study history.

- With the days of the week, when in English we use on:

    Voy al cine el sábado / I am going to the movies on Saturday.

- With parts of the body or articles of clothing, especially if the possessor is clearly stated:

    Me pongo el sombrero / I put on my hat.

- With common expressions, for example:

    a la escuela / to school; *en la iglesia* / in church
    la semana pasada / last week

- With the seasons of the year:

    en la primavera / in spring; *en el verano* / in summer;
    en el otoño / in autumn; *en el invierno* / in winter

- To show possession with the preposition *de* + a common noun:

    el libro del alumno / the pupil's book
    los libros de los alumnos / the pupils' books
    la muñeca de la chiquita / the little girl's doll

> Mnemonic Tip
>
> Note that when a proper noun is used, the definite article is not needed with *de* to show possession:
>
> *el libro de Juan* / John's book

- With names of some cities, countries and continents: *la Argentina, el Brasil, el Canadá, los Estados Unidos, la Habana, la América del Norte, la América Central, la América del Sur.*

- With a proper noun modified by an adjective:

    el pequeño José / Little Joseph

- With a noun in apposition with a pronoun:

    Nosotros los norteamericanos / We North Americans

- With an infinitive used as a noun, especially when it begins a sentence:

    El estudiar es bueno. / Studying is good.

Mnemonic Tip

There are some exceptions: *Ver es creer* / Seeing is believing; and other proverbs. But you do not normally use the definite article with an infinitive if it does not begin a sentence:

Es bueno estudiar / It is good to study.

- When telling time:

  Es la una / It is one o'clock; *Son las dos* / It is two o'clock.

**§4.1–2
The Definite
Article Is Not
Used:**

- In direct address with the rank, profession, title of the person to whom you are talking or writing:

  Buenos días, señora Molina. / Good morning, Mrs. Molina.

- After the verb *hablar* when the name of a language is right after a form of *hablar:*

  Hablo español / I speak Spanish.

- After the prepositions *en* and *de* with the name of a language or a subject matter:

  Estoy escribiendo en inglés. / I am writing in English.
  La señora Johnson es profesora de inglés. / Mrs. Johnson is a teacher of English.

- With a proper noun to show possession when using *de:*

  los libros de Marta / Martha's books

- With an infinitive if the infinitive does not begin the sentence:

  Es bueno trabajar. / It is good to work.
  Me gusta viajar. / I like to travel.

- With a noun in apposition with a noun:

  Madrid, capital de España, es una ciudad interesante.
  Madrid, capital of Spain, is an interesting city.

- With a numeral that denotes the order of succession of a monarch:

  Carlos V (Quinto) / Charles the Fifth

- With names of some countries and continents:

  España / Spain; *Francia* / France; *México* / Mexico;
  Europa / Europe

§4.2
INDEFINITE ARTICLE

In Spanish, there are four forms of the indefinite article (a, an, some, a few). They are:

	Singular	**Plural**
Masculine	*un*	unos
Feminine	*una*	unas

EXAMPLES:

un libro (a book); *unos libros* (some books, a few books)
una naranja (an orange); *unas naranjas* (some oranges, a few oranges)

An indefinite article agrees in gender and number with the noun it modifies.

Noun	**Article**
m. singular	*un*
m. plural	*unos*
f. singular	*una*
f. plural	*unas*

The plural of the indefinite article indicates an indefinite number:

unas treinta personas / some thirty persons.

§4.2–1
The Indefinite Article Is Used:

• When you want to say a or an. It is also used as a numeral to mean one:

un libro / a book or one book

If you want to make it clear that you mean one, you may use *solamente* (only) in front of *un* or *una:*

Tengo solamente un libro. / I have (only) one book.

• With a modified noun of nationality, profession, rank, or religion:

El doctor Gómez es un médico excelente. / Dr. Gómez is an excellent doctor.

• In front of each noun in a series, which we do not always do in English:

> *Tengo un libro, un cuaderno, y una pluma.* / I have a book, notebook, and pen.

• In the plural when an indefinite number is indicated:

> *Tengo unos dólares.* / I have some (a few) dollars.

§4.2–2
The Indefinite Article Is Not Used:

• With *cien* and *mil:*

> *cien libros* / a (one) hundred books
> *mil dólares* / a (one) thousand dollars

• With *cierto, cierta* and *tal:*

> *cierto lugar* / a certain place; *cierta persona* / a certain person
> *tal hombre* / such a man; *tal caso* / such a case

• With *otro, otra:*

> *otro libro* / another book; *otra pluma* / another pen

• With an unmodified noun of nationality, profession, rank, or religion:

> *Mi hijo es dentista.* / My son is a dentist.
> *Soy mexicano.* / I am Mexican.

• When you use *Qué* in an exclamation:

> *¡Qué hombre!* / What a man!

• With some negations, particularly with the verb *tener,* or in an interrogative statement before an unmodified noun object:

> *¿Tiene Ud. libro?* / Do you have a book?

• With a noun in apposition:

> *Martí, gran político y más grande poeta . . .* / Martí, a great politician and greatest poet . . .

§4.3
THE NEUTER ARTICLE *LO*

Lo has idiomatic uses, generally speaking.
It is used:

• With a masculine singular form of an adjective used as a noun:

> *lo bueno* / the good; *lo malo* / the bad
> *lo interesante* / what(ever) is interesting

• With a past participle:

> *lo dicho y lo escrito* / what has been said and what has been
> written

• With an adjective or adverb + *que,* meaning how:

> *Veo lo fácil que es.* / I see how easy it is.

EJERCICIOS/EXERCISES

The answers to these exercises begin right after the last
question in each group.

I. Write the words in Spanish for the English words.
    Example: the United Nations. You write on the line:
    Las Naciones Unidas.

    1. the capital (money) _____

    2. the capital (city) _____

    3. the young man _____

    4. the young men _____

    5. the girl _____

    6. the cute little girl _____

    7. the first time _____

    8. many times _____

II. Unscramble the Spanish words and write them in the
    correct order to get a meaningful sentence. Then
    translate the sentence into English. Example: ¿día, qué,
    hoy, es? You write on the line: **¿Qué día es hoy?**/ What
    day is it today?

    1. ¿hora, es, qué? ¿dos, las, son?_____

       _____

    2. contigo, puedo, no, ir, yo _____

       _____

    3. tengo, no, tiempo, mucho_____

       _____

III. Translate the following statements into Spanish. Refer to the preceding pages in this lesson if you have to.

1. I see how easy it is. _____

2. Do you have a book? (use Ud. for *you*) _____

3. I have only one book. _____

4. Dr. Gómez is an excellent doctor. _____

5. I have the book, notebook, and pen. _____

6. I am writing in Spanish. _____

7. I put on my hat._____

8. I like coffee. _____

9. I am going to the park. _____

10. I am coming from the park. _____

Answers to the preceding group of exercises.

I. 1. el capital   5. la chica (la muchacha)
   2. la capital   6. la chiquita
   3. el joven   7. la primera vez
   4. los jóvenes   8. muchas veces

II. 1. **¿Qué hora es?** What time is it? **Son las dos.** It is two o'clock.

   2. **Yo no puedo ir contigo.** I can't (I am unable to) go with you.

   3. **No tengo mucho tiempo porque tengo mucho trabajo.** I don't (do not) have much time because I have a lot of work to do.

III. 1. Veo lo fácil que es.

   2. ¿Tiene Ud. libro?

   3. Tengo solamente un libro.

   4. El doctor Gómez es un médico excelente.

   5. Tengo el libro, el cuaderno, y la pluma.

   6. Escribo (*or* Estoy escribiendo) en español.

   7. Me pongo el sombrero.

   8. Me gusta el café.

   9. Voy al parque.

   10. Vengo del parque.

§5.

Adjectives

DEFINITION

An adjective is a word that describes a noun or pronoun in some way.

§5.1 AGREEMENT

An adjective agrees in gender and number with the noun or pronoun it describes. Gender means masculine, feminine, or neuter. Number means singular or plural.

An adjective that ends in *o* in the masculine singular changes *o* to *a* to form the feminine: *rojo / roja, pequeño / pequeña.*

An adjective that expresses a person's nationality, which ends in a consonant, requires the addition of *a* to form the feminine singular:

Juan es español / María es española.

An adjective that ends in *e* generally does not change to form the feminine: *un muchacho inteligente / una muchacha inteligente.*

An adjective that ends in a consonant generally does not change to form the feminine: *una pregunta difícil / un libro difícil*—except for an adjective of nationality, as stated above, and adjectives that end in *-án, -ón, -ín, -or* (*trabajador / trabajadora,* industrious).

§5.2 POSITION

Normally, a descriptive adjective is placed after the noun it describes: *una casa amarilla.*

Two descriptive adjectives, *bueno* and *malo,* are sometimes placed in front of the noun. When placed in front of a masculine singular noun, the *o* drops: *un buen amigo; un mal alumno.*

A limiting adjective is generally placed in front of the noun: *algunos estudiantes; mucho dinero.*

In an interrogative sentence, the predicate adjective precedes the subject when it is a noun: *¿Es bonita María?*

Some adjectives have a different meaning depending on their position.

un nuevo sombrero / a new (different, another) hat *un sombrero neuvo* / a new (brand new) hat
un gran hombre / a great man *un hombre grande* / a large, big man
una gran mujer / a great woman *una mujer grande* / a large, big woman
la pobre niña / the poor girl (unfortunate, unlucky) *la niña pobre* / the poor girl (poor, not rich)

§5.3 PLURAL OF ADJECTIVES

Like nouns, to form the plural of an adjective, add *s* if the adjective ends in a vowel: *blanco / blancos; blanca / blancas.*

If an adjective ends in a consonant, add *es* to form the plural: *español / españoles; difícil / difíciles.*

Mnemonic Tip

Note that the accent on *difícil* remains in the plural in order to keep the stress there: *difíciles.*

Some adjectives drop the accent mark in the plural because it is not needed to indicate the stress. The stress falls naturally on the same vowel in the plural: *cortés / corteses; alemán / alemanes.*

Some adjectives add the accent mark in the plural because the stress needs to be kept on the vowel that was stressed in the singular where no accent mark was needed. In the singular, the stress falls naturally on that vowel: *joven / jóvenes.*

An adjective that ends in *z* changes *z* to *c* and adds *es* to form the plural: *feliz / felices.*

If an adjective describes or modifies two or more nouns that are all masculine, naturally the masculine plural is used: *Roberto y Felipe están cansados.*

If an adjective describes or modifies two or more nouns that are all feminine, naturally the feminine plural is used: *Elena y Marta están cansadas.*

If an adjective describes or modifies two or more nouns of different genders, the masculine plural is used: *María, Elena, Marta, y Roberto están cansados.*

§5.4
TYPES

§5.4–1
Descriptive Adjectives

A descriptive adjective is a word that describes a noun or pronoun: *casa blanca, chicas bonitas, chicos altos; Ella es bonita.*

Two or more descriptive adjectives of equal importance are placed after the noun. If there are two, they are joined by *y* (or *e*). If there are more than two, the last two are connected by *y* (or *e*):

> *un hombre alto y guapo* / a tall, handsome man
> *una mujer alta, hemosa e inteligente* / a tall, beautiful and
> intelligent woman

§5.4–2
Limiting Adjectives

A limiting adjective limits the number of the noun: *una casa, un libro, algunos muchachos, muchas veces.*

§5.4–3
Demonstrative Adjectives

A demonstrative adjective is used to point out someone or something. Like other adjectives, a demonstrative adjective agrees in gender and number with the noun it modifies. The demonstrative adjectives are:

English Meaning	Masculine	Feminine
this (here)	*este libro*	*esta pluma*
these (here)	*estos libros*	*estas plumas*
that (there)	*ese libro*	*esa pluma*
those (there)	*esos libros*	*esas plumas*
that (farther away or out of sight)	*aquel libro*	*aquella pluma*
those (farther away or out of sight)	*aquellos libros*	*aquellas plumas*

If there is more than one noun, a demonstrative adjective is ordinarily used in front of each noun:

> *este hombre y esta mujer* / this man and (this) woman

The demonstrative adjectives are used to form the demonstrative pronouns.

The answers to these exercises begin right after the last question in each group.

Translate the following English words into Spanish. Refer to the preceding pages in this lesson if you have to.

I. 1. José is Spanish and María is Spanish. _____
_____

   2. A yellow house is pretty. _____
_____

   3. Is Juanita pretty? _____
_____

   4. Roberto and Felipe are tired. _____
_____

   5. Elena and Marta are tired. _____
_____

II. 1. María, Elena, Marta and Roberto are tired. _____
_____

   2. a tall, handsome man and a tall, beautiful and intelligent woman _____
_____

   3. this man and this woman _____
_____

   4. this book, this pen, these books, these pens, that book, that pen _____
_____

   5. those books, those pens, that book (farther away), those pens (farther away) _____
_____

Answers to the preceding group of exercises.

I. 1. José es español y María es española.
   2. Una casa amarilla es bonita.
   3. ¿Es bonita Juanita?
   4. Roberto y Felipe están cansados.
   5. Elena y Marta están cansadas.

II. 1. María, Elena, Marta y Roberto están cansados.

 2. un hombre alto y guapo y una mujer alta, hermosa e inteligente.

 3. este hombre y esta mujer

 4. este libro, esta pluma, estos libros, estas plumas, ese libro, esa pluma

 5. esos libros, esas plumas, aquel libro, aquellas plumas

Mnemonic Tip	To distinguish between *este libro* (this book) and *ese libro* (that book), remember that the *t* in *este libro* (this book near me) falls off on its way to *ese libro* (that book near you).

§5.4–4 Possessive Adjectives

A possessive adjective is a word that shows possession and it agrees in gender and number with the noun, not with the possessor. A short form of a possessive adjective is placed in front of the noun. If there is more than one noun stated, a possessive adjective is needed in front of each noun:

mi madre y mi padre / my mother and (my) father

There are two forms for the possessive adjectives: the short form and the long form. The short form is placed in front of the noun. The short forms are:

English Meaning	Before a Singular Noun	Before a Plural Noun
1. my	*mi amigo, mi amiga*	*mis amigos, mis amigas*
2. your	*tu amigo, tu amiga*	*tus amigos, tus amigas*
3. your, his, her, its	*su amigo, su amiga*	*sus amigos, sus amigas*
1. our	*neustro amigo*	*nuestros amigos*
	nuestra amiga	*nuestras amigas*
2. your	*vuestro amigo*	*vuestros amigos*
	vuestra amiga	*vuestras amigas*
3. your, their	*su amigo, su amiga*	*sus amigos, sus amigas*

In order to clarify the meaning of *su* or *sus,* when there might be ambiguity, do the following: Replace *su* or *sus* with the definite article + the noun and add *de Ud., de él, de ella, de Uds., de ellos, de ellas:*

> *su libro* OR *el libro de Ud., el libro de él, el libro de ella; el libro de Uds., el libro de ellos, el libro de ellas*
>
> *sus libros* OR *los libros de Ud., los libros de él, los libros de ella; los libros de Uds., los libros de ellos, los libros de ellas*

The long form is placed after the noun. The long forms are:

English Meaning	After a Singular Noun	After a Plural Noun
1. my; (of) mine	*mío, mía*	míos, mías
2. your; (of) yours	*tuyo, tuya*	*tuyos, tuyas*
3. your, his her, its; (of yours, of his, of hers, of its)	*suyo, suya*	*suyos, suyas*
1. our; (of) ours	*neustro, nuestra*	*nuestros, nuestras*
2. your; (of) yours	*vuestro, vuestra*	*vuestros, vuestras*
3. your, their; (of yours, of theirs)	*suyo, suya*	*suyos, suyas*

EXAMPLES:

amigo mío / my friend; *un amigo mío* / a friend of mine

The long forms are used primarily:

- When you are talking directly to someone or when writing a letter to someone:
  ¡Hola, amigo mío! ¿Qué tal? / Hello, my friend! How are things?

- When you want to express "of mine," "of yours," "of his," "of hers," etc.
- With the verb *ser: Estos libros son míos* / These books are mine.
- In the expression: *¡Dios mío!* / My heavens! My God!

In order to clarify the meanings of *suyo, suya, suyos, suyas* (since they are third person singular or plural), do the same as for *su* and *sus* above: *dos amigos suyos* can be clarified as: *dos amigos de Ud., dos amigos de él,* (two friends of yours, of his).

The long forms of the possessive adjectives are used to serve as possessive pronouns.

A possessive adjective is ordinarily not used when referring to an article of clothing being worn or to parts of the body, particularly when a reflexive verb is used:

Me lavo las manos antes de comer / I wash my hands before eating.

§5.4–5 Interrogatives

¿Qué . . . ? and *¿cuál . . . ?*

- These two interrogative words both mean "what" or "which" but there is a difference in use:
- Use *¿Qué . . . ?* as a pronoun (when there is no noun right after it) if you are inquiring about something, if you want an explanation about something, if you want something defined or described:

  ¿Qué es esto? / What is this?

- Use *¿Qué . . . ?* as an adjective, when there is a noun right after it:

  ¿Qué día es hoy? / What day is it today?

- Use *¿Cuál . . . ?* as a pronoun, when there is no noun right after it. If by "what" you mean "which" or, "which one," it is better Spanish to use *¿Cuál . . . ?* For example:

  ¿Cuál de estos lápices es mejor? / Which (Which one) of these pencils is better?

- The same is true in the plural:

  ¿Cuáles son buenos? / Which ones are good?

- Do not use *cuál* if there is a noun right after it; in that case, you must use *qué*, as noted above.

§5.4–6 As Nouns

At times, an adjective is used as a noun if it is preceded by an article or a demonstrative adjective:

el viejo / the old man; *aquel viejo* / that old man;
la joven / the young lady; *estos jóvenes* / these young men;
este ciego / this blind man

§5.5 SHORTENED FORMS

Certain masculine singular adjectives drop the final *o* when in front of a masculine singular noun:

alguno: algún día	primero: el primer año
bueno: un buen amigo	tercero: el tercer mes
malo: mal tiempo	uno: un dólar
ninguno: ningún libro	

Note that when *alguno* and *ninguno* are shortened, an accent mark is required on the *u*.

Santo shortens to *San* before a masculine singular saint: *San Francisco, San José* but remains *Santo* in front of *Do-* or *To-*: *Santo Domingo, Santo Tomás*.

Grande shortens to *gran* when in front of any singular noun, whether masculine or feminine:

un gran hombre / a great (famous) man

Ciento shortens to *cien* when in front of any plural noun, whether masculine or feminine:

cien libros / one (a) hundred books
cien sillas / one (a) hundred chairs

Ciento shortens to *cien* except in the numbers 101 through 199:

cien mil / one hundred thousand
ciento tres dólares / one hundred three dollars

Note that in English we say one hundred or a hundred, but in Spanish no word is used in front of *ciento* or *cien* to express one or a; it is merely *ciento* or *cien*.

Cualquiera and *cualesquiera* lose the final *a* in front of a noun: *cualquier hombre*.

§5.6
COMPARATIVES
AND
SUPERLATIVES

§5.6–1
Comparatives

Of equality: *tan . . . como* (as . . . as) *María es tan alta como Elena* / Mary is as tall as Helen.
Of a lesser degree: *menos . . . que* (less . . . than) *María es menos alta que Anita.* / Mary is less tall than Anita.
Of a higher degree: *más. . . que* (more . . . than) *María es más alta que Isabel.* / Mary is taller than Elizabeth.

COMPARISON BETWEEN TWO CLAUSES

- Use *de lo que* to express "than" when comparing two clauses with different verbs if an adjective or adverb is the comparison:

  Esta frase es más fácil de lo que Ud. cree / This sentence is easier than you think.

EJERCICIOS/EXERCISES

The answers to these exercises begin right after the last question in each group.

Translate the following English sentences and words into Spanish. Refer to the preceding pages in this lesson if you have to.

I. 1. My mother and (my) father are good persons. ___
___

2. Hello, José, my friend! How are things? _____
___

3. These books are mine. _____

4. My heavens! My God! _____

5. I wash my hands before eating. _____
___

6. What is this? _____

7. What day is it today? _____

II. 1. Which (Which one) of these two pencils is better?
___

2. Which ones are good? _____

3. María is as tall as Helen. _____

4. Alicia is less tall than Anita. _____

5. Elena is taller than Isabel. _____

6. This sentence is easier than you think. _____

7. one (a) hundred books, one (a) hundred chairs, one hundred thousand _____

Answers to the preceding group of exercises.

I. 1. Mi madre y mi padre son buenas personas.

2. ¡Hola, José, amigo mío! ¿Qué tal?

3. Estos libros son míos.

4. ¡Dios mío!

5. Me lavo las manos antes de comer.

6. ¿Qué es esto?

7. ¿Qué día es hoy?

II. 1. ¿Cuál de estos dos lápices es mejor?

2. ¿Cuáles son buenos?

3. María es tan alta como Elena.

4. Alicia es menos alta que Anita.
5. Elena es más alta que Isabel.
6. Esta frase es más fácil de lo que Ud. cree.
7. cien libros, cien sillas, cien mil

• Use the appropriate form of *de lo que, de los que, de la que, de las que* when comparing two clauses with the same verbs if a noun is the comparison:

> *Tengo más dinero de lo que Ud. tiene* / I have more money than you have.
> *Roberto tiene más amigas de las que tiene Juan* / Robert has more girl friends than John has.

§5.6–2 Superlatives

To express the superlative degree, use the comparative forms given above with the appropriate definite article:

> With a proper noun. *Anita es la más alta* / Anita is the tallest.
> *Anita y Roberto son los más altos* / Anita and Robert are the tallest.
> With a common noun. *El muchacho más alto de la clase es Roberto* / The tallest boy in the class is Robert.

| Mnemonic Tip | Note that after a superlative in Spanish, "in" is expressed by *de,* not *en.* |

When two or more superlative adjectives describe the same noun, *más* or *menos* is used only once in front of the first adjective: *Aquella mujer es la más pobre y vieja.*

Absolute superlative: adjectives ending in *-ísimo, -ísima, -ísimos, -ísimas*

To express an adjective in a very high degree, drop the final vowel (if there is one) and add the appropriate ending among the following, depending on the correct agreement: *-ísimo, -ísima, -ísimos, -ísimas:*

> *María está contentísima.* / Mary is very (extremely) happy.
> *Los muchachos están contentísimos.*

These forms may be used instead of *muy* + adjective:

> *una casa grandísima* / una casa muy grande

Never use *muy* in front of *mucho.* Say *muchísimo.*

> *Muchísimas gracias.* / many thanks; thank you very, very much.

§5.6–3
Irregular Comparatives and Superlatives

Adjective	Comparative	Superlative
bueno (good)	*mejor* (better)	*el mejor* (best)
malo (bad)	*peor* (worse)	*el peor* (worst)
grande (large)	*más grande (larger)* *mayor* (greater, older)	*el más grande* (largest) *el mayor* (greatest, oldest)
pequeño (small)	*más pequeño* (smaller) *menor* (smaller, younger)	*el más pequeño* (smallest) *el menor* (smallest, youngest)

Note that you must be careful to make the correct agreement in gender and number.

- *Más que* (more than) or *menos que* (less than) becomes *más de, menos de* + a number:

  El Señor Gómez tiene más de cincuenta años.
  BUT: *No tengo más que dos dólares.* / I have only two dollars.

In this example, the meaning "only," expressed by *no* in front of the verb; in this case, you must keep *que* to express "only."

- *Tanto, tanta, tantos, tantas* + noun + *como:* as much (as many) . . . as

  Tengo tanto dinero como usted. / I have as much money as you.
  Tengo tantos libros como usted. / I have as many books as you.

- *Cuanto más (menos). . . tanto más (menos). /* the more (the less) . . . the more (less)
  A proportion or ratio is expressed by this phrase.

  Cuanto más dinero tengo, tanto más necesito. / The more money I have, the more I need.
  Cuanto menos dinero tengo, tanto menos necesito. / The less money I have, the less I need.

A note about the adjectives poco and pequeño:

These two adjectives mean "little," but note the difference.
Poco means "little" in terms of quantity:

Tenemos poco trabajo hoy. / We have little work today.

Pequeño means "little" in terms of size:

Mi casa es pequeña. / My house is small.

EJERCICIOS/EXERCISES

The answers to these exercises begin right after the last question in each group.

Translate the following Spanish sentences into English. **Then write the Spanish sentences for practice.** Refer to the preceding pages in this lesson if you have to.

I. 1. Tengo más dinero do lo que Ud. tiene. _____
_____

2. Roberto tiene más amigas de las que tiene Juan.
_____

3. Anita y Roberto son los más altos. _____
_____

4. El muchacho más alto de la clase es Roberto.
_____

5. María está contentísima. _____
_____

II. 1. Los muchachos están contentísimos. _____
_____

2. Muchísimas gracias. _____

3. El Señor Gómez tiene más de cincuenta años.
_____
_____

4. Cuanto más dinero tengo, tanto más necesito.
_____

5. Tenemos poco trabajo hoy. _____
_____

Answers to the preceding group of exercises.

I. 1. I have more money than you have.
2. Robert has more girl friends than John has.
3. Anita and Robert are the tallest.
4. The tallest boy in the class is Robert.
5. Mary is very (extremely) happy.

II. 1. The boys are very (extremely) happy.
2. Many thanks. Thank you very, very much.
3. Mr. Gómez is more than fifty years old.
4. The more money I have, the more I need.
5. We have little work today.

§6.

Pronouns

DEFINITION

A pronoun is a word that takes the place of a noun; for example, in English there are these common pronouns: I, you, he, she, it, we, they, me, him, her us, them—just to mention a few.

TYPES

Pronouns are divided into certain types: personal, prepositional, demonstrative, possessive, relative, interrogative, indefinite and negative.

§6.1 Personal Pronouns

A personal pronoun is used as the subject of a verb, direct or indirect object of a verb, as a reflexive pronoun object, and as object of a preposition.

§6.1–1 Subject Pronouns

Singular	Examples
yo / I	*Yo hablo.*
tú / you (familiar)	*Tú hablas.*
usted / you (polite)	*Usted habla.*
él / he, it	*Él habla.*
ella / she, it	*Ella habla.*

Plural	Examples
nosotros (nosotras) / we	*Nosotros hablamos.*
vosotros (vosotras) / you (fam.)	*Vosotros habláis.*
ustedes / you (polite)	*Ustedes hablan.*
ellos / they	*Ellos hablan.*
ellas / they	*Ellas hablan.*

In Spanish, subject pronouns are not used at all times. The ending of the verb tells you if the subject is 1st, 2nd, or 3rd person in the singular or plural. Of course, in the 3rd person singular and plural there is more than one possible subject with the same ending on the verb form. In that case, if there is any doubt as to what the subject is, it is mentioned for the sake of clarity. At other times, subject pronouns in Spanish are used when you want to be emphatic, to make a contrast between this person and that person, or out of simple courtesy.

§6.1–2 Direct Object Pronouns

Singular	Examples
me / me	*María me ha visto.* / Mary has seen me.
te / you (fam.)	*María te había visto.* / Mary had seen you.
lo, la / you	*María lo (la) ve.* / Mary sees you.
lo / him; *lo* / him, it	*María lo(lo) ve.* / Mary sees him (it).
la / her, it	*María la ve.* / Mary sees her (it).
Plural	Examples
nos / us	*María nos había visto.* / Mary had seen us.
os / you (fam.)	*María os ha visto.* / Mary has seen you.
los, las / you	*María los (las) ve.* / Mary sees you.
los / them	*María los ve.* / Mary sees them.
las / them	*María las ve.* / Mary sees them.

In Latin American countries, *lo* is generally used instead of *le* to mean "him."

Note that in the 3rd person plural, the direct objects *los* (m) and *las* (f) refer to people and things.

Also note that in the 3rd person singular, the direct object pronoun *lo* is masculine and *la* is feminine and both mean "you."

3d PERSON DIRECT OBJECT PRONOUNS		
Spanish	**English**	**Gender**
lo	him, it, you	m
la	her, you, it	f
los	you (pl.), them	m
las	you (pl.), them	f

There is also the neuter *lo* direct object pronoun. It usually refers to an idea or a statement:

¿Está Ud. enfermo? / Are you sick? *Sí, lo estoy* / Yes, I am.
¿Son amigos? / Are they friends? *Sí, lo son* / Yes, they are.

Of course, your reply could be *Sí, estoy enfermo* and *Sí, son amigos.* But because your verb is a form of *estar* or *ser,* you do not have to repeat what was mentioned; neuter *lo* takes its place as a direct object pronoun. This neuter *lo* direct object pronoun is also used with other verbs, e.g., *pedir, preguntar* and *parecer:*

María parece contenta / Mary seems happy.
Sí, lo parece / Yes, she does (Yes, she does seem so).

To make the examples in Spanish given above negative, place *no* in front of the direct object pronouns: *María no me ve.* To make the examples in §6.1 - 1 negative, place *no* in front of the verb.

§6.1–3 Indirect Object Pronouns

Singular	Examples
me / to me	*Pablo me ha hablado* / Paul has talked to me.
te / to you (fam.)	*Pablo te habla* / Paul talks to you.
le / to you, to him, to her, to it	*Pablo le habla* / Paul talks to you (to him, to her, to it).
Plural	Examples
nos / to us	*Pablo nos ha hablado* / Paul has talked to us.
os / to you (fam.)	*Pablo os habla* / Paul talks to you.
les / to you, to them	*Pabla les habla* / Paul talks to you (to them).

To make these sentences negative, place *no* in front of the indirect object pronouns:

Pablo no me habla / Paul does not talk to me.

Note that *me, te, nos, os* are direct object pronouns and indirect object pronouns.

Note that *le* as an indirect object pronoun has more than one meaning. If there is any doubt as to the meaning, merely add after the verb any of the following accordingly to clarify the meaning:

a Ud., a él, a ella: Pablo le habla a usted / Paul is talking to you.

> Note that *les* has more than one meaning. If there is any doubt as to the meaning, merely add after the verb any of the following, accordingly:
>
> *a Uds., a ellos, a ellas: Pablo no les habla a ellos* / Paul is not talking to them.

As you can see in the examples given above, an indirect object pronoun ordinarily is placed in front of the main verb. Other positions are discussed later in this chapter.

An indirect object pronoun is needed when you use a verb that indicates a person is being deprived of something, e.g., to steal something from someone, to take something off or from someone, to buy something from someone, and actions of this sort. The reason an indirect object pronoun is needed is that you are dealing with the preposition *a +* noun or pronoun and it must be accounted for.

Los ladrones le robaron todo el dinero a él / The robbers stole all the money from him.

La madre le quitó al niño el sombrero / The mother took off the child's hat.

The indirect object pronouns are used with the verb *gustar* and with the following verbs: *bastar, faltar or hacer falta, quedarle (a uno), tocarle (a uno), placer, parecer.*

A Ricardo le gusta el helado / Richard likes ice cream (i.e., Ice cream is pleasing to him, to Richard).

A Juan le bastan cien dólares / One hundred dollars are enough for John.

A los muchachos les faltan cinco dólares / The boys need five dollars (i.e., Five dollars are lacking to them, to the boys).

OR

A la mujer le hacen falta cinco dólares / The woman needs five dollars (i.e., Five dollars are lacking to her, to the woman).

§6.1–4 Position of Object Pronouns

Let's review the normal position of a single object pronoun when dealing with a simple tense or a compound tense.

Attach the single object pronoun to an infinitive:

Juan quiere escribirlo. / John wants to write it.

EJERCICIOS/EXERCISES

The answers to these exercises begin right after the last question in each group.

I. Write the five subject pronouns in Spanish **in the singular.** Also write the English translation for each one. Refer to the preceding pages in this lesson in section **§6. Pronouns.** Pay special attention to the familiar use of the subject pronoun **tú** (meaning *you*), which is used when you are talking to a member of your family, a friend, someone younger than you, or to a pet.

_____

_____

_____

II. Now, write the five subject pronouns in Spanish **in the plural.** Also write the English translation for each one. Refer to the preceding pages in this lesson in section **§6. Pronouns**. Pay special attention to the familiar use of the subject pronoun **vosotros** (masculine form) and **vosotras** (feminine form). They both mean *you* in the plural. They are the plural forms of the singular **tú,** which you just practiced in I. here above.

_____

_____

_____

III. Translate the following Spanish sentences into English. **Then write the Spanish sentences for practice.** Refer to the preceding pages in this lesson if you have to check your work.

1. María me ha visto. _____

_____

2. María te había visto. _____

_____

3. María nos había visto. _____

_____

4. ¿Está usted (Ud.) enfermo? Sí, lo estoy. _____

_____

5. ¿Son amigos? Sí, lo son. _____

_____

6. Pablo me habla, José te habla, Clara le habla.

   _____

7. Cristina nos habla, Alfredo os habla, y Carlos les habla. _____

   _____

8. Juana no me habla. _____

   _____

9. Los ladrones le robaron todo el dinero a él. _____

   _____

10. A Ricardo le gusta el helado. _____

   _____

Answers to the preceding group of exercises.

I. This is an exercise to practice writing the Spanish **subject pronouns** in the **singular** with their English translations. You can review them at the beginning of this lesson, which is **§6. Pronouns.** When you find them, write the forms on the blank lines under the question.

II. This, too, is an exercise to practice writing the Spanish **subject pronouns** but this time in the plural. They are also at the beginning of this lesson, which is **§6. Pronouns.**

III. 1. María has seen me.
   2. María had seen you.
   3. María had seen us.
   4. Are you sick (ill)? Yes, I am.
   5. Are they friends? Yes, they are.
   6. Pablo talks to me, José talks to you, Clara talks to you (to him, to her, to it).
   7. Cristina talks to us, Alfred talks to you, and Carlos talks to you (plural), _or_ to them.
   8. Juana does not talk to me.
   9. The robbers stole all the money from him.
   10. Ricardo likes ice cream.

If the main verb is *poder, querer, saber, ir a,* you may place the object pronoun in front of the main verb:

Juan lo quiere escribir. / John wants to write it.
¿Puedo levantarme? OR *¿Me puedo levantar?* / May I get up?

Attach the single object pronoun to a present participle:

Juan está escribiéndolo. / John is writing it.

Note that when you attach an object pronoun to a present participle, you must add an accent mark on the vowel that was stressed in the present participle before the object pronoun was attached.

If the main verb is a progressive form with *estar* or another auxiliary, you may place the object pronoun in front of the main verb:

Juan lo está escribiendo. / John is writing it.

When you are dealing with a verb form in the affirmative imperative (command), you must attach the single object pronoun to the verb form and add an accent mark on the vowel that was stressed in the verb form before the single object pronoun was added.

¡Hábleme Ud., por favor! / Talk to me, please!

When you are dealing with a verb form in the negative imperative (command), you must place the object pronoun in front of the verb form.

¡No me hable Ud., por favor! / Do not talk to me, please!

§6.1–5 Position of Double Object Pronouns: A Summary

An indirect object pronoun is always placed in front of a direct object pronoun.

With a verb in a simple tense or in a compound tense in the affirmative or negative:

The indirect object pronoun is placed in front of the direct object pronoun and both are placed in front of the verb form.

Juan me lo da / John is giving it to me.
Juan nos los dio / John gave them to us.
María no me lo ha dado / Mary has not given it to me.

With a verb in a simple tense or in a compound tense in the interrogative:

The indirect object pronoun remains in front of the direct object pronoun and both remain in front of the verb form. The subject (whether a noun or pronoun) is placed after the verb form.

¿Nos la dio Juan? / Did John give it to us?

With a verb in the affirmative imperative (command):

The object pronouns are still in the same order (indirect object + direct object) but they are attached to the verb form and an accent mark is added on the vowel that was stressed in the verb form before the two object pronouns were added.

¡Dígamelo Ud., por favor! / Tell it to me, please!

With a verb in the negative imperative (command):

The position of *no* and the two object pronouns is the same as usual, in front of the verb form.

¡No me lo diga Ud., por favor! / Don't tell it to me, please!

When dealing with an infinitive, attach both object pronouns (indirect, direct) to the infinitive.

Juan quiere dármelo / John wants to give it to me.

OR

If the main verb is *poder, querer, saber, ir a,* you may place the two object pronouns in front of the main verb.

Juan me lo quiere dar / John wants to give it to me.

When dealing with a present participle, attach both object pronouns (indirect, direct) to the present participle:

Juan está escribiéndomelo / John is writing it to me.

OR

If the main verb is a progressive form with *estar* or another auxiliary, you may place the two object pronouns (indirect, direct) in front of the main verb:

Juan me lo está escribiendo / John is writing it to me.
Juana me lo estaba escribiendo / Jane was writing it to me.

When an indirect object pronoun and a direct object pronoun are both 3rd person, the indirect object pronoun (*le* or *les*) changes to *se* because it cannot stand as *le* or *les* in front of a direct object pronoun beginning with the letter "l."

Juan se lo da / John is giving it to you (to him, to her, to it, to you [plural], to them).
¡Dígaselo Ud.! / Tell it to him!
¡No se lo diga Ud.! / Don't tell it to him!
Juan quiere dárselo.
Juan se lo quiere dar. } John wants to give it to her.
Juan está escribiéndoselo.
Juan se lo está escribiendo. } John is writing it to them.

Since the form *se* can have more than one meaning (to him, to her, to them, etc.), in addition to the fact that it looks exactly like the reflexive pronoun *se,* any doubt as to its meaning can be clarified merely by adding any of the following accordingly: *a Ud., a él, a ella, a Uds., a ellos, a ellas.*

| Mnemonic Tip |

When you are dealing with double object pronouns (one direct and the other indirect), remember that people are more important than things; therefore, the indirect object pronoun (usually referring to a person) goes in front of the direct object pronoun (usually referring to a thing).

§6.1–6 Reflexive Pronouns

Singular	Examples
me / myself	*Me lavo* / I wash myself.
te / yourself	*Te lavas* / You wash yourself.
se / yourself, himself, herself, itself	*Ud. se lava* / You wash yourself; *Pablo se lava* / Paul washes himself, etc.
Plural	Examples
nos / ourselves	*Nosotros (-as) nos lavamos.*
os / yourselves	*Vosotros (-as) os laváis.*
se / yourselves, themselves	*Uds. se lavan* / You wash yourselves; *Ellos (Ellas) se lavan* / They wash themselves.

A reflexive verb contains a reflexive pronoun, and the action of the verb falls on the subject and its reflexive pronoun either directly or indirectly. For that reason the reflexive pronoun must agree with the subject: *yo me . . . , tú te . . . , Ud. se . . . , él se . . . , ella se . . . , nosotros nos . . . , vosotros os . . . , Uds. se . . . , ellos se . . . , ellas se . . . .*

A reflexive pronoun is ordinarily placed in front of the verb form, as you can see in the examples given above.

To make these sentences negative, place *no* in front of the reflexive pronoun: *Yo no me lavo, Tú no te lavas, Ud. no se lava,* etc.

Note that *me, te, nos, os* are not only reflexive pronouns but they are also direct object pronouns and indirect object pronouns.

A reflexive verb in Spanish is not always reflexive in English.

Spanish	English
levantarse	to get up
sentarse	to sit down

There are some reflexive verbs in Spanish that are also reflexive in English.

Spanish	English
bañarse	to bathe oneself
lavarse	to wash oneself

The following reflexive pronouns are also used as reciprocal pronouns, meaning "each other" or "to each other": *se, nos, os.*

Ayer por la noche, María y yo nos vimos en el cine / Yesterday evening, Mary and I saw each other at the movies.
Roberto y Teresa se escriben todos los días / Robert and Teresa write to each other every day.

If the meaning of these three reflexive pronouns is not clear when they are used in a reciprocal meaning, any of the following may be added accordingly to express the idea of "each other" or "to each other": *uno a otro, una a otra, unos a otros,* etc.

If you are dealing with a reflexive pronoun, it is normally placed in front of an object pronoun.

Yo me lo puse / I put it on (me, on myself).

§6.2 Prepositional Pronouns

Pronouns that are used as objects of prepositions are called prepositional pronouns or disjunctive pronouns. They are:

Singular	Plural
para mí / for me, for myself	*para nosotros (nosotras)* / for us, for ourselves
para ti / for you, for yourself	*para vosotros (vosotras)* / for you, for yourselves
para usted (Ud.) / for you	*para ustedes (Uds.)* / for you
para él / for him, for it	*para ellos* / for them
para ella / for her, for it	*para ellas* / for them

Note the following exceptions with the prepositions *con, entre,* and *menos:*

conmigo / with me   *entre tú y yo* / between you and me
contigo / with you (fam.)   *menos yo* / except me
consigo / with yourself, with yourselves, with himself, with herself, with themselves

EJERCICIOS/EXERCISES

The answers to these exercises begin right after the last question in each group.

I. Translate the following Spanish sentences into English. **Then write the Spanish sentences for practice.** Refer to the preceding pages in this lesson if you have to check your work.

    1. Juan lo quiere escribir. _____

    2. Juan quiere escribirlo. _____

    3. Juan está escribiéndolo. _____

    4. ¿Peudo levantarme? _____

    5. ¿Me puedo levantar? _____

    6. ¡Hábleme Ud., por favor! _____

    7. ¡No me hable Ud., por favor! _____

    8. ¿Nos la dio Juan? _____

    9. ¡Dígamelo Ud., por favor! _____

    10. ¡No me lo diga Ud., por favor! _____

II. Match the following. On the blank line write the number of the Spanish sentence or phrase that matches the English.

    1. Juan quiere dármelo.   ___ Come with me.

    2. Juan está escribiéndomelo.   ___ This is for you.

    3. Yo me lavo las manos.   ___ They write to each other.

    4. Tú te lavas las manos.   ___ You wash your hands.

    5. Estos son para él.   ___ John wants to give me it.

    6. Ellas se escriben.   ___ John is writing it to me.

    7. Yo me lo puse.   ___ These are for him.

    8. Esto es para ti.   ___ I put it on.

    9. Eso es para mí.   ___ That is for me.

    10. Venga conmigo.   ___ I wash my hands.

Answers to the preceding group of exercises.

I.   1. Juan wants to write it.
     2. Juan wants to write it.
     3. Juan is writing it.
     4. May I get up?
     5. May I get up?
     6. Talk (Speak) to me, please!
     7. Don't talk (speak) to me, please!
     8. Did John give it to us?
     9. Tell it to me, please!
    10. Don't tell it to me, please!

II. 10, 8, 6, 4, 1, 2, 5, 7, 9, 3

§6.3 Demonstrative Pronouns

Demonstrative pronouns are formed from the demonstrative adjectives. To form a demonstrative pronoun write an accent mark on the stressed vowel of a demonstrative adjective. A demonstrative pronoun takes the place of a noun. It agrees in gender and number with the noun it replaces. The demonstrative pronouns are:

Masculine	Feminine	Neuter	English Meaning	
éste	ésta	esto	this one (here)	
éstos	éstas		these (here)	
ése	ésa	eso	that one (there)	
ésos	ésas		those (there)	
aquél	aquélla	aquello	that one	(farther away or out of sight)
aquéllos	aquéllas		those	

EXAMPLES:
Me gustan este cuadro y ése / I like this picture and that one.
Estas camisas y aquéllas son hermosas / These shirts and those are beautiful.

Mnemonic Tip	To help you remember that a demon-strative pronoun is formed from a demonstrative adjective, regard the written accent mark (´) over the stressed vowel in the demonstrative pronoun as a marker that makes the word stand alone as a pronoun. As such, there is no noun after it; but there is a noun after the demonstrative adjective: *este libro* / this book; *éste* / this one.

§6.3–1 Neuter Forms

Note that the neuter forms do not have an accent mark. They are not used when you are referring to a particular noun. They are used when referring to an idea, a statement, a situation, a clause, a phrase. Never use the neuter pronouns to refer to a person.

¿Qué es esto? / What is this?
Eso es fácil de hacer / That is easy to do.
Juan no estudia y esto me inquieta / John does not study and
                                        this worries me.

Note also that the English term "the latter" is expressed in Spanish as *éste, ésta, éstos,* or *éstas;* and "the former" is expressed in Spanish as *aquél, aquélla, aquéllos, aquéllas*—depending on the gender and number of the noun referred to.

The pronouns *el de, la de, los de, las de; el que, la que, los que, las que* are used in place of nouns.

EXAMPLES:

mi hermano y el (hermano) de mi amigo / my brother and my
    friend's
mi hermana y la (hermana) de mi amigo / my sister and my
    friend's
mis hermanos y los (hermanos) del muchacho / my brothers
    and the boy's
El (muchacho) que baila con María es mi hermano / The one
    (boy) who is dancing with Mary is my brother.
La (muchacha) que baila con Roberto es mi hermana / The
    one (girl) who is dancing with Robert is my sister.
Las (muchachas) que bailan son mis amigas / The ones (girls)
    who are dancing are my friends.

§6.4 Possessive Pronouns

A possessive pronoun is a word that takes the place of a noun to show possession, as in English: mine, yours, etc.

You form a possessive pronoun by using the appropriate definite article *(el, la, los, las)* + the long form of the possessive adjective. A possessive pronoun agrees in gender and number with the noun it replaces. It does not agree with the possessor.

The possessive pronouns are:

English Meaning	Singular Form (agrees in gender and number with the noun it replaces)	Plural Form (agrees in gender and number with the noun it replaces)
mine	*el mío, la mía*	*los míos, las mías*
yours (fam. sing.)	*el tuyo, la tuya*	*los tuyos, las tuyas*
yours, his, hers, its	*el suyo, la suya*	*los suyos, las suyas*
ours	*el nuestro, la neustra*	*los nuestros, las nuestras*
yours (fam. pl.)	*el vuestro, la vuestra*	*los vuestros, las vuestras*
yours, theirs	*el suyo, la suya*	*los suyos, las suyas*

EXAMPLES:

Mi hermano es más alto que el suyo / My brother is taller than yours (his, hers, theirs).

Su hermana es más alta que la mía / Your sister is taller than mine.

In order to clarify the meanings of *el suyo, la suya, los suyos, las suyas* (since they can mean yours, his, hers, its, theirs), drop the *suyo* form, keep the appropriate definite article *(el, la, los, las),* and add any of the following: *de Ud., de él, de ella, de Uds., de ellos, de ellas.*

mi libro y el de Ud., mi casa y la de él, mis amigos y los de ella, mis amigas y las de Uds. / my book and yours, my house and his, my friends and hers, my friends and yours, etc.

§6.4–1 *¿De quién es . . . ? ¿De quiénes es . . . ? / Whose is . . . ?*
¿De quién son . . . ? ¿De quiénes son . . . ? / Whose are . . . ?

"Whose," when asking a question (usually at the beginning of a sentence), is expressed by any of the above. If you believe that the possessor is singular, use *¿De quién es . . . ?* If you think that the possessor is plural, use

¿De quiénes es . . . ? And if the noun you have in mind (whose . . .) is plural, use the third person plural form of *ser:*

> *¿De quién es esta casa?* / Whose is this house?
> *Es de mi tío* / It is my uncle's.
> *¿De quiénes es esta casa?* / Whose is this house?
> *Es de mis amigos* / It is my friends'.
> *¿De quién son estos guantes?* / Whose are these gloves?
> *Son de Juan* / They are John's.
> *¿De quiénes son estos niños?* / Whose are these children?
> *Son de los Señores Pardo* / They are Mr. and Mrs. Pardo's.

Note that the verb *ser* is used in these expressions showing possession.

Also note that if a possessive pronoun is used with the verb *ser,* the definite article is dropped:

> *¿De quién es este lápiz?* / Whose is this pencil?
> *Es mío* / It is mine.
> *¿De quién son estas camisas?* / Whose are these shirts?
> *Son suyas* / They are theirs (yours, his, hers).

OR,

> *Son de Ud., Son de él, Son de ella* / They are yours, They are his, They are hers.

EJERCICIOS/EXERCISES

The answers to these exercises begin right after the last question in each group.

I. **Culture.   Appreciation of Spanish Art. Speaking and Writing**

Situation. You and your classmates are on a field trip to The National Gallery of Art in Washington, D.C. You are admiring a painting by **El Greco** (1541-1614), a great Spanish artist / **un gran artista español.** It is entitled *The Virgin with Saint Inés and Saint Tecla.* Imagine the picture in your mind and say aloud a few words in Spanish that come to you. You may use your own words and those on the preceding pages since the first lesson, or, for starters, you may use the following vocabulary:

Este cuadro de El Greco es magnífico / This painting by El Greco is magnificent. How about a few more adjectives? For example, **impresionante** / impressive; **interesante** / interesting; **espléndido** / splendid; **bello** / beautiful; **gracioso** / gracious; **extático** / ecstatic. Some nouns: **el éxtasis** / ecstasy; **La Virgen** / The Virgin; **el nene** / the baby; **el ángel, los ángeles** / the angel, angels; **las alas** / the wings; **el cordero blanco** / the white lamb; **las manos bellas** / the beautiful hands; **la cabeza de un león** / the head of a lion. A few verbs: **mirar** / to look at; **Yo miro** or **Yo estoy mirando** / I am looking at; **ver** / to see; **yo veo** / I see; **Me gusta mucho** / I like it a lot; **apreciar** / to appreciate; **Yo aprecio muchísimo este cuadro** / I appreciate this painting very much; **admirar** / to admire; **Yo admiro** / I admire. If you want to use other verbs, check them out in the tables of regular and irregular verbs beginning a few pages farther on. Now, practice writing in Spanish what you said on these lines:

_____

_____

_____

_____

_____

Answers to the preceding group of exercises.

I. Note to the student. The exercise on the preceding page on the topic of culture is to encourage you to speak and write about an appreciation of Spanish art. The exercise gives you many words and expressions in Spanish and English that you can use on the lines provided under the exercise. To help get you started, let's look at the paragraph in Spanish and English and let's use some of the vocabulary there. For example:

> **Este cuadro de El Greco es magnífico. Me gusta mucho. En este momento, estoy mirándolo y veo muchas cosas muy interesantes. Yo lo admiro mucho. Yo aprecio muchísimo este cuadro. Es muy impresionante y espléndido.**

Now, if you wish, for practice, you may write the above paragraph in Spanish on the lines provided under the exercise on the preceding page. Or, if you prefer, you may write your own ideas and words. You may want to begin by writing the above short paragraph as an example just to get yourself started. Feel at ease and use your imagination.

§6.5
Relative
Pronouns

A pronoun is a word that takes the place of a noun. A relative pronoun is a pronoun that refers to an antecedent. An antecedent is something that comes before something; it can be a word, a phrase, or a clause that is replaced by a pronoun or some other substitute. Example: "Is it Mary who did that?" In this sentence, "who" is the relative pronoun and "Mary" is the antecedent.

In Spanish, a relative pronoun can refer to an antecedent that is a person or a thing, or an idea. A relative pronoun can be subject or object of a verb, or object of a preposition.

§6.5–1 *que* / who, that, whom, which

• As subject referring to a person:

> *La muchacha que habla con Juan es mi hermana* / The girl who is talking with John is my sister.

The relative pronoun *que* is subject of the verb *habla* and refers to *la muchacha,* which is the subject of *es.*

• As subject referring to a thing:

> *El libro que está en la mesa es mío* / The book which (that) is on the table is mine.

The relative pronoun *que* is subject of the verb *está* and refers to *el libro,* which is the subject of *es.*

• As direct object of a verb referring to a person:

> *El señor Molina es el profesor que admiro* / Mr. Molina is the professor whom I admire.

The relative pronoun *que* is object of the verb form *admiro.* It refers to *el profesor.*

• As direct object of a verb referring to a thing:

> *La composición que Ud. lee es mía* / The composition (that, which) you are reading is mine.

Note in the English translation of this example, that we do not always use a relative pronoun in English. In Spanish, it must be stated.

• As object of a preposition referring only to a thing:

> *La cama en que duermo es grande* / The bed in which I sleep is large.

The relative pronoun *que* is object of the preposition *en.* It refers to *la cama.* Other prepositions used commonly with *que* are *a, con, de.*

• As object of a preposition, *que* refers to a thing only—not to a person. Use *quien* or *quienes* as object of a preposition referring to persons.

§6.5–2 *quien* / who, whom

• As subject of a verb referring only to persons:

Yo sé quien lo hizo / I know who did it.

Quien is the subject of *hizo.* It does not refer to a specific antecedent. Here, *quien* includes its antecedent.

When used as a subject, *quien* (or *quienes,* if plural) can also mean he who, she who, the one who, the ones who, those who. In place of *quien* or *quienes* in this sense, you can also use *el que, la que, los que, las que.*

Quien escucha oye. / Who listens hears. He who listens hears. She who listens hears.

OR:

El que escucha oye. / He who listens hears.
La que escucha oye. / She who listens hears.
Quienes escuchan oyen. / Who listen hear. Those who listen hear. The ones who listen hear.

OR:

Los que escuchan oyen. Las que escuchan oyen. / Those who listen hear.

• As subject of a verb, the relative pronoun *quien* may be used instead of *que* referring only to persons when it is subject of a nonrestictive dependent clause set off by commas:

La señora Gómez, quien (or que) es profesora, conoce a mi madre / Mrs. Gómez, who is a teacher, knows my mother.

• As direct object of a verb referring only to persons, the relative pronoun *quien* or *quienes* may be used with the personal *a (a quien, a quienes)* instead of *que:*

La muchacha que (or a quien) Ud. vio en el baile es mi hermana / The girl whom you saw at the dance is my sister.

• As object of a preposition referring only to persons:

> *¿Conoces a la chica con quien tomé el almuerzo?* / Do you
>   know the girl with whom I had lunch?
> *¿Conoces a los chicos con quienes María tomó el almuerzo?* /
>   Do you know the boys with whom Mary had lunch?
> *¿Conoce Ud. a los hombres de quienes hablo?* / Do you know
>   the men of whom (about whom) I am talking?

§6.5–3 *el cual, la cual, los cuales, las cuales* / who, that, whom, which, the one which, the ones which, the one who, the ones who

These relative pronouns may be used in place of *que* to clarify the gender and number of *que:*

> *La madre de José, la cual es muy inteligente, es dentista* /
>   Joseph's mother, who is very intelligent, is a dentist.

These substitute relative pronouns may also refer to things:

> *El libro, el cual está sobre la mesa, es mío* / The book, which is
>   on the table, is mine.

These relative pronouns are also used as substitutes for *el que, la que, los que, las que* when used as the subject of a nonrestrictive dependent clause set off by commas:

> *La señora Gómez, la cual (or la que, or quien, or que) es
>   profesora, conoce a mi madre* / Mrs. Gómez, who is a teacher,
>   knows my mother.

These relative pronouns, as well as *el que, la que, los que, las que,* are used as objects of prepositions except with *a, con, de, en*—in which case the relative pronoun *que* is preferred with things. These relative pronouns *(el cual, la cual, los cuales, las cuales* and *el que, la que, los que, las que)* are commonly used with the following prepositions: *para, por, sin, delante de, cerca de,* and *sobre:*

> *En este cuarto, hay una gran ventana por la cual se ve el sol
>   por la mañana* / In this room, there is a large window through
>   which you (one, anyone) can see the sun in the morning.

These compound relative pronouns refer to persons as well as things and can be used as subject of a verb or direct object of a verb when used in a nonrestrictive dependent clause separated from its antecedent and set off with commas.

§6.5 – 4 *lo cual* / which; *lo que* / what, that which

These are neuter compound relative pronouns. They do not refer to an antecedent of any gender or number.

Lo cual and *lo que* refer to a statement, a clause, an idea:

Mi hijo Juan estudia sus lecciones todos los días, lo cual es bueno / My son John studies his lessons every day, which is good.

Mi hija recibió buenas notas, lo que me gustó / My daughter received good marks, which pleased me.

Lo que is also used to express "what" in the sense of "that which:"

Comprendo lo que Ud. dice / I understand what (that which) you say.

Lo que Ud. dice es verdad / What (That which) you say is true.

§6.5–5 *cuanto = todo lo que* / all that

As a relative pronoun, *cuanto* may be used in place of *todo lo que:*

Todo lo que Ud. dice es verdad;

OR

Cuanto Ud. dice es verdad / All that (All that which) you say is true.

§6.5–6 *cuyo, cuya, cuyos, cuyas* / whose

This word (and its forms as given) refers to persons and things. Strictly speaking, *cuyo,* etc. is not regarded as a relative pronoun but rather as a relative possessive adjective. It agrees in gender and number with what is possessed (whose . . .), not with the possessor. Its position is directly in front of the noun it modifies.

El señor García, cuyos hijos son inteligentes, es profesor / Mr. García, whose children are intelligent, is a professor.

El muchacho, cuya madre es profesora, es inteligente / The boy, whose mother is a professor, is intelligent.

| Mnemonic Tip | The forms of *cuyo* cannot be used as an interrogative when you ask "Whose is . . . ?" You must use *de quién: ¿De quién es este libro?* |

When referring to parts of the body, use a *quien* instead of *cuyo:*

> *La niña, a quien la madre lavó las manos, es bonita* / The child, whose hands the mother washed, is pretty.

§6.6 Interrogative Pronouns

See also specific interrogatives (*qué, cuál,* etc.) in the index.

Here are a few common interrogatives that you should be aware of. Note the required accent mark on these words when used in a question.

¿qué . . . ? / what . . . ?
¿cuál . . . ? / which, which one . . . ?
¿cuáles . . . ? / which, which ones . . . ?
¿quién . . . ? ¿quiénes . . . ? / who . . . ?
¿a quién . . . ? ¿a quiénes . . . ? / whom . . . ? to whom . . . ?
¿de quién . . . ? / of whom, from whom, by whom, whose . . . ?
¿De quién es este lápiz? / Whose is this pencil?

---

§6.7 Indefinite Pronouns

algo / something, anything
(with *sin,* use *nada: sin nada* / without anything)
alguien / anybody, anyone, someone, somebody
(with *sin,* use *nadie: sin nadie* / without anyone)
alguno, alguna, algunos, algunas / some, any

§6.8 Negative Pronouns

nada / nothing: *sin nada* / without anything
(after *sin, nada* is used instead of *algo: Ella no quiere nada* / She does not want anything.)
nadie / nobody, no one, not anyone, not anybody: *sin nadie* / without anybody
(after *sin, nadie* is used instead of *alguien*)
ninguno, ninguna / no one, none, not any, not anybody

EJERCICIOS/EXERCISES

The answers to these exercises begin right after the last question in each group.

I. Translate the following Spanish sentences into English. **Then write the Spanish sentences for practice on the lines.** Refer to the preceding pages in this lesson to check your work.

1. La muchacha que habla con Juan es mi hermana.

   _____

2. El libro que está en la mesa es mío. _____

   _____

3. El señor Molina es el profesor que admiro. _____

   _____

4. La composición que Ud. lee es mía. _____

   _____

5. La cama en que duermo es grande. _____

   _____

6. Yo sé quien lo hizo. _____

   _____

7. Quien escucha oye. _____

   _____

8. La señora Gómez, quien (*or* que) es profesora, conoce a mi hermano. _____

   _____

   _____

9. La muchacha que (*or* a quien) Ud. vio en el baile es mi hermana. _____

   _____

   _____

10. ¿Conoces a los chicos con quienes María tomó el almuerzo? _____

    _____

11. La madre de José, la cual es muy inteligente, es dentista. _____

    _____

12. Comprendo lo que Ud. dice. _____

_____

13. Todo lo que Ud. dice es verdad. _____

_____

14. El señor García, cuyos hijos son inteligentes,
    trabaja mucho. _____

_____

15. ¿De quién es este lápiz? _____

_____

**II. Vocabulary. Several words in a single word. Seek
and find.**

How many Spanish words can you find in the Spanish
word **nombres** / nouns? You may use the letters in the
word **nombres** more than once, in any order, and you
may add accent signs or a tilde (ñ), if necessary, in
order to form new words; for example, just to get you
started, the Spanish words **me** and **es** are in the word
nombres. So is the word **señor** if you add the tilde on n
(ñ). **Find at least ten Spanish words** and write them
on the lines below.

1. _____   7. _____
2. _____   8. _____
3. _____   9. _____
4. _____ 10. _____
5. _____ 11. _____
6. _____ 12. _____

**III. Vocabulary. Several words in a single word. Here is
another word.**

How many Spanish words can you find in the Spanish
word **adjetivos** / adjectives? **Find at least six Spanish
words** and write them on the lines below.

1. _____   5. _____
2. _____   6. _____
3. _____   7. _____
4. _____   8. _____

Answers to the preceding group of exercises.

I.   1. The girl who is talking with John is my sister.
     2. The book which (that) is on the table is mine.
     3. Mr. Molina is the professor whom (that) I admire.
     4. The composition (that, which) you are reading is mine.
     5. The bed in which I sleep is large (big).
     6. I know who did it.
     7. Who listens hears. He who listens hears. She who listens hears.
     8. Mrs. Gómez, who is a teacher, knows my brother.
     9. The girl whom you saw at the dance is my sister.
    10. Do you know the boys with whom Mary had lunch?
    11. Joseph's mother, who is very intelligent, is a dentist.
    12. I understand what (that which) you say (you are saying).
    13. All that (All that which) you say is true.
    14. Mr. García, whose children are intelligent, works a lot.
    15. Whose is this pencil?

II. Vocabulary.

1.	no	7.	menos
2.	se	8.	menor
3.	es	9.	mes
4.	me	10.	ser
5.	sobre	11.	sé
6.	son	12.	señor

III. Vocabulary.

1.	se	5.	sí
2.	sé	6.	da
3.	es	7.	días
4.	si	8.	adiós

§7.

Verbs

§7.1
AGREEMENT

§7.1–1
Subject and Verb

A subject and verb form must agree in person and number. By person is meant 1st, 2nd, or 3rd; by number is meant singular or plural. To get a picture of the three persons in the singular and in the plural, see subject pronouns in §6.

§7.1–2
Subject and Reflexive Pronoun of a Reflexive Verb

A subject and reflexive pronoun must agree in person and number. To get a picture of the correct reflexive pronoun that goes with the subject, according to the person you need (1st, 2nd or 3rd, singular or plural), see reflexive pronouns in §6.

§7.2
TYPES

§7.2–1
Auxiliary (or helping) Verb *haber* / to have

The auxiliary (helping) verb *haber* is used in any of the seven simple tenses + the past participle of the main verb to form the seven compound tenses.

§7.2–2
Transitive Verbs

A transitive verb is a verb that takes a direct object. It is transitive because the action passes over from the subject and directly affects someone or something in some way.

> *Veo a mi amigo.* / I see my friend.
> *Abro la ventana.* / I open the window.

When the direct object of the verb is a pronoun, it is placed in front of the verb most of the time; at other times it is attached to an infinitive; if the main verb is *poder, querer, saber, ir a* + infinitive, the direct object pronoun may be

77

placed in front of the main verb instead of attaching it to the infinitive; at other times, the direct object pronoun is attached to a present participle. For an in-depth analysis of the word order of elements in Spanish sentences, particularly pronouns, review §6.

Here are the same sentences. as above, but with direct object pronouns instead of direct object nouns:

> *(Yo) lo veo.* / I see him.
> *(Yo) la abro.* / I open it.

For the position of pronouns in other types of sentences in Spanish, review position of object pronouns in §6.

§7.2–3 Intransitive Verbs

An intransitive verb is a verb that does not take a direct object. It is called intransitive because the action does not pass over from the subject and directly affect anyone or anything.

> *La profesora está hablando.* / The teacher is talking.
> *La señora Gómez salió temprano.* / Mrs. Gómez left early.

An intransitive verb takes an indirect object.

> *La profesora está hablando a los alumnos* / The teacher is talking to the students.

The indirect object noun is *alumnos* because it is preceded by a *los* (to the).

> *La profesora les está hablando.* / The teacher is talking to them.

The indirect object is the pronoun *les,* to them.

For a review of direct object pronouns and indirect object pronouns, see §6.

A transitive verb can take an indirect object.

> *La profesora da los libros a los alumnos.* / The teacher is giving the books to the pupils.

The direct object is *los libros;* the indirect object is a *los alumnos.*

> *La profesora los da a los alumnos.* / The teacher is giving them to the pupils.

The direct object pronoun is *los* (meaning *los libros*) and the indirect object noun is still *a los alumnos.*

> *La profesora les da los libros.* / The teacher is giving the books to them.

The indirect object pronoun is *les* (meaning "to them," i.e., *a los alumnos*).

La profesora se los da. / The teacher is giving them to them.

The indirect object pronoun *les* changes to *se* because *les* is 3rd person and it is followed by *los,* a direct object pronoun, which is also 3rd person. For a review of this point in Spanish grammar, see position of double object pronouns in §6.

You may clarify the indirect object pronoun *se* in this sentence by adding *a ellos* or *a los alumnos.*

§7.3 PARTICIPLES

§7.3–1 Past Participle

A past participle is regularly formed as follows:

Infinitive	Drop	Add	To the Stem	You Get
trabajar	*-ar*	*ado*	*trabaj*	*trabajado*
comer	*-er*	*ido*	*com*	*comido*
recibir	*-ir*	*ido*	*recib*	*recibido*

COMMON IRREGULAR PAST PARTICIPLES	
Infinitive	**Past Participle**
abrir / to open	*abierto* / opened
caer / to fall	*caído* / fallen
creer / to believe	*creído* / believed
cubrir / to cover	*cubierto* / covered
decir / to say, to tell	*dicho* / said, told
devolver / to return (something)	*devuelto* / returned (something)
escribir / to write	*escrito* / written
hacer / to do, to make	*hecho* / done, made
ir / to go	*ido* / gone
leer / to read	*leído* / read
morir / to die	*muerto* / died
oír / to hear	*oído* / heard
poner / to put	*puesto* / put
reír / to laugh	*reído* / laughed
resolver / to resolve, to solve	*resuelto* / resolved, solved
romper / to break	*roto* / broken
traer / to bring	*traído* / brought
ver / to see	*visto* / seen
volver / to return	*vuelto* / returned

Uses of the Past Participle

To form the compound tenses:

As in English, the past participle is needed to form the compound tenses in Spanish, of which there are seven. For the complete conjugation showing the forms of the six persons in each of the following compound tenses and for an explanation of how they are formed, see the specific name of each tense in the index.

THE COMPOUND TENSES	
Name of tense	**Example (1st person, singular)**
Present Perfect Indicative	*he hablado*
Pluperfect Indicative	*había hablado*
Preterit Perfect	*hube hablado*
Future Perfect	*habré hablado*
Conditional Perfect	*habría hablado*
Present Perfect Subjunctive	*haya hablado*
Pluperfect Subjunctive	*hubiera hablado* or *hubiese hablado*

To form the Perfect Infinitive:

haber hablado / to have spoken

To form the Perfect Participle:

habiendo hablado / having spoken

To serve as an adjective, which must agree in gender and number with the noun it modifies:

El señor Molina es muy respetado de todos los alumnos. / Mr. Molina is very respected by all the students.
La señora González es muy conocida. / Mrs. González is very well known.

To express the result of an action with *estar:*

La puerta está abierta. / The door is open.
Las cartas están escritas. / The letters are written.

To express the passive voice with *ser:*

La ventana fue abierta por el ladrón. / The window was opened by the robber.

**§7.3–2
Present
Participle**

A present participle is a verb form which, in English, ends in -ing: singing, eating, receiving. In Spanish, a present participle is regularly formed as follows:

drop the *ar* of an *-ar* ending verb, like *cantar,* and add *-ando:*
cantando / singing
drop the *er* of an *-er* ending verb, like *comer,* and add *-iendo:*
comiendo / eating
drop the *ir* of an *-ir* ending verb, like *recibir,* and add *-iendo:*
recibiendo / receiving

Gerunds and Present Participles

In English, a gerund also ends in -ing but there is a distinct difference in use between a gerund and a present participle. When a present participle is used as a noun it is called a gerund; for example: Reading is good. As a present participle: The boy fell asleep while reading.

In the first example (Reading is good), reading is a gerund because it is the subject of the verb "is." In Spanish, however, we must not use the present participle form as a noun to serve as a subject; we must use the infinitive form of the verb: *Leer es bueno.*

COMMON REGULAR PRESENT PARTICIPLES	
Infinitive	**Present Participle**
caer / to fall	*cayendo* / falling
construir / to construct	*construyendo* / constructing
corregir / to correct	*corrigiendo* / correcting
creer / to believe	*creyendo* / believing
decir / to say, to tell	*diciendo* / saying, telling
despedirse / to say good-bye	*despidiéndose* / saying good-bye
divertirse / to enjoy oneself	*divirtiéndose* / enjoying oneself
dormir / to sleep	*durmiendo* / sleeping
ir / to go	*yendo* / going
leer / to read	*leyendo* / reading
mentir / to lie (tell a falsehood)	*mintiendo* / lying
morir / to die	*muriendo* / dying
oír / to hear	*oyendo* / hearing
pedir / to ask (for), to request	*pidiendo* / asking (for), requesting
poder / to be able	*pudiendo* / being able
reír / to laugh	*riendo* / laughing
repetir / to repeat	*repitiendo* / repeating
seguir / to follow	*siguiendo* / following
sentir / to feel	*sintiendo* / feeling
servir / to serve	*sirviendo* / serving
traer / to bring	*trayendo* / bringing
venir / to come	*viniendo* / coming
vestir / to dress	*vistiendo* / dressing

Uses of the Present Participle

To form the progressive tenses:

The progressive present is formed by using *estar* in the present tense plus the present participle of the main verb you are using.

Estoy hablando. / I am talking.

The progressive past is formed by using *estar* in the imperfect indicative plus the present participle of the main verb you are using.

Estaba hablando. / I was talking.

Instead of using *estar,* as noted above, to form these two progressive tenses, sometimes *ir* is used:

Va hablando. / He (she) keeps right on talking.
Iba hablando. / He (she) kept right on talking.

To express vividly an action that occurred (preterit + present participle):

El niño entró llorando en la casa. / The little boy came crying into the house.

To express the English use of "by" + present participle in Spanish, we use the gerund form, which has the same ending as a present participle.

Trabajando se gana dinero. / By working, one earns (a person earns) money.
Estudiando mucho, Pepe recibió buenas notas. / By studying hard, Joe received good grades.

No preposition is used in front of the present participle (the Spanish gerund) even though it is expressed in English as "by" + present participle.

In Spanish we us *al* + infinitive (not + present participle) to express "on" or "upon" + present participle:

Al entrar en la casa, el niño comenzó a llorar. / Upon entering the house, the little boy began to cry.

To form the perfect participle:

habiendo hablado / having talked

§7.4
VERBS AND
PREPOSITIONS

A verb right after a preposition is in the infinitive form:

Pablo salió sin hablar. / Paul went out without talking.

§7.4–1
Verbs of
Motion
Take the
Preposition *a*
+ Infinitive

ir a / to go to
regresar a / to return to
salir a / to go out to
venir a / to come to
volver a / to return to

EXAMPLE:

> *María fue a comer.* Mary went to eat.

§7.4–2
Verbs That
Take the
Preposition *a*
+ Infinitive

aprender a / to learn to, to learn how to
aspirar a / to aspire to
ayudar a (hacer algo) / to help to
comenzar a / to begin to
decidirse a / to decide to
dedicarse a / to devote oneself to
detenerse a / to pause to, to stop to
empezar a / to begin to, to start to
enseñar a / to teach to
invitar a / to invite to
negarse a / to refuse to
ponerse a / to begin to, to start to
prepararse a / to prepare (oneself) to
principiar a / to begin to, to start to
venir a / to end up by
volver a / to do something again

EXAMPLES:

> *El señor Gómez se negó a ir.* / Mr. Gómez refused to go.
> *Juana se puso a correr.* / Jane began to run.
> *El muchacho volvió a jugar.* / The boy played again.

§7.4–3
Verbs That
Take the
Preposition *a*
+ Noun (or
Pronoun)

acercarse a / to approach
asistir a / to attend, to be present at
asomarse a / to appear at
dar a / to face, to overlook, to look out upon, to look out over
dedicarse a / to devote oneself to
echar una carta al correo / to mail, to post a letter
jugar a / to play (a game, sport, cards)

llegar a ser / to become
querer a / to love
ser aficionado a / to be fond of, to be a fan of
subir a / to get on, to get into (a bus, a train, a vehicle)

EXAMPLES:

> *Nos acercamos a la ciudad.* / We are approaching the city.
> *Una muchacha bonita se asomó a la puerta.* / A pretty girl
>   appeared at the door.
> *Mi cuarto da al jardín.* / My room faces the garden.
> *Me dedico a mis estudios.* / I devote myself to my studies.

§7.4–4 Verbs That Take the Preposition *con* + Infinitive

contar con / to count on, to rely on
soñar con / to dream of, to dream about

EXAMPLES:

> *Cuento con tener éxito.* / I am counting on being successful.
> *Sueño con ir a Chile.* / I dream of going to Chile.

§7.4–5 Verbs That Take the Preposition *con* + Noun (or Pronoun)

casarse con / to marry, to get married to
cumplir con / to fulfill
dar con / to meet, to find, to come upon
encontrarse con / to run into, to meet by chance

EXAMPLE:

> *José se casó con Ana.* / Joseph married Anna.

§7.4–6 Verbs That Take the Preposition *de* + Infinitive

acabar de / to have just
acordarse de / to remember to
alegrarse de / to be glad to
cansarse de / to become tired of
dejar de / to stop, to fail to
ocuparse de / to be busy with, to attend to
olvidarse de / to forget to
tratar de / to try to

EXAMPLES:

> *Guillermo acaba de llegar.* / William has just arrived.
> *Me alegro de hablarle.* / I am glad to talk to you.
> *Me canso de esperar el autobús.* / I'm getting tired of waiting
>   for the bus.

§7.4–7
Verbs That Take the Preposition *de* + Noun (or Pronoun)

acordarse de / to remember
aprovecharse de / to take advantage of
bajar de / to get out of, to descend from, to get off
burlarse de / to make fun of
cambiar de / to change (trains, buses, clothes, etc.)
cansarse de / to become tired of

EXAMPLES:

Me acuerdo de aquel hombre. / I remember that man.
Vamos a aprovecharnos de esta oportunidad. / Let's take advantage of this opportunity.
Después de bajar del tren, fui a comer. / After getting off the train, I went to eat.
Todos los días cambio de ropa. / Every day I change my clothes.
Me canso de este trabajo. / I am getting tired of this work.

§7.4–8
Verbs That Generally Take the Preposition *en* + Infinitive

consentir en / to consent to
convenir en / to agree to, to agree on
empeñarse en / to persist in, to insist on
insistir en / to insist on
quedar en / to agree to, to agree on
tardar en / to be late / (to delay) / in

EXAMPLES:

El muchacho se empeñó en salir. / The boy insisted on going out.
El avión tardó en llegar. / The plane was late in arriving.

§7.4–9
Verbs That Generally Take the Preposition *en* + Noun (or Pronoun)

apoyarse en / to lean against, to lean on
confiar en / to rely on, to trust in
consistir en / to consist of
entrar en / to enter (into), to go into
fijarse en / to stare at, to notice, to take notice, to observe
pensar en / to think of, to think about (*pensar en* is used when asking or when stating what or whom a person is thinking of)
ponerse en camino / to set out, to start out

EXAMPLES:

Me apoyé en la puerta. / I leaned against the door.
Entré en el restaurante. / I entered (I went in) the restaurant.
¿En qué piensa Ud.? / What are you thinking of?
Pienso en mi trabajo. / I am thinking of my work.

§7.4–10
Verbs That Generally Take the Preposition *por* + Infinitive, Noun, Pronoun, Adjective

acabar por / to end up by
dar por / to consider, to regard as
darse por / to pretend (to be something), to think oneself (to be something)
estar por / to be in favor of
interesarse por / to take an interest in
preguntar por / to ask for, to inquire about

EXAMPLES:

Domingo acabó por casarse con Elena. / Dominic finally ended up by marrying Helen.
¿Mi libro de español? Lo doy por perdido. / My Spanish book? I consider it lost.
La señorita López se da por actriz. / Miss López pretends to be an actress.

§7.4–11
Verb + No Preposition + Infinitive

Verbs That Do Not Ordinarily Take a Preposition When Followed by an Infinitive

deber + infinitive / must, ought to

Debo hacer mis lecciones. / I must (ought to) do my lessons.

decidir + infinitive / to decide
dejar + infinitive / to allow to, to let

Mi madre me dejó salir. / My mother allowed me to go out.
Dejé caer mi libro. / I dropped my book (I let my book fall).

desear + infinitive / to desire to, to wish to

Deseo tomar un café. / I wish to have a cup of coffee.

esperar + infinitive / to expect to, to hope to

Espero ir a la América del Sur este invierno. / I expect to go to South America this winter.

hacer + infinitive / to do, to make, to have something made or done

Tú me haces reír. / You make me laugh.

necesitar + infinitive / to need

> *Necesito pasar una hora en la biblioteca.* / I need to spend an hour in the library.

oír + infinitive / to hear

> *Le oí entrar por la ventana.* / I heard him enter through the window.

pensar + infinitive / to intend to, to plan to

> *Pienso hacer un viaje a México.* / I plan to take a trip to Mexico.

poder + infinitive / to be able to, can

> *Puedo venir a verle a la una.* / I can come to see you at one o'clock.

preferir + infinitive / to prefer

> *Prefiero quedarme en casa esta noche.* / I prefer to stay at home this evening.

prometer + infinitive / to promise

> *Prometo venir a verle a las ocho.* / I promise to come to see you at eight o'clock.

querer + infinitive / to want to, to wish to

> *Quiero comer ahora.* / I want to eat now.

saber + infinitive / to know how to

> *¿Sabe Ud. nadar?* / Do you know how to swim?
> *Sí, yo sé nadar.* / Yes, I know how to swim.

ver + infinitive / to see

> *Veo venir el tren.* / I see the train coming.

EJERCICIOS/EXERCISES

The answers to these exercises begin right after the last question in each group.

I. Write the **past participle** for each of the following verbs. The first six are formed regularly and easily. The rest of them are irregular and you must make an effort to memorize their unusual irregular forms as past participles. Study again the preceding pages to help yourself.

1. trabajar _____	11. hacer _____
2. hablar _____	12. poner _____
3. comer _____	13. volver _____
4. aprender _____	14. ver _____
5. recibir _____	15. traer _____
6. vivir _____	16. romper _____
7. abrir _____	17. resolver _____
8. caer _____	18. reír _____
9. decir _____	19. morir _____
10. ir _____	20. oír _____

II. Here, write the **present participle** (**gerundio** in Spanish) for each of the following verbs. The first three are formed regularly and easily. The rest of them are irregular and you must make an effort to memorize their unusual irregular forms as present participles. Study again the preceding pages to help yourself.

1. cantar _____	9. ir _____
2. comer _____	10. leer _____
3. recibir _____	11. mentir _____
4. caer _____	12. morir _____
5. decir _____	13. oír _____
6. despedirse _____	14. pedir _____
7. divertirse _____	15. traer _____
8. dormir _____	16. venir _____

Answers to the preceding group of exercises.

I. Past participles

1.	trabajado	11.	hecho
2.	hablado	12.	puesto
3.	comido	13.	vuelto
4.	aprendido	14.	visto
5.	recibido	15.	traído
6.	vivido	16.	roto
7.	abierto	17.	resuelto
8.	caído	18.	reído
9.	dicho	19.	muerto
10.	ido	20.	oído

II. Present participles (gerundio in Spanish)

1.	cantando	9.	yendo
2.	comiendo	10.	leyendo
3.	recibiendo	11.	mintiendo
4.	cayendo	12.	muriendo
5.	diciendo	13.	oyendo
6.	despidiéndose	14.	pidiendo
7.	divirtiéndose	15.	trayendo
8.	durmiendo	16.	viviendo

**§7.4–12
Verbs That Do Not Ordinarily Require a Preposition Whereas in English a Preposition Is Used**

buscar / to look for, to search for

> Busco mi libro. / I am looking for my book.

escuchar / to listen to

> Escucho la música. / I am listening to the music.

esperar / to wait for

> Espero el autobús. / I am waiting for the bus.

guardar cama / to stay in bed

> La semana pasada guardé cama. / Last week I stayed in bed.

mirar / to look at

> *Miro el cielo.* / I am looking at the sky.

pagar / to pay for

> *Pagué los billetes.* / I paid for the tickets.

pedir / to ask for

> *Pido un libro.* / I am asking for a book.

§7.5
TENSES AND MOODS

§7.5–1
Present Indicative

This tense is used most of the time in Spanish and English. It indicates:

• An action or a state of being at the present time.

EXAMPLES:

> *Hablo español.* / I speak Spanish.
> *Creo en Dios.* / I believe in God.

• Habitual action.

EXAMPLE:

> *Voy a la biblioteca todos los días.* / I go to the library every day.

• A general truth, something which is permanently true.

EXAMPLE:

> *Seis menos dos son cuatro.* / Six minus two are four.

- Vividness when talking or writing about past events.

  EXAMPLE:

  > *El asesino se pone pálido. Tiene miedo. Sale de la casa y corre a lo largo del río.* / The murderer turns pale. He is afraid. He goes out of the house and runs along the river.

- A near future.

  EXAMPLE:

  > *Mi hermano llega mañana.* / My brother arrives tomorrow.

- An action or state of being that occurred in the past and continues up to the present. In Spanish this is an idiomatic use of the present tense of a verb with *hace,* which is also in the present.

  EXAMPLE:

  > *Hace tres horas que miro la televisión.* / I have been watching television for three hours.

- The meaning of "almost" or "nearly" when used with *por poco.*

  EXAMPLE:

  > *Por poco me matan.* / They almost killed me.

This tense is regularly formed as follows:

Drop the *ar* ending of an infinitive, like *hablar,* and add: *o, as, a; amos, áis, an.*

| Tip | You then get: *hablo, hablas, habla; hablamos, habláis, hablan.* |

Drop the *er* ending of an infinitive, like *beber,* and add: *o, es, e; emos, éis, en.*

> | Tip | *You then get:* bebo, bebes, bebe;
> bebemos, bebéis, beben. |

Drop the *ir* / ending of an infinitive, like *recibir,* and add: *o, es, e; imos, ís, en.*

> | Tip | You then get: *recibo, recibes, recibe;*
> *recibimos, recibís, reciben.* |

§7.5–2 Imperfect Indicative

This is a past tense. Imperfect suggests incomplete. The Imperfect tense expresses an action or a state of being that was continuous in the past and its completion is not indicated. It expresses:

- An action that was going on in the past at the same time as another action.

    EXAMPLE:

    > *Mi hermano leía y mi padre hablaba.* / My brother was reading and my father was talking.

- An action that was going on in the past when another action occurred.

    EXAMPLE:

    > *Mi hermana cantaba cuando yo entré.* / My sister was singing when I came in.

- An action that a person did habitually in the past.

    EXAMPLE:

    > *Cuando estábamos en Neuva York, íbamos al cine todos los sábados.* / When we were in New York, we went to the movies every Saturday; When we were in New York, we used to go to the movies every Saturday.

- A description of a mental, emotional, or physical condition in the past.

EXAMPLES:

> (mental condition)   *Quería ir al cine.* / I wanted to go to the movies.
> (emotional condition)   *Estaba contento de verlo.* / I was happy to see him.
> (physical condition)   *Mi madre era hermosa cuando era pequeña.* / My mother was beautiful when she was young.

- The time of day in the past.

  EXAMPLES:

> *¿Qué hora era?* / What time was it?
> *Eran las tres.* / It was three o'clock.

- An action or state of being that occurred in the past and lasted for a certain length of time prior to another past action.

  EXAMPLE:

> *Hacía tres horas que miraba la televisión cuando mi hermano entró.* / I had been watching television for three hours when my brother came in.

- An indirect quotation in the past.

  EXAMPLE:

> Present: *Dice que quiere venir a mi casa.* / He says he wants to come to my house.
> Past: Dijo que quería venir a mi casa. / He said he wanted to come to my house.

This tense is regularly formed as follows:

Drop the *-ar* ending of an infinitive, like *hablar,* and add: *aba, abas, aba; ábamos, abais, aban*

You then get: *hablaba, hablabas, hablaba;*
hablábamos, hablabais, hablaban.

The usual equivalent in English is: I was talking, I used to talk, I talked.

Drop the *-er* ending of an infinitive, like *beber,* or the *-ir* ending of an infinitive, like *recibir,* and add: *ía, ías, ía; íamos, íais, ían*

You then get: *bebía, bebías, bebía;*
bebíamos, bebíais, bebían.

The usual equivalent in English is: I was drinking, I used to drink, I drank.

The answers to these exercises begin right after the last question in each group.

Sharing information. Proficiency in Speaking and Writing

Situation: You are planning to spend a summer session studying Spanish at the **Universidad de Madrid.** You are looking for an apartment. Read the newspaper announcement of an apartment vacancy that is given below.

You are sharing this information with Richard, a student in your Spanish class, who is also making plans to study Spanish in Madrid. Maybe you can share the apartment with him.

While talking with Richard, you may add words and ideas of your own. Refer to the following vocabulary below and on the next page, according to your needs, while providing responses to the seven questions.

GRAN APARTAMENTO
en Madrid
buena vista del parque El Retiro
2 dormitorios—2 cuartos de baño
cocina moderna, gran balcón
cerca del Museo del Prado
tel. 12-34-56-78

---

1. After your conversation with Richard, write on the chalkboard in your Spanish classroom or on a sheet of paper what you and he said. You may practice writing on the lines below. Answer the questions in complete sentences in Spanish.

1. ¿En qué ciudad está situado el apartamento?
   _____

2. ¿Cuántos dormitorios hay en el apartamento?
   _____

3. ¿Cuántos baños hay? _____

4. ¿Es grande o pequeño el apartamento?
   _____

5. ¿Cómo se llama el parque cerca del apartamento?

_____

_____

6. ¿Cómo se llama el museo cerca del apartamento?

_____

7. ¿Cuál es el número de teléfono?　_____

Vocabulario

apartamento _n.m._
　apartment
balcón _n.m._ balcony
baño _n.m._ bath
buena _adj., f.s._ good
cerca _adv._ near, **cerca del**
　near the
ciudad _n.f._ city
cocina _n.f._ kitchen
¿Cómo se llama el parque?
　What is the name of the
　park?
cuál _pron._ what, which
cuántos _adj., m.pl._ how
　many, how much
cuarto _n.m._ room

del of the **(de + el > del)**
dormitorio _n.m._ bedroom
en _prep._ in; **¿en qué?** in
　what?
está situado is situated,
　located
gran, grande _adj._ big, large
hay there is, there are
moderna _adj., f.s._ modern
museo _n.m._ museum
número _n.m._ number
o _conj._ or
parque _n.m._ park
pequeño _adj. m.s._ small
teléfono _n.m._ telephone
vista _n.f._ view

Answers to the preceding group of exercises.

1. El apartamento está situado en Madrid.

2. Hay dos dormitorios en el apartamento.

3. Hay dos cuartos _(rooms)_ de baño.

4. El apartamento es grande.

5. El parque cerca del apartamento se llama El Retiro.

6. El museo cerca del apartamento se llama el Museo del Prado.

7. El número de teléfono es 12-34-56-78.

§7.5–3
Preterit

This tense expresses an action that was completed at some time in the past.

EXAMPLES:

> *Mi padre llegó ayer.* / My father arrived yesterday.
> *María fue a la iglesia esta mañana.* / Mary went to church this morning.
> *¿Qué pasó?* / What happened?
> *Tomé el desayuno a las siete.* / I had breakfast at seven o'clock.
> *Salí de casa, tomé el autobús y llegué a la escuela a las ocho.* / I left the house, I took the bus and I arrived at school at eight o'clock.

In Spanish, some verbs have a different meaning when used in the preterit.

EXAMPLES:

> *La conocí la semana pasada en el baile.* / I met her last week at the dance.
> *Pude hacerlo.* / I succeeded in doing it.
> *No pude hacerlo.* / I failed to do it.
> *Quise llamarlo.* / I tried to call you.
> *No quise hacerlo.* / I refused to do it.
> *Supe la verdad.* / I found out the truth.
> *Tuve una carta de mi amigo Roberto.* / I received a letter from my friend Robert.

This tense is regularly formed as follows:

- Drop the *-ar* ending of an infinitive, like *hablar,* and add: *é, aste, ó; amos, asteis, aron.*

 Tip

> You then get: *hablé, hablaste, habló, hablamos, hablasteis, hablaron*

The usual equivalent in English is: I talked, I did talk; you talked, you did talk, etc. I spoke, I did speak; you spoke, you did speak, etc.

- Drop the -er ending of an infinitive, like *beber,* or the -ir ending of an infinitive, like *recibir,* and add:
  í, iste, ió; imos, isteis, ieron.

Tip

> You then get: *bebí, bebiste, bebió,*
> *bebimos, bebisteis, bebieron.*

§7.5–4
Future

In Spanish and English, the future tense is used to express an action or a state of being that will take place at some time in the future.

> *Lo haré.* / I shall do it; I will do it.

Also, in Spanish the future tense is used to indicate:

- Conjecture regarding the present.

> *¿Qué hora será?* / I wonder what time it is.
> *¿Quién será?* / Who can that be? I wonder who that is.

- Probability regarding the present.

> *Serán las cinco.* / It is probably five o'clock; It must be five
> o'clock.
> *Tendrá muchos amigos.* / He probably has many friends; He
> must have many friends.

- An indirect quotation.

> *María dice que vendrá mañana.* / Mary says that she will come
> tomorrow.

Remember that the future is never used in Spanish after *si* when *si* means "if."
This tense is regularly formed as follows:
   Add the following endings to the whole infinitive:
é, ás, á; emos, éis, án.

Tip

> You then get: *hablaré, hablarás, hablará,*
> *hablaremos, hablaréis, hablarán.*

§7.5–5
Conditional

The conditional is used in Spanish and in English to express:

- An action that you would do if something else were possible.

  Iría a España si tuviera dinero. / I would go to Spain if I had money.

- A conditional desire. This is a conditional of courtesy.

  Me gustaría tomar una limonada. / I would like to have a lemonade.

- An indirect quotation.

  María dijo que vendría mañana. / Mary said that she would come tomorrow.
  María decía que vendría mañana. / Mary was saying that she would come tomorrow.

- Conjecture regarding the past.

  ¿Quién sería? / I wonder who that was.

- Probability regarding the past.

  Serían las cinco cuando salieron. / It was probably five o'clock when they went out.

This tense is regularly formed as follows:

Add the following endings to the whole infinitive: *ía, ías, ía; íamos, íais, ían.*

 Tip

> You then get: *hablaría, hablarías, hablaría, hablaríamos, hablaríais, hablarían.*

§7.5–6
Present
Subjunctive

The subjunctive mood is used in Spanish much more than in English. In Spanish the present subjunctive is used:

- To express a command in the *usted* or *ustedes* form, either in the affirmative or negative.

  Siéntese Ud. / Sit down.
  No se siente Ud. / Don't sit down.

- To express a negative command in the familiar form *(tú).*

  No te sientes. / Don't sit down.
  No duermas. / Don't sleep.

- To express a command in the first person plural, either in the affirmative or negative *(nosotros)*.

  Sentémonos. / Let's sit down.
  No entremos. / Let's not go in.

- After a verb that expresses some kind of wish, insistence, preference, suggestion, or request.

  Quiero que María lo haga. / I want Mary to do it.
  Insisto en que María lo haga. / I insist that Mary do it.

- After a verb that expresses doubt, fear, joy, hope, sorrow, or some other emotion.

  Dudo que María lo haga. / I doubt that Mary is doing it; I doubt
  that Mary will do it.
  No creo que María venga. / I don't believe (I doubt) that Mary is
  coming; I don't believe (I doubt)
  that Mary will come.

- After certain impersonal expressions that show necessity, doubt, regret, importance, urgency, or possibility.

  Es necesario que María lo haga. / It is necessary for Mary to
  do it; It is necessary that
  Mary do it.
  No es cierto que María venga. / It is doubtful (not certain) that
  Mary is coming; It is
  doubtful (not certain) that
  Mary will come.

- After certain conjunctions of time, such as *antes (de) que, cuando, en cuanto, después (de) que, hasta que, mientras,* and the like.

  Le hablaré a María cuando venga. / I shall talk to Mary when
  she comes.
  Vámonos antes (de) que llueva. / Let's go before it rains.

- After certain conjunctions that express a condition, negation, purpose, such as *a menos que, con tal que, para que, a fin de que, sin que, en caso (de) que,* and the like.

  Démelo con tal que sea bueno. / Give it to me provided that it
  is good.
  Me voy a menos que venga. / I'm leaving unless he comes.

- After certain adverbs, such as *acaso, quizá,* and *tal vez.*

  Acaso venga mañana / Perhaps he will come tomorrow.
  Perhaps he is coming tomorrow.

- After *aunque* if the action has not yet occurred.

  Aunque María venga esta noche, no me quedo. / Although
  Mary may come tonight, I'm not staying; Although Mary is
  coming tonight, I'm not staying.

- In an adjectival clause if the antecedent is something or someone that is indefinite, negative, vague, or nonexistent.

  Busco un libro que sea interesante. / I'm looking for a book that is interesting.

  ¿Hay alguien aquí que hable francés? / Is there anyone here who speaks French?

  No hay nadie que pueda hacerlo. / There is no one who can do it.

- After *por más que* or *por mucho que.*

  Por más que hable usted, no quiero escuchar. / No matter how much you talk, I don't want to listen.

- After the expression *ojalá (que),* which expresses a great desire. This interjection means "would to God!" or "may God grant!" It is derived from the Arabic.

  ¡Ojalá que vengan mañana! / Would to God that they come tomorrow!

Tip	Finally, remember that the present subjunctive is never used in Spanish after *si* when *si* means "if."

The present subjunctive of regular verbs and many irregular verbs is normally formed as follows:

Go to the present indicative, 1st person singular of the verb you have in mind, drop the ending *o,* and

- for an *-ar* ending type, add: *e, es, e; emos, éis, en*
- for an *-er* or *-ir* ending type, add: *a, as, a; amos, áis, an*

Tip

You then get, for example: *hable, hables, hable; hablemos, habléis, hablen*

beba, bebas, beba; bebamos, bebáis, beban

reciba, recibas, reciba; recibamos, recibáis, reciban

Central Islip Public Library
33 Hawthorne Avenue
Central Islip, NY 11722

§7.5–7
Imperfect
Subjunctive

This past tense is used for the same reasons as the *presente de subjuntivo*—that is, after certain verbs, conjunctions, impersonal expressions, etc., which were explained and illustrated above. The main difference between these two tenses is the time of the action.

If the verb in the main clause is in the present indicative or future or present perfect indicative or imperative, the present subjunctive or the present perfect subjunctive is used in the dependent clause—provided, of course, that there is some element which requires the use of the subjunctive.

However, if the verb in the main clause is in the imperfect indicative, preterit, conditional, or pluperfect indicative, the imperfect subjunctive (this tense) or pluperfect subjunctive is ordinarily used in the dependent clause—provided, of course, that there is some element which requires the use of the subjunctive.

EXAMPLES:

Insistí en que María lo hiciera. / I insisted that Mary do it.
Se lo explicaba a María para que lo comprendiera. / I was explaining it to Mary so that she might understand it.

Note that the imperfect subjunctive is used after *como si* to express a condition contrary to fact.

EXAMPLE:

Me habla como si fuera un niño. / He speaks to me as if I were a child.

Finally, note that *quisiera* (the imperfect subjunctive of *querer*) can be used to express in a very polite way, I would like:

Quisiera hablar ahora. / I would like to speak now.

The imperfect subjunctive is regularly formed as follows:
For all verbs, drop the -*ron* ending of the 3rd person plural of the preterit and add the following endings:

ra, ras, ra;	OR	se, ses, se;
ramos, rais, ran		semos, seis, sen

EXAMPLES:

Preterit, 3rd Person Plural	Imperfect Subjunctive
bebieron (beber)	*bebiera, bebieras, bebiera; bebiéramos, bebierais, bebieran*
	OR
	bebiese, bebieses, bebiese; bebiésemos, bebieseis, bebiesen
dijeron (decir)	*dijera, dijeras, dijera; dijéramos, dijerais, dijeran*
	OR
	dijese, dijeses, dijese; dijésemos, dijeseis, dijesen
fueron (ir)	*fuera, fueras, fuera; fuéramos, fuerais, fueran*
	OR
	fuese, fueses, fuese; fuésemos, fueseis, fuesen

§7.5–8 Present Perfect Indicative

This tense expresses an action that took place at no definite time in the past. It is a compound tense because it is formed with the present indicative of *haber* (the auxiliary or helping verb) plus the past participle of the verb you have in mind.

(Yo) he hablado. / I have spoken.
(Tú) no has venido a verme. / You have not come to see me.
Elena ha ganado el premio. / Helen has won the prize.

§7.5–9 Pluperfect OR Past Perfect Indicative

In Spanish and English, this past tense is used to express an action which happened in the past before another past action. Since it is used in relation to another past action, the other past action is ordinarily expressed in the preterit.

In Spanish, this tense is formed with the imperfect indicative of *haber* plus the past participle of the verb you have in mind.

Cuando llegué a casa, mi hermano había salido. / When I arrived home, my brother had gone out.
Juan lo había perdido en la calle. / John had lost it in the street.

§7.5–10
Past Anterior
OR Preterit
Perfect

This past tense is compound because it is formed with the preterit of *haber* plus the past participle of the verb you are using. It is translated into English like the pluperfect indicative explained above.

This tense is ordinarily used in formal writing, such as history and literature. It is normally used after certain conjunctions of time, e.g., *después que, cuando, apenas, luego que, en cuanto.*

EXAMPLE:

Después que hubo hablado, salió. / After he had spoken, he left.

§7.5–11
Future Perfect
OR Future
Anterior

This compound tense is formed with the future of *haber* plus the past participle of the verb you have in mind. In Spanish and in English, this tense is used to express an action that will happen in the future before another future action. In English, this tense is formed by using "shall have" or "will have" plus the past participle of the verb you have in mind.

EXAMPLE:

María llegará mañana y habré terminado mi trabajo. / Mary will arrive tomorrow and I will have finished my work.

Also, in Spanish the future perfect is used to indicate conjecture or probability regarding recent past time.

EXAMPLES:

María se habrá acostado. / Mary has probably gone to bed; Mary must have gone to bed.
José habrá llegado. / Joseph has probably arrived; Joseph must have arrived.

§7.5–12
Conditional
Perfect

This is formed with the conditional of *haber* plus the past participle of the verb you have in mind. It is used in Spanish and English to express an action that you would have done if something else had been possible; that is, you would have done something on condition that something else had been possible.

In English it is formed by using *would have* plus the past participle of the verb you have in mind.

EXAMPLE:

Habría ido a España si hubiera tenido dinero. / I would have gone to Spain if I had had money.

Also, in Spanish the conditional perfect is used to indicate probability or conjecture in the past.

EXAMPLES:

Habrían sido las cinco cuando salieron. / It must have been five o'clock when they went out.

¿Quién habría sido? / Who could that have been? (or I wonder who that could have been).

§7.5–13 Present Perfect OR Past Subjunctive

This is formed by using the present subjunctive of *haber* as the helping verb plus the past participle of the verb you have in mind.

María duda que yo le haya hablado al profesor. / Mary doubts that I have spoken to the professor.

Siento que tú no hayas venido a verme. / I am sorry that you have not come to see me.

§7.5–14 Pluperfect OR Past Perfect Subjunctive

This is formed by using the imperfect subjunctive of *haber* as the helping verb plus the past participle of the verb you have in mind.

EXAMPLES:

Sentí mucho que no hubiera venido María. / I was very sorry that Mary had not come.

Me alegraba de que hubiera venido María. / I was glad that Mary had come.

§7.5–15 Progressive Forms of Tenses

• In Spanish, there are also progressive forms of tenses. They are the progressive present and the progressive past.

• The progressive present is formed by using *estar* in the present tense plus the present participle of your main verb: *Estoy hablando* (I am talking).

• The progressive past is formed by using *estar* in the imperfect indicative plus the present participle of your main verb: *Estaba hablando* (I was talking).

• The progressive forms are used when you want to emphasize or intensify an action: *Estoy hablando; Estaba hablando.*

§7.5–16
Passive Voice

Passsive voice means that the action of the verb falls on the subject; in other words, the subject receives the action:

> *La ventana fue abierta por el ladrón.* / The window was opened by the robber.

Note that *abierta* (really a form of the past participle *abrir / abierto*) is used as an adjective and it must agree in gender and number with the subject that it describes.

Active voice means that the subject performs the action and the subject is always stated:

> *El ladrón abrió la ventana.* / The robber opened the window.

To form the true passive, use *ser* + the past participle of the verb you have in mind; the past participle then serves as an adjective and it must agree in gender and number with the subject that it describes, as in the example given above. In the true passive, the agent (the doer) is always expressed with the preposition *por* in front of it. The formula for the true passive construction is: subject + tense of *ser* + past participle + *por* + the agent (the doer):

> *Estas composiciones fueron escritas por Juan.* / These compositions were written by John.

The reflexive pronoun *se* may be used to substitute for the true passive voice construction. When you use the *se* construction, the subject is a thing (not a person) and the doer (agent) is not stated:

> *Aquí se habla español.* / Spanish is spoken here.
> *Aquí se hablan español e inglés.* / Spanish and English are spoken here.
> *Se venden libros en esta tienda.* / Books are sold in this store.

There are a few standard idiomatic expressions that are commonly used with the pronoun *se.* These expressions are not truly passive, the pronoun *se* is not truly a reflexive pronoun, and the verb form is in the 3rd person singular only. In this construction, there is no subject expressed; the subject is contained in the use of *se* + the 3rd person singular of the verb at all times and the common translations into English are: it is . . . , people . . . , they . . . , one . . . .

> *Se cree que . . .* / It is believed that . . . , people believe that . . . , they believe that . . . , one believes that . . .

EJERCICIOS/EXERCISES

The answers to these exercises begin right after the last question in each group.

I. Translate the following Spanish sentences into English. **Then write the Spanish sentences for practice.** Refer to the preceding pages in this lesson if you have to.

1. Mi padre llegó ayer. _____

2. María fue a la iglesia esta mañana. _____
   _____

3. ¿Qué pasó? _____

4. Salí de casa, tomé el autobús, y llegué a la escuela a las ocho. _____
   _____
   _____

5. ¿Ana? La conocí la semana pasada en el baile.
   _____

6. Tuve una carta de mi amigo Roberto. _____
   _____

7. Lo haré. _____

8. María dice que vendrá mañana. _____
   _____

9. Yo iría a España si tuviera dinero. _____
   _____

10. Me gustaría tomar una limonada. _____
    _____

11. Isabel decía que vendría mañana. _____
    _____

12. Siéntese Ud., por favor _____

13. No se siente Ud. _____

14. No te sientes, por favor. _____

15. Sentémonos. _____

II.   1. Quiero que María lo haga. _____

_____

2. No creo que María venga. _____

_____

3. Démelo con tal que sea bueno. _____

_____

4. Vámonos antes (de) que llueva. _____

_____

5. ¿Hay alguien aquí que hable francés? _____

_____

6. ¡Ojalá que vengan mañana! _____

_____

7. Se lo explicaba a María para que lo comprendiera.

_____

_____

8. Este hombre me habla como si fuera un niño.

_____

_____

9. Yo he hablado. _____

10. Elena ha ganado el premio. _____

_____

11. Juan lo había perdido en la calle. _____

_____

12. María llegará mañana y yo habré terminado mi
    trabajo. _____

_____

13. Yo habría ido a España si hubiera tenido bastante
    dinero. _____

_____

14. Siento que tú no hayas venido a verme. _____

_____

15. Sentí mucho que no hubiera venido María. _____

_____

Answers to the preceding group of exercises.

I. 1. My father arrived yesterday.
    2. Mary went to church this morning.
    3. What happened?
    4. I left the house, I took the bus, and I arrived at school at eight o'clock.
    5. Anna? I met her last week at the dance.
    6. I received a letter from my friend Robert.
    7. I will (shall) do it.
    8. Mary says that she will come tomorrow.
    9. I would go to Spain if I had money.
    10. I would like to have a lemonade.
    11. Isabel was saying that she would come tomorrow.
    12. Sit down, please.
    13. Don't sit down.
    14. Don't sit down, please.
    15. Let's sit down.

II. 1. I want Mary to do it.
    2. I don't believe (I doubt) that Mary is coming; I don't believe (I doubt) that Mary will come.
    3. Give it to me provided that it is good.
    4. Let's go before it rains.
    5. Is there anyone here who speaks French?
    6. Would to God that they come tomorrow!
    7. I was explaining it to Mary so that she might understand it.
    8. This man talks to me as if I were a child.
    9. I have spoken.
    10. Helen has won the prize.
    11. John had lost it in the street.
    12. Mary will arrive tomorrow and I will have finished my work.
    13. I would have gone to Spain if I had had enough money.
    14. I am sorry that you have not come to see me.
    15. I was very sorry that Mary had not come.

> *Se cree que este criminal es culpable.* / It is believed that
>   this criminal is guilty.

Se dice que . . . . / It is said that . . . , people say that . . . , they
say that . . . , one says that . . . , you say . . .

> *Se dice que va a nevar esta noche.* / They say that it's going
>   to snow tonight.
> *¿Cómo se dice en español* ice cream? / How do you say "ice
>   cream" in Spanish?

Se sabe que . . . / It is known that . . . , people know that . . . ,
they know that . . . , one knows that . . .

> *Se sabe que María va a casarse con Juan.* / People know
>   that Mary is going to marry John.

The *se* reflexive pronoun construction is avoided if the subject is a person because there can be ambiguity in meaning. For example, how would you translate into English the following: *Se da un regalo.* Which of the following two meanings is intended? She (he) is being given a present, or She (he) is giving a present to himself (to herself). In correct Spanish you would have to say: *Le da (*a María, a Juan, etc.) un regalo. / He (she) is giving a present to Mary (to John, etc.). Avoid using the *se* construction in the passive when the subject is a person; change your sentence around and state it in the active voice to make the meaning clear. Otherwise, the pronoun *se* seems to go with the verb, as if the verb itself is reflexive, which gives an entirely different meaning. Another example: *Se miró* would mean "He (she) looked at himself (herself)," not "He (she) was looked at!" If you mean to say He (she) looked at him (at her), say: *La miró* or, if in the plural, say *La miraron. /* They looked at her.

§7.5–17 Imperative OR Command Mood

The imperative mood is used in Spanish and in English to express a command. We saw earlier that the subjunctive mood is used to express commands in the *Ud.* and *Uds.* forms, in addition to other uses of the subjunctive mood.

Here are other points you ought to know about the imperative.

• An indirect command or deep desire expressed in the third person singular or plural is in the subjunctive. Notice the use of "Let" or "May" in the English translations. *Que* introduces this kind of command.

¡Que lo haga Jorge! / Let George do it!
¡Que Dios se lo pague! / May God reward you!
¡Que entre Roberto! / Let Robert enter!
¡Que salgan! / Let them leave!

- In some indirect commands, *que* is omitted. Here, too, the subjunctive is used.

  ¡Viva el presidente! / Long live the president!

- The verb form of the affirmative singular familiar *(tú)* is the same as the 3rd person singular of the present indicative when expressing a command.

  ¡Entra pronto! / Come in quickly!
  ¡Sigue leyendo! / Keep on reading! OR Continue reading!

- There are some exceptions, however. The following verb forms are irregular in the affirmative singular imperative *(tú* form only).

di (decir)	*sal (salir)*	*val (valer)*
haz (hacer)	*sé (ser)*	*ve (ir)*
he (haber)	*ten (tener)*	*ven (venir)*
pon (poner)		

- In the affirmative command, 1st person plural, instead of using the present subjunctive command, *vamos a* (Let's or Let us) + infinitive may be used.

  Vamos a comer. OR *Comamos.* / Let's eat.
  Vamos a cantar. OR *Cantemos.* / Let's sing.

- In the affirmative command, 1st person plural, *vamos* may be used to mean "Let's go:"

  Vamos al cine. / Let's go to the movies.

- However, if in the negative (Let's not go), the present subjunctive of *ir* must be used:

  No vayamos al cine. / Let's not go to the movies.

- Note that *Vámonos* (1st person plural of *irse,* imperative) means "Let's go" or "Let's go away" or "Let's leave."

- Also note that *no nos vayamos* (1st person plural of *irse,* present subjunctive) means "Let's not go" or "Let's not go away" or "Let's not leave."

- The imperative in the affirmative familiar plural *(vosotros, vosotras)* is formed by dropping the final *r* of the infinitive and adding *d.*

  ¡Hablad! / Speak!   *¡Id!* / Go!
  ¡Comed! / Eat!   *¡Venid!* / Come!

- When forming the affirmative familiar plural *(vosotros, vosotras)* imperative of a reflexive verb, the final *d* on the infinitive must be dropped before the reflexive pronoun *os* is added, and both elements are joined to make one word.

    ¡Levantaos! / Get up!   *¡Sentaos!* / Sit down!

- When the final d is dropped in a reflexive verb ending in -ir, an accent mark must be written on the *i.*

    ¡Vestíos! / Get dressed!   *¡Divertíos!* / Have a good time!

- When forming the 1st person plural affirmative imperative of a reflexive verb, the final *s* must drop before the reflexive pronoun *os* is added, and both elements are joined to make one word. This requires an accent mark on the vowel of the syllable that was stressed before *os* was added. *Vamos + nos* changes to:

    ¡Vámonos! / Let's go! or Let's go away! or Let's leave!

- All negative imperatives in the familiar 2nd person singular *(tú)* and plural *(vosotros, vosotras)* are expressed in the present subjunctive.

    ¡No corras (tú)! / Don't run!
    ¡No corráis (vosotros or vosotras)! / Don't run!

- Object pronouns (direct, indirect, or reflexive) with an imperative verb form in the affirmative are attached to the verb form. Examples:

    ¡Hágalo (Ud.)! / Do it!
    ¡Díganoslo (Ud.)! / Tell it to us!
    ¡Dímelo (tú)! / Tell it to me!
    ¡Levántate (tú)! / Get up!

- Object pronouns (direct, indirect, or reflexive) with an imperative verb form in the negative are placed in front of the verb form. Compare the following examples with those given above:

    ¡No lo haga (Ud.)! / Don't do it!
    ¡No nos lo diga (Ud.)! / Don't tell it to us!
    ¡No me lo digas (tú)! / Don't tell it to me!
    ¡No te levantes (tú)! / Don't get up!

- Note that in Latin America the 2nd person plural familiar *(vosotros, vosotras)* forms are avoided. In place of them, the 3rd person plural *Uds.* forms are customarily used.

§7.5–18
Subjunctive

The subjunctive is not a tense; it is a mood or mode. Usually, when we speak in Spanish or English, we use the indicative mood. We use the subjunctive mood in Spanish for certain reasons.

Uses

7.5–18.1 AFTER CERTAIN CONJUNCTIONS

When the following conjunctions introduce a new clause, the verb in that new clause is in the subjunctive mood:

a fin de que / so that, in order that
a menos que / unless
como si / as if
con tal que or *con tal de que* / provided that
para que / in order that, so that
sin que / without

EXAMPLES:

Se lo explico a ustedes a fin de que puedan comprenderlo. / I am explaining it to you so that (in order that) you may be able to understand it.
Saldré a las tres y media a menos que esté lloviendo. / I will go out at three thirty unless it is raining.

When the following conjunctions introduce a new clause, the verb in that new clause is sometimes in the indicative mood, sometimes in the subjunctive mood. Use the subjunctive mood if what is being expressed indicates some sort of anxious anticipation, doubt, indefiniteness, vagueness, or uncertainty. If these are not implied and if the action was completed in the past, use the indicative mood:

a pesar de que / in spite of the fact that
así que / as soon as, after
aunque / although, even if, even though
cuando / when
de manera que / so that, so as
de modo que / so that, in such a way that
después que or *después de que* / after
en cuanto / as soon as
hasta que / until
luego que / as soon as, after
mientras / while, as long as
siempre que / whenever, provided that

EXAMPLES:

Le daré el dinero a Roberto cuando me lo pida. / I shall give
   the money to Robert when he asks me for it. (*Pida* is in the
   subjunctive mood because some doubt or uncertainty is
   suggested and Robert may not ask for it.)

EJERCICIOS/EXERCISES

**The answers to these exercises begin right after the
last question in each group.**

I. Translate the following Spanish sentences into English.
    Then write the Spanish sentences for practice. Refer
    to the preceding pages in this lesson if you have to.

    1. Se cree que este criminal es culpable. _____
        _____

    2. Se dice que va a nevar esta noche. _____
        _____

    3. Se sabe que Juana va a casarse con Juan. _____
        _____

    4. ¡Que lo haga Jorge! _____

    5. ¡Que Dios se lo pague! _____

    6. ¡Entra (tú) pronto! _____

    7. ¡Sigue (tú) leyendo! _____

II. 1. ¡Di (tú) la verdad! _____ (la verdad/the truth)
        _____

    2. Vamos al cine. _____

    3. ¡Levantaos! _____ ¡Sentaos!
        _____

    4. ¡No corras (tú)! _____

    5. ¡Hágalo (Ud.)! _____ ¡No lo haga (Ud.)!
        _____

    6. Se lo explico a ustedes a fin de que puedan
        comprenderlo. _____
        _____

    7. Saldré a las tres y media a menos que esté
        lloviendo. _____
        _____

Answers to the preceding group of exercises.

I. 1. It is believed that this criminal is guilty.
2. They say that it's going to snow tonight.
3. People know that Juana is going to marry Juan.
4. Let George do it!
5. May God reward you!
6. Come in quickly!
7. Keep on reading! *or* Continue reading!

II. 1. Tell the truth!
2. Let's go to the movies.
3. Get up! Sit down!
4. Don't run!
5. Do it! Don't do it!
6. I am explaining it to you so that (in order that) you may be able to understand it.
7. I will go out at three thirty unless it is raining.

BUT

Se lo di a Roberto cuando me lo pidió. / I gave it to Robert when he asked me for it. (No subjunctive of *pedir* here because he actually did ask me for it.)

Esperaré hasta que llegue el autobús. / I shall wait until the bus arrives. (*Llegue* is in the subjunctive mood here because some doubt or uncertainty is suggested and the bus may never arrive.)

BUT

Esperé hasta que llegó el autobús. / I waited until the bus arrived. (No subjunctive of *llegar* here because the bus actually did arrive.)

7.5–18.2 AFTER CERTAIN ADVERBS

acaso	
quizá or *quizás*	perhaps, maybe
tal vez	

Tal vez hayan perdido. / Perhaps they have lost. (Subjunctive is used here because some degree of uncertainty or pessimism is implied.)

Tal vez han ganado. / Perhaps they have won. (No subjunctive is used here because some degree of certainty or optimism is implied.)

Por + adjective or adverb + *que* / however, no matter how

Por (más) interesante que sea, no quiero ver esa película. / No matter how interesting it may be, I do not want to see that film.

7.5–18.3 AFTER CERTAIN INDEFINITE EXPRESSIONS

> *cualquier, cualquiera, cualesquier, cualesquiera* / whatever,
>   whichever, any (the final *a* drops in *cualquiera* and
>   *cualesquiera* when the word is in front of a noun)
> *cuandoquiera* / whenever
> *dondequiera* / wherever; *adondequiera* / to wherever
> *quienquiera, quienesquiera* / whoever

EXAMPLES:

Dondequiera que Ud. esté escríbame. / Wherever you may be,
    write to me.
Adondequiera que Ud. vaya, dígamelo. / Wherever you may
    go, tell me.

7.5–18.4 AFTER AN INDEFINITE OR NEGATIVE ANTECEDENT

The reason why the subjunctive is needed after an indefinite or negative antecedent is that the person or thing desired may possibly not exist; or, if it does exist, you may never find it.

EXAMPLES:

> *Busco un libro que sea interesante.* / I am looking for a book
>   that is interesting.
>
> BUT
>
> *Tengo un libro que es interesante.* / I have a book that is
>   interesting.

> *¿Conoce Ud. a alguien que tenga paciencia?* / Do you know
>   someone who has patience?
>
> BUT
>
> *Conozco a alguien que tiene paciencia.* / I know someone
>   who has patience.

> *No encontré a nadie que supiera la respuesta.* / I did not find
>   anyone who knew the answer.
>
> BUT
>
> *Encontré a alguien que sabe la respuesta.* / I found
>   someone who knows the answer.

7.5–18.5 AFTER ¡Que . . . !

In order to express indirectly a wish, an order, a command in the 3rd person singular or plural, you may use the exclamatory *¡Que . . . !* alone to introduce the subjunctive clause.

¡Que lo haga Jorge! / Let George do it!
¡Que entre! / Let him enter!

7.5–18.6 AFTER *¡Ojalá que . . . !*

The exclamatory expression *Ojalá* is one of Arabic origin meaning "Oh, God!"

¡Ojalá que vengan! / If only they would come!
¡Ojalá que lleguen! / If only they would arrive!

7.5–18.7 AFTER CERTAIN IMPERSONAL EXPRESSIONS

> *Basta que . . .* / It is enough that . . . ; It is sufficient that . . .
> *Conviene que . . .* / It is fitting that . . . ; It is proper that . . .
> *Importa que . . .* / It is important that . . .
> *Más vale que . . .* / It is better that . . .
> *Es aconsejable que . . .* / It is advisable that . . .

EXAMPLES:

Basta que sepan la verdad. / It is sufficient that they know the truth.
Conviene que venga ahora mismo. / It is proper that she come right now.
Es aconsejable que salga inmediatamente. / It is advisable that she leave immediately.

7.5–18.8 AFTER VERBS OR EXPRESSIONS THAT INDICATE DENIAL, DOUBT OR LACK OF BELIEF, AND UNCERTAINTY

> *dudar que . . .* / to doubt that . . .
> *negar que . . .* / to deny that . . .
> *no creer que . . .* / not to believe that . . .
> *Es dudoso que . . .* / It is doubtful that . . .
> *Es incierto que . . .* / It is uncertain that . . .
> *Hay duda que . . .* / There is doubt that . . .
> *No es cierto que . . .* / It is not certain that . . .
> *No estar seguro que . . .* / Not to be sure that . . .

EXAMPLES:

Dudo que mis amigos vengan. / I doubt that my friends are coming.
No creo que sea urgente. / I do not believe that it is urgent.

7.5–18.9 AFTER VERBS OR EXPRESSIONS THAT INDICATE AN EMOTION

estar contento que . . . / to be happy that . . . , to be pleased that . . .
estar feliz que . . . / to be happy that . . .
estar triste que . . . / to be sad that . . .
alegrarse (de) que . . . / to be glad that . . .
sentir que . . . / to regret that . . . , to feel sorry that . . .

EXAMPLES:

Estoy muy contento de que mis amigos vengan a verme / I am very pleased that my friends are coming (will come) to see me.
Me alegro de que ellos hayan venido / I am glad that they have come.

EJERCICIOS/EXERCISES

The answers to these exercises begin right after the last question in each group.

I. **Volunteering. Proficiency in Speaking and Writing Practice**

Situation: Your Spanish teacher is asking for a volunteer to go to the chalkboard and write one sentence in Spanish using one object pronoun. You are playing the role of **Tú.** Write your statements on the lines.

You may vary and extend this dialogue with your own words and ideas. Review the preceding pages if you have to.

La maestra
(El maestro):   **¿Quién quiere escribir una frase con un pronombre de complemento en la pizarra hoy?**

Ramón: **¡Yo! ¡Yo! Yo quiero escribirla en la pizarra.**

Tú:

    (Me! Me! I want to write it on the board. Ramón wrote it on the board yesterday.)

La maestra
(El maestro):   **Está bien. Tú puedes pasar a la pizarra y escribirla.**

Tú:

    (May I get up?)

La maestra
(El maestro):   **Claro que sí. Tú puedes levantarte.**
¿Qué vas a escribir?

Tú:
_____

(I'm going to write: "Let's write it in Spanish!")

II. Putting it all together. Speaking and Writing Practice

Situation: Today it is your turn (**te toca a ti**) to go to the front of the class and say a few sentences in Spanish. Look at and examine the five sentences below. The words are scrambled. Put them together in the right order and read them aloud to your teacher and classmates. For practice, write them on the lines and memorize them if you want to. **Also, translate the sentences into English.**

1. hijos / dos / de / José / tiene / el padre / y / hijas / tres.

   _____

2. el hijo mayor / que / se / llama / Andrés / veinte / tiene / años.

   _____

3. la hija menor / que / se / llama / Elena / dieciocho / años / tiene.

   _____

4. Andrés / hacerse / quiere / médico.

   _____

5. hacerse / Elena / quiere / profesora.

   _____

Answers to the preceding group of exercises.

I.   ¡Yo! ¡Yo! Yo quiero escribirla en la pizarra. Ramón la escribió en la pizarra ayer.

   ¿Puedo levantarme? _or_ Me puedo levantar?

   Voy a escribir: "¡Vamos a escribirlo en español!"

II. 1. El padre de José tiene dos hijos y tres hijas.

   2. El hijo mayor, que se llama Andrés, tiene veinte años.

   3. La hija menor, que se llama Elena, tiene dieciocho años.

   4. Andrés quiere hacerse médico.

   5. Elena quiere hacerse profesora.

7.5–18.10 AFTER CERTAIN VERBS THAT IMPLY A WISH OR DESIRE THAT SOMETHING BE DONE, INCLUDING A COMMAND, ORDER, PREFERENCE, ADVICE, PERMISSION, REQUEST, PLEA, INSISTENCE, SUGGESTION

> *aconsejar* / to advise
> *decir* / to tell (someone to do something)
> *desear* / to want, to wish
> *mandar* / to order, to command
> *pedir* / to ask, to request
> *preferir* / to prefer
> *prohibir* / to forbid, to prohibit
> *querer* / to want, to wish
> *rogar* / to beg, to request
> *sugerir* / to suggest

EXAMPLES:

> *Les aconsejo a ellos que hagan el trabajo.* / I advise them to do the work.
> *Les digo a ellos que escriban los ejercicios.* / I am telling them to write the exercises.
> *Mi madre quiere que yo vaya a la escuela.* / My mother wants me to go to school.

BUT

Yo quiero ir a la escuela. / I want to go to school.

Note: In this example, there is no change in subject; therefore, the infinitive *ir* is used. But in the example above, beginning with *Mi madre quiere que . . . ,* there is a new subject *(yo)* in the dependent clause and *ir* is in the subjunctive because the verb *querer* is used in the main clause.

> *El capitán me manda que yo entre* / The captain orders me to come in.

7.5–18.11 SEQUENCE OF TENSES WHEN THE SUBJUNCTIVE IS REQUIRED: A SUMMARY

When the verb in the main clause is in the:	The verb in the following clause (the dependent clause) most likely will be in the:

Present Indicative or Future or Present Perfect Indicative or Imperative (Command)	Present Subjunctive or Present Perfect Subjunctive
Conditional or a past tense (Imperfect Indicative or Preterit or Pluperfect Indicative)	Imperfect Subjunctive or Pluperfect Subjunctive

EXAMPLES:

Deseo que Ana cante. / I want Anna to sing.
Le diré a Ana que baile. / I will tell Anna to dance.
Le he dicho a Ana que cante y baile. / I have said to Anna to
   sing and dance.
Dígale a Ana que cante y baile. / Tell Anna to sing and dance.
Dudo que mi madre tome el tren. / I doubt that my mother is
   taking the train.

§7.5–19 The Names of Tenses and Moods

The Simple Tenses	The Compound Tenses
Present indicative	Present perfect indicative
Imperfect indicative	Pluperfect OR Past perfect indicative
Preterit	Past anterior OR Preterit perfect
Future	Future perfect OR Future anterior
Conditional	Conditional perfect
Present subjunctive	Present perfect OR Past subjunctive
Imperfect subjunctive	Pluperfect OR Past perfect subjunctive
Imperative OR Command	

Haber (helping verb) in the 7 simple tenses

Present participle: *habiendo*
Past participle: *habido*
Infinitive: *haber*

Present indicative	*he, has, ha; hemos, habéis, han* I have, you have, you or he or she or it has; we have, you have, you or they have
Imperfect indicative	*había, habías, había; habíamos, habíais, habían* I had, you had, you or he or she or it had; we had, you had, you or they had
Preterit	*hube, hubiste, hubo; hubimos, hubisteis, hubieron* I had, you had, you or he or she or it had; we had, you had, you or they had

Haber (helping verb) in the 7 simple tenses

Present participle: *habiendo*
Past participle: *habido*
Infinitive: *haber*

Future	*habré, habrás, habrá; habremos, habréis, habrán*
	I shall have, you will have, you or he or she or it will have; we shall have, you will have, you or they will have
Conditional	*habría, habrías, habría; habríamos, habríais, habrían*
	I would have, you would have, you or he or she or it would have; we would have, you would have, you or they would have
Present subjunctive	*haya, hayas, haya; hayamos, hayáis, hayan*
	that I may have, that you may have, that you or he or she or it may have; that we may have, that you may have, that you or they may have
Imperfect subjunctive	(the -*ra* form): *hubiera, hubieras, hubiera; hubiéramos, hubierais, hubieran*
	OR
	(the -*se* form): *hubiese, hubieses, hubiese; hubiésemos, hubieseis, hubiesen*
	that I might have, that you might have, that you or he or she or it might have; that we might have, that you might have, that you or they might have

Note: The subject pronouns in Spanish were omitted above in order to emphasize the verb forms.

Singular: *yo, tú, Ud.* OR *él* OR *ella;*
Plural: *nosotros (nosotras), vosotros (vosotras), Uds.* OR *ellos* OR *ellas*

§7.6
SPECIAL CASES AND VERBS WITH SPECIAL MEANINGS

§7.6–1
Si Clause: A Summary of Contrary-to-Fact Conditions

When the verb in the *Si* clause is:	The verb in the main or result clause is:
Present Indicative	Future

EXAMPLE:
Si tengo bastante tiempo, vendré a verle. / If I have enough time, I will come to see you.

Note that the present subjunctive form of a verb is never used in a clause beginning with the conjunction *si.*

Imperfect Subjunctive (*-se* form or *-ra* form)	Conditional or Imperfect Subjunctive (*-ra* form)

EXAMPLE:
Si yo tuviese (or *tuviera*) *bastante tiempo, vendría a verle.* / If I had enough time, I would come to see you.

OR

Si yo tuviese (or *tuviera*) *bastante tiempo, viniera a verle.* / If I had enough time, I would come to see you.

Pluperfect Subjunctive (*-se* form or *-ra* form)	Conditional Perfect or Pluperfect Subjunctive (*-ra* form)

EXAMPLE:
Si yo hubiese tenido (or *hubiera tenido*) *bastante tiempo, habría venido a verle.* / If I had had enough time, I would have come to see you.

OR

Si yo hubiese tenido (or *hubiera tenido*) *bastante tiempo, hubiera venido a verle.* / If I had had enough time, I would have come to see you.

§7.6–2
Acabar de + Infinitive

In the present indicative:

> *María acaba de llegar.* / Mary has just arrived.
> *Acabo de comer.* / I have just eaten.
> *Acabamos de terminar la lección.* / We have just finished the lesson.

When you use *acabar* in the present tense, it indicates that the action of the main verb (+ infinitive) has just occurred now in the present. In English, we express this by using have just + the past participle of the main verb.

In the imperfect indicative:

> *María acababa de llegar.* / Mary had just arrived.
> *Acababa de comer.* / I had just eaten.
> *Acabábamos de terminar la lección.* / We had just finished the lesson.

When you use *acabar* in the imperfect indicative, it indicates that the action of the main verb (+ infinitive) had occurred at some time in the past when another action occurred. In English, we express this by using had just + the past participle of the main verb.

§7.6–3
Conocer and *saber*

These two verbs mean to know, but they are used differently.

• *Conocer* means to know in the sense of being acquainted with a person, a place, or a thing:

> *¿Conoce Ud. a María?* / Do you know Mary?
> *¿Conoce Ud. bien los Estados Unidos?* / Do you know the United States well?
> *¿Conoce Ud. este libro?* / Do you know (Are you acquainted with) this book?

In the preterit tense, *conocer* means met in the sense of first met, first became acquainted with someone:

> *¿Conoce Ud. a Elena?* / Do you know Helen?
> *Sí, (yo) la conocí anoche en casa de un amigo mío.* / Yes, I met her [for the first time] last night at the home of one of my friends.

• *Saber* means to know a fact, to know something thoroughly:

> *¿Sabe Ud. qué hora es?* / Do you know what time it is?

When you use *saber* + infinitive, it means to know how:

> *¿Sabe Ud. nadar?* / Do you know how to swim?
> *Sí, (yo) sé nadar.* / Yes, I know how to swim.

In the preterit tense, *saber* means found out:

> *¿Lo sabe Ud.?* / Do you know it?
> *Sí, lo supe ayer.* / Yes, I found it out yesterday.

§7.6–4
Deber, deber de and *tener que*

Generally speaking, use *deber* when you want to express a moral obligation, something you ought to do but you may or may not do it:

> *Debo estudiar esta noche pero estoy cansado y no me siento bien.* / I ought to study tonight but I am tired and I do not feel well.

Generally speaking, *deber de* + infinitive is used to express a supposition, something that is probable:

> *La señora Gómez debe de estar enferma porque sale de casa raramente.* / Mrs. Gómez must be sick (is probably sick) because she goes out of the house rarely.

Generally speaking, use *tener que* when you want to say that you have to do something:

> *No puedo salir esta noche porque tengo que estudiar.* / I cannot go out tonight because I have to study.

§7.6–5
Dejar, salir and *salir de*

These verbs mean to leave, but notice the uses:
Use *dejar* when you leave someone or when you leave something behind you:

> *El alumno dejó sus libros en la sala de clase.* / The pupil left his books in the classroom.

Dejar also means to let or to allow or to let go:

> *¡Déjelo!* / Let it! (Leave it!)

Use *salir de* when you mean to leave in the sense of to go out of (a place):

> *El alumno salió de la sala de clase.* / The pupil left the classroom.
> *¿Dónde está su madre? Mi madre salió.* / Where is your mother? My mother went out.

§7.6–6
Dejar de + Infinitive and *dejar caer*

Use *dejar de* + infinitive when you mean to stop or to fail to:

> *Los alumnos dejaron de hablar.* / The students stopped talking.
> *¡No deje Ud. de llamarme!* / Don't fail to call me!

Dejar caer means to drop:

> *Luis dejó caer sus libros.* / Louis dropped his books.

§7.6–7
Ir, irse

Use *ir* when you simply mean to go:

> *Voy al cine.* / I am going to the movies.

Use *irse* when you mean to leave in the sense of to go away:

> *Mis padres se fueron al campo para visitar a mis abuelos.* / My parents left for (went away to) the country to visit my grandparents.

§7.6–8
Gastar and *pasar*

These two verbs mean to spend, but notice the uses:
Use *gastar* when you spend money:

> *No me gusta gastar mucho dinero.* / I don't like to spend much money.

Use *pasar* when you spend time:

> *Me gustaría pasar un año en España.* / I would like to spend a year in Spain.

§7.6–9
Gustar

- Essentially, the verb *gustar* means to be pleasing to . . .
- In English, we say, for example, I like ice cream. In Spanish, we say *Me gusta el helado.*
- In English, the thing that you like is the direct object. In Spanish, the thing that you like is the subject. Also, in Spanish, the person who likes the thing is the indirect object: to me, to you, etc.:

> *A Roberto le gusta el helado.* / Robert likes ice cream; in other words, "To Robert, ice cream is pleasing to him."

- In Spanish, therefore, the verb *gustar* is used in the third person, either in the singular or plural, when you talk about something that you like—something that is pleasing to you. Therefore, the verb form must agree with the subject; if the thing liked is singular, the verb is third person singular; if the thing liked is plural, the verb *gustar* is third person plural:

> *Me gusta el café.* / I like coffee.
> *Me gustan el café y la leche.* / I like coffee and milk.

- When you mention the person or the persons who like something, you must use the preposition *a* in front of the person; you must also use the indirect object pronoun of the noun which is the person:

> *A los muchachos y a las muchachas les gusta jugar.* / Boys and girls like to play; that is to say, "To play is pleasing to them, to boys and girls."

• Review the indirect object pronouns, which are *me, te, le; nos, os, les*.

EXAMPLES:

Me gusta leer. / I like to read.
Te gusta leer. / You (familiar) like to read.
A Felipe le gusta el helado. / Philip likes ice cream.
Al chico le gusta la leche. / The boy likes milk.
A Carlota le gusta bailar. / Charlotte likes to dance.
A las chicas les gustó el libro. / The girls liked the book.
Nos gustó el cuento. / We liked the story.

§7.6–10
Haber, haber de + Infinitive and *tener*

The verb *haber* (to have) is used as an auxiliary verb (or helping verb) in order to form the seven compound tenses.

The verb *haber* is also used to form the perfect (or past) infinitive: *haber hablado* (to have spoken). This is formed by using the infinitive form of *haber* + the past participle of the main verb.

The verb *haber* is also used to form the perfect participle: *habiendo hablado* (having spoken). This is formed by using the present participle of *haber* + the past participle of the main verb.

The verb *haber* + *de* + infinitive is equivalent to the English use of "to be supposed to . . ." or "to be to . . .".

EXAMPLE:

María ha de traer un pastel, yo he de traer el helado, y mis amigos han de traer sus discos. / Mary is supposed to bring a pie, I am supposed to bring the ice cream, and my friends are to bring their records.

The verb *tener* is used to mean to have in the sense of to possess or to hold:

Tengo un perro y un gato. / I have a dog and a cat.

In the preterit tense, *tener* can mean received:

Ayer mi padre tuvo un choque. / Yesterday my father received a shock.

§7.6–11
Jugar and *tocar*

Both these verbs mean to play but they have different uses. *Jugar a* is used to play a sport, a game:

¿Juega Ud. al tenis? / Do you play tennis?
Me gusta jugar a la pelota. / I like to play ball.

The verb *tocar* is used to play a musical instrument:

Carmen toca muy bien el piano. / Carmen plays the piano very well.

The verb *tocar* has other meanings: to be one's turn, in which case it takes an indirect object:

¿A quién le toca? / Whose turn is it?
Le toca a Juan. / It is John's turn.

to knock on a door:

tocar a la puerta; Alguien toca a la puerta. / Someone is knocking on (at) the door.

Essentially, *tocar* means to touch.

§7.6–12
Llegar a ser, hacerse and *ponerse*

These three verbs mean to become. Note the uses:
Use *llegar a ser* + a noun: to become a doctor, to become a teacher; in other words, the noun indicates the goal that you are striving for:

Quiero llegar a ser doctor. / I want to become a doctor.

Hacerse is used similarly:

Juan se hizo abogado. / John became a lawyer.

Use *ponerse* + an adjective: to become pale, to become sick; in other words, the adjective indicates the state or condition (physical or mental) that you have become:

Cuando vi el accidente, me puse pálido. / When I saw the accident, I became pale.
Mi madre se puso triste al oír la noticia desgraciada. / My mother became sad upon hearing the unfortunate news.

§7.6–13
Llevar and *tomar*

These two verbs mean to take but note the uses:
Llevar means to take in the sense of carry or transport from place to place:

José llevó la silla de la cocina al comedor. / Joseph took the chair from the kitchen to the dining room.

The verb *llevar* is also used when you take someone somewhere:

Pedro llevó a María al baile anoche. / Peter took Mary to the dance last night.

As you probably know, *llevar* also means to wear:

María, ¿por qué llevas la falda nueva? / Mary, why are you wearing your new skirt?

EJERCICIOS/EXERCISES

The answers to these exercises begin right after the last question in each group.

Translate the following Spanish sentences into English. **Then write the Spanish sentences for practice.** Refer to the preceding pages in this lesson if you have to.

I.   1. Les aconsejo a ellos que hagan el trabajo. _____
   _____

   2. Le he dicho a Ana que cante y baile. _____

   3. Si tengo bastante tiempo, vendré a verle. _____
   _____

   4. Si yo tuviese (*or* tuviera) bastante tiempo, vendría a verle. _____
   _____

   5. Si yo hubiese tenido (*or* hubiera tenido) bastante tiempo, habría venido a verle. _____
   _____

   6. Acabo de comer. _____
   _____

   7. Acabamos de terminar la lección. _____
   _____

   8. ¿Conoce Ud. a Lola? ¿Conoce Ud. este libro?
   _____

   9. ¿Sabe Ud. qué hora es? _____
   _____

   10. ¿Sabe Ud. nadar? _____
   _____

II. 1. María acababa de llegar. _____
   _____

   2. Debo estudiar esta noche pero estoy cansado y no me siento bien. _____
   _____

   3. Luis dejó caer sus libros. _____
   _____

   4. Voy al cine. _____
   5. Mis padres se fueron al campo para visitar a mis abuelos. _____
   _____

   6. No me gusta gastar mucho dinero. _____
   _____

7. Me gustaría pasar un año en España. _____
   _____

8. A Roberto le gusta el helado. _____
   _____

9. A los muchachos y a las muchachas les gusta
   jugar. _____
   _____

10. ¿A quién le toca? Le toca a Juan. _____
    _____

Answers to the preceding group of exercises.

I. 1. I advise them to do the work.
    2. I have said to Anna to sing and dance.
    3. If I have enough time, I will come to see you.
    4. If I had enough time, I would come to see you.
    5. If I had had enough time, I would have come to see you.
    6. I have just eaten.
    7. We have just finished the lesson.
    8. Do you know Lola? Do you know (Are you acquainted) with this book?
    9. Do you know what time it is?
    10. Do you know how to swim?

II. 1. Mary had just arrived.
    2. I ought to study tonight but I am tired and I do not feel well.
    3. Louis dropped his books.
    4. I am going to the movies.
    5. My parents left for (went away to) the country to visit my grandparents.
    6. I don't like to spend much money.
    7. I would like to spend a year in Spain.
    8. Robert likes ice cream.
    9. Boys and girls like to play.
    10. Whose turn is it? It's John's turn.

Tomar means to take in the sense of grab or catch:

> *La profesora tomó el libro y comenzó a leer a la clase.* / The teacher took the book and began to read to the class.
> *Mi amigo tomó el tren esta mañana a las siete.* / My friend took the train this morning at seven o'clock.

§7.6–14
Pedir and *preguntar*

Both these verbs mean to ask but note the uses:
Pedir means to ask for something or to request:

El alumno pidió un lápiz al profesor. / The pupil asked the teacher for a pencil.

Preguntar means to inquire, to ask a question:

La alumna preguntó a la profesora cómo estaba. / The pupil asked the teacher how she was.

§7.6–15
Pensar de and *pensar en*

Both these verbs mean to think of but note the uses:
Pensar is used with the preposition *de* when you ask someone what he/she thinks of someone or something, when you ask for someone's opinion:

¿Qué piensa Ud. de este libro? / What do you think of this book?
Pienso que es bueno. / I think that it is good.

Pensar is used with the preposition *en* when you ask someone what or whom he/she is thinking about:

Miguel, no hablas mucho; ¿en qué piensas? / Michael, you are not talking much; of what are you thinking? (what are you thinking of?
Pienso en las vacaciones de verano. / I'm thinking of summer vacation.

§7.6–16
Poder and *saber*

Both these verbs mean can, but note the uses:
Poder means can in the sense of ability:

No puedo ayudarle; lo siento. / I cannot (am unable to) help you; I'm sorry.

Saber means can in the sense of to know how:

Este niño no sabe contar. / This child can't (does not know how to) count.

In the preterit tense, *poder* has the special meaning of succeeded:

Después de algunos minutos, Juan pudo abrir la puerta. / After a few minutes, John succeeded in opening the door.

In the preterit tense, *saber* has the special meaning of found out:

Lo supe ayer. / I found it out yesterday.

§7.6–17
Ser and *estar*

These two verbs mean to be but note the uses:

Generally speaking, use *ser* when you want to express to be.

Use *estar* when to be is used in the following ways:

Health:

¿Cómo está Ud.? / How are you?
Estoy bien. / I am well.
Estoy enfermo (enferma). / I am sick.

Location: persons, places, things:

Estoy en la sala de clase. / I am in the classroom.
La escuela está lejos. / The school is far.
Barcelona está en España. / Barcelona is (located) in Spain.

State or condition: persons

Estoy contento (contenta). / I am happy.
Los alumnos están cansados. (Las alumnas están cansadas).
    The students are tired.
María está triste hoy. / Mary is sad today.
Estoy listo (lista). / I am ready.
Estoy pálido (pálida). / I am pale.
Estoy ocupado (ocupada). / I am busy.

State or condition: things and places

La ventana está abierta. / The window is open.
La taza está llena. / The cup is full.
El té está caliente. / The tea is hot.

To form the progressive present of a verb, use the present tense of *estar* + the present participle of the main verb.

Estoy estudiando en mi cuarto y no puedo salir esta noche. /
    I am studying in my room and I cannot go out tonight.

To form the progressive past of a verb, use the imperfect tense of *estar* + the present participle of the main verb.

Mi hermano estaba leyendo cuando (yo) entré en el cuarto. /
    My brother was reading when I entered (came into) the room.

§7.6–18
Volver and *devolver*

These two verbs mean to return but note the uses:

Volver means to return in the sense of to come back:

Voy a volver a casa. / I am going to return home.

A synonym of *volver* is *regresar:*

Los muchachos regresaron a las ocho de la noche. / The boys came back at eight o'clock in the evening.

Devolver means to return in the sense of to give back:

Voy a devolver el libro a la biblioteca. / I am going to return the book to the library.

§7.7 COMMONLY USED BASIC IRREGULAR VERBS

§7.7–1 Present Indicative

acordarse / to remember
me acuerdo, te acuerdas, se acuerda; nos acordamos, os acordáis, se acuerdan

acostarse / to go to bed, to lie down
me acuesto, te acuestas, se acuesta; nos acostamos, os acostáis, se acuestan

almorzar / to lunch, to have lunch
almuerzo, almuerzas, almuerza; almorzamos, almorzáis, almuerzan

aparecer / to appear, to show up
aparezco, apareces, aparece; aparecemos, aparecéis, aparecen

caber / to fit, to be contained
quepo, cabes, cabe; cabemos, cabéis, caben

caer / to fall
caigo, caes, cae; caemos, caéis, caen

cerrar / to close
cierro, cierras, cierra; cerramos, cerráis, cierran

cocer / to cook
cuezo, cueces, cuece; cocemos, cocéis, cuecen

coger / to seize, to grasp, to grab, to catch
cojo, coges, coge; cogemos, cogéis, cogen

comenzar / to begin, to start, to commence
comienzo, comienzas, comienza; comenzamos, comenzáis, comienzan

conducir / to conduct, to lead, to drive
conduzco, conduces, conduce; conducimos, conducís, conducen

conocer / to know, to be acquainted with
conozco, conoces, conoce; conocemos, conocéis, conocen

contar / to count, to relate
cuento, cuentas, cuenta; contamos, contáis, cuentan

corregir / to correct
corrijo, corriges, corrige; corregimos, corregís, corrigen

costar / to cost
cuesta; cuestan

dar / to give
doy, das, da; damos, dais, dan

decir / to say, to tell
digo, dices, dice; decimos, decís dicen

despertarse / to awaken, to wake up (oneself)
me despierto, te despiertas, se despierta; nos despertamos, os despertáis, se despiertan

devolver / to return, to give back (something)
devuelvo, devuelves, devuelve; devolvemos, devolvéis, devuelven

divertirse / to have a good time, to enjoy oneself
me divierto, te diviertes, se divierte; nos divertimos, os divertís, se divierten

doler / to ache, to pain, to hurt, to cause grief, to cause regret
duelo, dueles, duele; dolemos, doléis, duelen

dormir / to sleep
duermo, duermes, duerme; dormimos, dormís, duermen

dormirse / to fall asleep
me duermo, te duermes, se duerme; nos dormimos, os dormís, se duermen

empezar / to begin, to start
empiezo, empiezas, empieza; empezamos, empezáis, empiezan

encontrar / to meet, to encounter, to find
encuentro, encuentras, encuentra; encontramos, encontráis, encuentran

entender / to understand
entiendo, entiendes, entiende; entendemos, entendéis, entienden

enviar / to send
envío, envías, envía; enviamos, enviáis, envían

estar / to be
estoy, estás, está; estamos, estáis, están

haber / to have (as an auxiliary or helping verb)
he, has, ha; hemos, habéis, han

hacer / to do, to make
hago, haces, hace; hacemos, hacéis, hacen

helar / to freeze
hiela OR está helando (in the present progressive form)

ir / to go
voy, vas, va; vamos, vais, van

irse / to go away
me voy, te vas, se va; nos vamos, os vais, se van

jugar / to play
juego, juegas, juega;
jugamos, jugáis, juegan

llover / to rain
llueve OR está lloviendo
(in the present
progressive form)

morir / to die
muero, mueres, muere;
morimos, morís, mueren

mostrar / to show, to point
out
muestro, muestras,
muestra; mostramos,
mostráis, muestran

nacer / to be born
nazco, naces, nace;
nacemos, nacéis, nacen

nevar / to snow
nieve OR está nevando
(in the present
progressive form)

obtener / to obtain, to get
obtengo, obtienes,
obtiene; obtenemos,
obtenéis, obtienen

oír / to hear
oigo, oyes, oye; oímos,
oís, oyen

pedir / to ask for, to request
pido, pides, pide;
pedimos, pedís, piden

pensar / to think
pienso, piensas, piensa;
pensamos, pensáis,
piensan

perder / to lose
pierdo, pierdes, pierde;
perdemos, perdéis,
pierden

poder / to be able, can
puedo, puedes, puede;
podemos, podéis,
pueden

poner / to put, to place
pongo, pones, pone;
ponemos, ponéis, ponen

querer / to want, to wish
quiero, quieres, quiere;
queremos, queréis,
quieren

recordar / to remember
recuerdo, recuerdas,
recuerda; recordamos,
recordáis, recuerdan

reír / to laugh
río, ríes, ríe; reímos,
reís, ríen

repetir / to repeat
repito, repites, repite;
repetimos, repetís,
repiten

saber / to know, to know
how
sé, sabes, sabe;
sabemos, sabéis, saben

salir / to go out
salgo, sales, sale;
salimos, salís, salen

seguir / to follow, to pursue,
to continue
sigo, sigues, sigue;
seguimos, seguís,
siguen

sentarse / to sit down
me siento, te sientas, se
sienta; nos sentamos, os
sentáis, se sientan

sentir / to feel sorry, to
regret, to feel, to
experience, to sense
siento, sientes, siente;
sentimos, sentís, sienten

sentirse / to feel (well, sick)
me siento, te sientes, se
siente; nos sentimos, os
sentís, se sienten

ser / to be
soy, eres, es; somos,
sois, son

servir / to serve
sirvo, sirves, sirve;
servimos, servís, sirven

soñar / to dream
sueño, sueñas, sueña;
soñamos, soñáis, sueñan

sonreír / to smile
sonrío, sonríes, sonríe;
sonreímos, sonreís,
sonríen

tener / to have, to hold
tengo, tienes, tiene;
tenemos, tenéis, tienen

traer / to bring
traigo, traes, trae;
traemos, traéis, traen

venir / to come
vengo, vienes, viene;
venimos, venís, vienen

ver / to see
veo, ves, ve; vemos,
veis, ven

volver / to return
vuelvo, vuelves, vuelve;
volvemos, volvéis,
vuelven

§7.7–2 Imperfect Indicative

ir / to go (I was going, I
used to go, etc.)
iba, ibas, iba; íbamos,
ibais, iban

ser / to be (I was, I used to
be, etc.)
era, eras, era; éramos,
erais, eran

ver / to see (I was seeing, I
used to see, etc.)
veía, veías, veía;
veíamos, veíais, veían

§7.7–3 Preterit

acercarse / to approach, to
draw near
me acerqué, te
acercaste, se acercó;
nos acercamos, os
acercasteis, se
acercaron

almorzar / to have lunch, to
eat lunch
almorcé, almorzaste,
almorzó; almorzamos,
almorzasteis,
almorzaron

andar / to walk
anduve, anduviste,
anduvo; anduvimos,
anduvisteis, anduvieron

buscar / to look for, to
search, to seek
busqué, buscaste,
buscó; buscamos,
buscasteis, buscaron

caber / to fit, to be
contained
cupe, cupiste, cupo;
cupimos, cupisteis,
cupieron

caer / to fall
caí, caíste, cayó; caímos, caísteis, cayeron

comenzar / to begin, to commence, to start
comencé, comenzaste, comenzó; comenzamos, comenzasteis, comenzaron

conducir / to conduct, to lead, to drive
conduje, condujiste, condujo; condujimos, condujisteis, condujeron

creer / to believe
creí, creíste, creyó; creímos, creísteis, creyeron

dar / to give
di, diste, dio; dimos, disteis, dieron

decir / to say, to tell
dije, dijiste, dijo; dijimos, dijisteis, dijeron

detener / to detain, to stop (someone or something)
detuve, detuviste, detuvo; detuvimos, detuvisteis, detuvieron

detenerse / to stop (oneself or itself)
me detuve, te detuviste, se detuvo; nos detuvimos, os detuvisteis, se detuvieron

estar / to be
estuve, estuviste, estuvo; estuvimos, estuvisteis, estuvieron

haber / to have (as an auxiliary or helping verb)
hube, hubiste, hubo; hubimos, hubisteis, hubieron

hacer / to do, to make
hice, hiciste, hizo; hicimos, hicisteis, hicieron

ir / to go
fui, fuiste, fue; fuimos, fuisteis, fueron

irse / to go away
me fui, te fuiste, se fue; nos fuimos, os fuisteis, se fueron

leer / to read
leí, leíste, leyó; leímos, leísteis, leyeron

llegar / to arrive
llegué, llegaste, llegó; llegamos, llegasteis, llegaron

oír / to hear (sometimes can mean "to understand")
oí, oíste, oyó; oímos, oísteis, oyeron

poder / to be able, can
pude, pudiste, pudo; pudimos, pudisteis, pudieron

poner / to put, to place
puse, pusiste, puso; pusimos, pusisteis, pusieron

querer / to want, to wish
quise, quisiste, quiso; quisimos, quisisteis, quisieron

reír / to laugh
reí, reíste, rió; reímos,
reísteis, rieron

saber / to know, to know
how
supe, supiste, supo;
supimos, supisteis,
supieron

ser / to be
fui, fuiste, fue; fuimos,
fuisteis, fueron
Note that these forms
are the same for *ir* in the
preterit.

tener / to have, to hold
tuve, tuviste, tuvo;
tuvimos, tuvisteis,
tuvieron

traer / to bring
traje, trajiste, trajo;
trajimos, trajisteis,
trajeron

venir / to come
vine, viniste, vino;
vinimos, vinisteis,
vinieron

ver / to see
vi, viste, vio; vimos,
visteis, vieron

§7.7–4 Future

caber / to fit, to be
contained
cabré, cabrás, cabrá;
cabremos, cabréis,
cabrán

decir / to say, to tell
diré, dirás, dirá; diremos,
diréis, dirán

haber / to have (as an
auxiliary or helping verb)
habré, habrás, habrá;
habremos, habréis,
habrán

hacer / to do, to make
haré, harás, hará;
haremos, haréis, harán

poder / to be able, can
podré, podrás, podrá;
podremos, podréis,
podrán

poner / to put, to place
pondré, pondrás,
pondrá; pondremos,
pondréis, pondrán

querer / to want, to wish
querré, querrás, querrá;
querremos, querréis,
querrán

saber / to know, to know
how
sabré, sabrás, sabrá;
sabremos, sabréis,
sabrán

salir / to go out
saldré, saldrás, saldrá;
saldremos, saldréis,
saldrán

tener / to have, to hold
tendré, tendrás, tendrá;
tendremos, tendréis,
tendrán

valer / to be worth, to be
worthy
valdré, valdrás, valdrá;
valdremos, valdréis,
valdrán

venir / to come
vendré, vendrás, vendrá;
vendremos, vendréis,
vendrán

§7.7–5 Conditional

caber / to fit, to be contained
cabría, cabrías, cabría; cabríamos, cabríais, cabrían

decir / to say, to tell
diría, dirías, diría; diríamos, diríais, dirían

haber / to have (as an auxiliary or helping verb)
habría, habrías, habría; habríamos, habríais, habrían

hacer / to do, to make
haría, harías, haría; haríamos, haríais, harían

poder / to be able, can
podría, podrías, podría; podríamos, podríais, podrían

poner / to put, to place
pondría, pondrías, pondría; pondríamos, pondríais, pondrían

querer / to want, to wish
querría, querrías, querría; querríamos, querríais, querrían

saber / to know, to know how
sabría, sabrías, sabría; sabríamos, sabríais, sabrían

salir / to go out
saldría, saldrías, saldría; saldríamos, saldríais, saldrían

tener / to have, to hold
tendría, tendrías, tendría; tendríamos, tendríais, tendrían

valer / to be worth, to be worthy
valdría, valdrías, valdría; valdríamos, valdríais, valdrían

venir / to come
vendría, vendrías, vendría; vendríamos, vendríais, vendrían

§7.7–6 Present Subjunctive

dar / to give
dé, des, dé; demos, deis, den

estar / to be
esté, estés, esté; estemos, estéis, estén

haber / to have (as an auxiliary or helping verb)
haya, hayas, haya; hayamos, hayáis, hayan

ir / to go
vaya, vayas, vaya; vayamos, vayáis, vayan

saber / to know, to know how
sepa, sepas, sepa; sepamos, sepáis, sepan

ser / to be
sea, seas, sea; seamos, seáis, sean

§7.7–7 Imperfect Subjunctive

beber / to drink
bebiera, bebieras, bebiera; bebiéramos, bebierais, bebieran

OR

bebiese, bebieses, bebiese; bebiésemos, bebieseis, bebiesen

dar / to give
diera, dieras, diera; diéramos, dierais, dieran

OR

diese, dieses, diese; diésemos, dieseis, diesen

hablar / to speak
hablara, hablaras, hablara; habláramos, hablarais, hablaran

OR

hablase, hablases, hablase; hablásemos, hablaseis, hablasen

leer / to read
leyera, leyeras, leyera; leyéramos, leyerais, leyeran

OR

leyese, leyeses, leyese; leyésemos, leyeseis, leyesen

recibir / to receive
recibiera, recibieras, recibiera; recibiéramos, recibierais, recibieran

OR

recibiese, recibieses, recibiese; recibiésemos, recibieseis, recibiesen

tener / to have
tuviera, tuvieras, tuviera; tuviéramos, tuvierais, tuvieran

OR

tuviese, tuvieses, tuviese; tuviésemos, tuvieseis, tuviesen

§7.7–8 Complete Conjugations

Here are four commonly used irregular verbs conjugated fully in all the tenses and moods.

In the format of the verbs that follow, the subject pronouns have been omitted in order to emphasize the verb forms. The subject pronouns are:

Singular	Plural
yo	*nosotros (nosotras)*
tú	*vosotros (vosotras)*
Ud. (él, ella)	*Uds. (ellos, ellas)*

estar / to be

gerundio	Present Participle: *estando*	Past Participle: *estado*

THE SEVEN SIMPLE TENSES	THE SEVEN COMPOUND TENSES

Singular	Plural	Singular	Plural
Present Indicative		**Present Perfect Indicative**	
estoy	estamos	he estado	hemos estado
estás	estáis	has estado	habéis estado
está	están	ha estado	han estado
Imperfect Indicative		**Pluperfect OR Past Perfect Indicative**	
estaba	estábamos	había estado	habíamos estado
estabas	estabais	habías estado	habíais estado
estaba	estaban	había estado	habían estado
Preterit		**Past Anterior OR Preterit Perfect**	
estuve	estuvimos	hube estado	hubimos estado
estuviste	estuvisteis	hubiste estado	hubisteis estado
estuvo	estuvieron	hubo estado	hubieron estado
Future		**Future Perfect OR Future Anterior**	
estaré	estaremos	habré estado	habremos estado
estarás	estaréis	habrás estado	habréis estado
estará	estarán	habrá estado	habrán estado
Conditional		**Conditional Perfect**	
estaría	estaríamos	habría estado	habríamos estado
estarías	estaríais	habrías estado	habríais estado
estaría	estarían	habría estado	habrían estado
Present Subjunctive		**Present Perfect OR Past Subjunctive**	
esté	estemos	haya estado	hayamos estado
estés	estéis	hayas estado	hayáis estado
esté	estén	haya estado	hayan estado
Imperfect Subjunctive		**Pluperfect OR Past Perfect Subjunctive**	
estuviera	estuviéramos	hubiera estado	hubiéramos estado
estuvieras	estuvierais	hubieras estado	hubierais estado
estuviera	estuvieran	hubiera estado	hubieran estado
OR		OR	
estuviese	estuviésemos	hubiese estado	hubiésemos estado
estuvieses	estuvieseis	hubieses estado	hubieseis estado
estuviese	estuviesen	hubiese estado	hubiesen estado

Imperative	
—	estemos
está; no estés	estad; no estéis
esté	estén

Common Idiomatic Expressions Using This Verb

¿Cómo está Ud.?	estar para + infinitive / to be about + infinitive
Estoy muy bien, gracias. ¿Y usted?	*Estoy para salir.* / I am about to go out.
Estoy enfermo hoy.	estar por / to be in favor of

hacer / to do, to make

gerundio   Present Participle: *haciendo*   Past Participle: *hecho*

THE SEVEN SIMPLE TENSES		THE SEVEN COMPOUND TENSES	
Singular	**Plural**	**Singular**	**Plural**
Present Indicative		Present Perfect Indicative	
hago	hacemos	he hecho	hemos hecho
haces	hacéis	has hecho	habéis hecho
hace	hacen	has hecho	han hecho
Imperfect Indicative		Pluperfect OR Past Perfect Indicative	
hacía	hacíamos	había hecho	habíamos hecho
hacías	hacíais	habías hecho	habíais hecho
hacía	hacían	había hecho	habían hecho
Preterit		Past Anterior OR Preterit Perfect	
hice	hicimos	hube hecho	hubimos hecho
hiciste	hicisteis	hubiste hecho	hubisteis hecho
hizo	hicieron	hubo hecho	hubieron hecho
Future		Future Perfect OR Future Anterior	
haré	haremos	habré hecho	habremos hecho
harás	haréis	habrás hecho	habréis hecho
hará	harán	habrá hecho	habrán hecho
Conditional		Conditional Perfect	
haría	haríamos	habría hecho	habríamos hecho
harías	haríais	habrías hecho	habríais hecho
haría	harían	habría hecho	habrían hecho
Present Subjunctive		Present Perfect OR Past Subjunctive	
haga	hagamos	haya hecho	hayamos hecho
hagas	hagáis	hayas hecho	hayáis hecho
haga	hagan	haya hecho	hayan hecho
Imperfect Subjunctive		Pluperfect OR Past Perfect Subjunctive	
hiciera	hiciéramos	hubiera hecho	hubiéramos hecho
hicieras	hicierais	hubieras hecho	hubierais hecho
hiciera	hicieran	hubiera hecho	hubieran hecho
OR		OR	
hiciese	hiciésemos	hubiese hecho	hubiésemos hecho
hicieses	hicieseis	hubieses hecho	hubieseis hecho
hiciese	hiciesen	hubiese hecho	hubiesen hecho

Imperative	
—	hagamos
haz; no hagas	haced; no hagáis
haga	hagan

Common Idiomatic Expressions Using This Verb

Dicho y hecho. / No sooner said than done.
La práctica hace maestro al novicio. / Practice makes perfect.

ir / to go

gerundio　　　Present Participle: *yendo*　　　　　　　Past Participle: *ido*

THE SEVEN SIMPLE TENSES	THE SEVEN COMPOUND TENSES

Singular	Plural	Singular	Plural
Present Indicative		Present Perfect Indicative	
voy	vamos	he ido	hemos ido
vas	vais	has ido	habéis ido
va	van	ha ido	han ido
Imperfect Indicative		Pluperfect OR Past Perfect Indicative	
iba	íbamos	había ido	habíamos ido
ibas	ibais	habías ido	habíais ido
iba	iban	había ido	habían ido
Preterit		Past Anterior OR Preterit Perfect	
fui	fuimos	hube ido	hubimos ido
fuiste	fuisteis	hubiste ido	hubisteis ido
fue	fueron	hubo ido	hubieron ido
Future		Future Perfect OR Future Anterior	
iré	iremos	habré ido	habremos ido
irás	iréis	habrás ido	habréis ido
irá	irán	habrá ido	habrán ido
Conditional		Conditional Perfect	
iría	iríamos	habría ido	habríamos ido
irías	iríais	habrías ido	habríais ido
iría	irían	habría ido	habrían ido
Present Subjunctive		Present Perfect OR Past Subjunctive	
vaya	vayamos	haya ido	hayamos ido
vayas	vayáis	hayas ido	hayáis ido
vaya	vayan	haya ido	hayan ido
Imperfect Subjunctive		Pluperfect OR Past Perfect Subjunctive	
fuera	fuéramos	hubiera ido	hubiéramos ido
fueras	fuerais	hubieras ido	hubierais ido
fuera	fueran	hubiera ido	hubieran ido
OR		OR	
fuese	fuésemos	hubiese ido	hubiésemos ido
fueses	fueseis	hubieses ido	hubieseis ido
fuese	fuesen	hubiese ido	hubiesen ido

Imperative	
—	vamos (no vayamos)
ve; no vayas	id; no vayáis
vaya	vayan

Common Idiomatic Expressions Using This Verb

ir de compras / to go shopping　　*ir a caballo* / to ride horseback　　*un billete de ida y vuelta* / round trip ticket
ir de brazo / to walk arm in arm　*¡Qué va!* / Nonsense!　　　　　*¿Cómo le va?* / How goes it? How are you?
Cuando el gato va a sus devociones, bailan los ratones. / When the cat is away, the mice will play.

ser / to be

gerundio	Present Participle: *siendo*	Past Participle: *sido*

THE SEVEN SIMPLE TENSES		THE SEVEN COMPOUND TENSES	
Singular	**Plural**	**Singular**	**Plural**
Present Indicative		Present Perfect Indicative	
soy	somos	he sido	hemos sido
eres	sois	has sido	habéis sido
es	son	ha sido	han sido
Imperfect Indicative		Pluperfect OR Past Perfect Indicative	
era	éramos	había sido	habíamos sido
eras	erais	habías sido	habíais sido
era	eran	había sido	habían sido
Preterit		Past Anterior OR Preterit Perfect	
fui	fuimos	hube sido	hubimos sido
fuiste	fuisteis	hubiste sido	hubisteis sido
fue	fueron	hubo sido	hubieron sido
Future		Future Perfect OR Future Anterior	
seré	seremos	habré sido	habremos sido
serás	seréis	habrás sido	habréis sido
será	serán	habrá sido	habrán sido
Conditional		Conditional Perfect	
sería	seríamos	habría sido	habríamos sido
serías	seríais	habrías sido	habríais sido
sería	serían	habría sido	habrían sido
Present Subjunctive		Present Perfect OR Past Subjunctive	
sea	seamos	haya sido	hayamos sido
seas	seáis	hayas sido	hayáis sido
sea	sean	haya sido	hayan sido
Imperfect Subjunctive		Pluperfect OR Past Perfect Subjunctive	
fuera	fuéramos	hubiera sido	hubiéramos sido
fueras	fuerais	hubieras sido	hubierais sido
fuera	fueran	hubiera sido	hubieran sido
OR		OR	
fuese	fuésemos	hubiese sido	hubiésemos sido
fueses	fueseis	hubieses sido	hubieseis sido
fuese	fuesen	hubiese sido	hubiesen sido

Imperative	
—	seamos
sé; no seas	sed; no seáis
sea	sean

Common Idiomatic Expressions Using This Verb

Dime con quien andas y te diré quien eres. / Tell me who your friends are and I will tell you who you are.
es decir / that is, that is to say; *Si yo fuera usted . . .* / If I were you . . .
¿Qué hora es? / What time is it? *Es la una* / It is one o'clock. *Son las dos* / It is two o'clock.

§7.8
INFINITIVES
DEFINITION

In English, an infinitive is identified as a verb with the preposition "to" in front of it: to talk, to eat, to live. In Spanish, an infinitive is identified by its ending; those that end in *-ar, -er, -ir: hablar* (to talk, to speak), *comer* (to eat), *vivir* (to live).

Negation

To make an infinitive negative, place *no* in front of it.

No entrar. / Do not enter.

As a Verbal Noun

A verbal noun is a verb used as a noun. In Spanish, an infinitive may be used as a noun. This means that an infinitive may be used as a subject, a direct object, a predicate noun, or object of a preposition.

• As a subject:

Ser o no ser es la cuestión. / To be or not to be is the question.
El estudiar es bueno. OR *Estudiar es bueno.* / Studying (to study) is good.

Here, when the infinitive is a subject and it begins the sentence, you may use the definite article *el* in front of the infinitive or you may omit it.

If the sentence does not begin with the infinitive, do not use the definite article *el* in front of it:

Es bueno estudiar. / It is good to study.

• As a direct object:

No deseo comer. / I do not want to eat.

• As a predicate noun:

Ver es creer. / Seeing is believing (To see is to believe).

• As object of a preposition:

después de llegar. / after arriving.

Here, the infinitive (verbal noun) *llegar* is object of the preposition *de*.

In Spanish, an infinitive is ordinarily used after such verbs as *dejar, hacer, mandar,* and *permitir* with no preposition needed:

Luis dejó caer sus libros. / Louis dropped his books.
Mi madre me hizo leerlo. / My mother made me read it.
Mi profesor me permitió hacerlo. / My teacher permitted me to do it.

Note that when *dejar* is followed by the preposition *de* it means to stop or to cease:

Luis dejó de trabajar. / Louis stopped working.

The verb *pensar* is directly followed by an infinitive with no preposition required in front of the infinitive when its meaning is "to intend":

Pienso ir a Chile. / I intend to go to Chile.

Ordinarily, the infinitive form of a verb is used right after a preposition:

Antes de estudiar, Rita telefoneó a su amiga Beatriz. / Before studying, Rita telephoned her friend Beatrice.
El alumno salió de la sala de clase sin decir nada. / The pupil left the classroom without saying anything.

The infinitive form of a verb is ordinarily used after certain verbs of perception, such as *ver* and *oír:*

Las vi salir. / I saw them go out.
Lsa oí cantar. / I heard them singing.

After *al,* a verb is used in the infinitive form:

Al entrar en la escuela, Dorotea fue a su clase de español. Upon entering the school, Dorothy went to her Spanish class.

The perfect infinitive (also known as the past infinitive) is formed by using *haber* in its infinitive form + the past participle of the main verb:

haber hablado / to have spoken
haber comido / to have eaten
haber escrito / to have written

EJERCICIOS/EXERCISES

The answers to these exercises begin right after the last question in each group.

I. **La palabra misteriosa. Usando el vocabulario dado más abajo,**
   The mystery word. Using the vocabulary given below,

   busque las palabras españolas en el árbol.
   look for the Spanish words in the tree.

   Las palabras están escritas horizontalmente,
   The words are written horizontally,

   verticalmente, y a la inversa. Raye las palabras encontradas.
   vertically, and in reverse. Draw a line through the words you find.

   Ponga en orden las siete letras que quedan para hallar la palabra misteriosa.
   Put in correct order the seven letters that remain in order to find the mystery word.

   Feliz / Merry, Happy   **Navidad** / Christmas

   regalo / gift   **amor** / love

   nieve / snow   **luz** / light

II. Complete este crucigrama

Complete this crossword puzzle.

Horizontales:

2. Una persona duerme sobre una _____.

3. Sinónimo de **esposa.**

4. Forma del verbo **ser,** tercera persona, singular, en el presente de indicativo.

6. Gerundio *(present participle)* de **hablar.**

7. Una persona se sienta en una _____.

8. Forma del verbo **saber,** primera persona, singular, en el presente de indicativo.

9. Contrario de **hermoso.**

Verticales:

1. Contrario de **último.**

2. Sinónimo de **andar.**

5. Sinónimo de **esposo.**

Answers to the preceding group of exercises.

I.

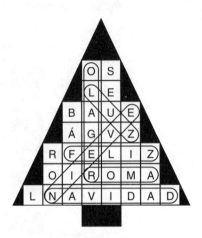

La palabra misteriosa es árboles.
The mystery word is **árboles** (trees).
The seven letters that remain are LORABSE.
Unscramble them and you get ARBOLES.

II.

§8.

Adverbs

An adverb is a word that modifies a verb, an adjective, or another adverb.

An adverb is regularly formed by adding the ending *mente* to the feminine singular form of an adjective.

lento, lenta / lentamente: slow / slowly
rápido, rápida / rápidamente: rapid / rapidly

If the form of the adjective is the same for the feminine singular and masculine singular *(fácil, feliz),* add *mente* to that form.

> *fácil* (easy) / *fácilmente* (easily)
> *feliz* (happy) / *felizmente* (happily)

Note that an accent mark on an adjective remains when the adjective is changed to an adverb. And note that the Spanish ending *mente* is equivalent to the ending -ly in English.

An adverb remains invariable; that is to say, it does not agree in gender and number and therefore does not change in form.

There are many adverbs that do not end in *mente.* Some common ones are:

abajo / below	*arriba* / above
bien / well	*mal* / badly
hoy / today	*mañana* / tomorrow
siempre / always	*nunca* / never
aquí / here	*allí* / there

The adverbial ending *ísimo*
Never use *muy* in front of *mucho.* Say *muchísimo:*

Elene trabaja muchísimo / Helen works a great deal; Helen works very, very much.

§8.2
COMPARISON

Regular comparison of adverbs
An adverb is compared regularly as an adjective.

María corre tan rápidamente como Elena / Mary runs as rapidly as Helen.
María corre menos rápidamente que Anita / Mary runs less rapidly than Anita.
María corre más rápidamente que Isabel / Mary runs more rapidly than Elizabeth.

Irregular comparative adverbs

mucho, poco / much, little: *Roberto trabaja mucho; Felipe trabaja poco.*
bien, mal / well, badly: *Juan trabaja bien; Lucas trabaja mal.*
más, menos / more, less: *Carlota trabaja más que Casandra; Elena trabaja menos que Marta.*
mejor, peor / better, worse: *Paula trabaja mejor que Anita; Isabel trabaja peor que Elena.*

In the comparative and superlative

rápidamente	**más rápidamente**	**lo más rápidamente**
rapidly	more rapidly	most rapidly

§8.3
INTERROGA-TIVE ADVERBS COMMONLY USED

Some common interrogative adverbs are:

¿cómo? / how? *¿cuándo?* / when?
¿cuánto?, ¿cuánta?, ¿cuántos?, ¿cuántas? / how much? how many?
¿por qué? / why? *¿para qué?* / why? *¿dónde?* / where?
¿adónde? / where to? (to where?)

§8.4
NEGATIVE ADVERBS COMMONLY USED

jamás / ever, never, not ever
nada / nothing (*sin nada* / without anything); after *sin, nada* is used instead of *algo; Ella no quiere nada* / She does not want anything.

ni / neither, nor	*también* / also, too
ni . . . ni / neither . . . nor	*tampoco* / neither
ni siquiera / not even	*ni yo tampoco* / nor I either
nunca / never, not ever, ever	*unos cuantos, unas cuantas* /
siempre / always	a few, some several

**§8.5
SPECIAL
USES**

Adverbs replaced by adjectives
　　An adverb may sometimes be replaced by an adjective whose agreement is with the subject, especially if the verb is one of motion:

> *Las muchachas van y vienen silenciosas.* / The girls come and
> go silently.

Ahí, allí, allá
　　These three adverbs all mean "there" but they have special uses:

- *ahí* means there, not too far away from the person who says it:

> *El libro que Ud. quiere está ahí sobre esa mesa.* / The book
> that you want is there on that table.

- allí means there, farther away from the person who says it, or even at a remote distance:

> *¿Quiere Ud. ir a Chicago? Sí, porque mi padre trabaja allí.*
> Do you want to go to Chicago? Yes, because my father
> works there.

- allá means there, generally used with a verb of motion:

> *Me gustaría mucho ir allá.* / I would like very much to go there.
> *Bueno, ¡vaya allá!* / Good, go there!

Aquí and acá
　　These two adverbs both mean "here" but they have special uses:

- *aquí* means here, a place close to the person who says it:

> *Aquí se habla español.* / Spanish is spoken here.

- *acá* means here, a place close to the person who says it, but it is used with a verb of motion:

> *Señor Gómez, ¡venga acá, por favor!* / Mr. Gómez, come here,
> please!

Con, sin + noun
　　At times, an adverb can be formed by using the preposition *con* (with) or *sin* (without) + a noun:

con cuidado / carefully	con dificultad / with difficulty
sin cuidado / carelessly	sin dificultad / without difficulty

　　The adverb *recientemente* (recently) becomes *recién* before a past participle:

> *los recién llegados* / the ones recently arrived; the recently
> arrived (ones)

§9.

Prepositions

A preposition is a word that connects words and, according to the thought expressed in the sentence, serves to indicate the relationship between the words.

a / at, to	*hacia* / toward
ante / before, in the presence of	*hasta* / until, up to, as far as
	menos / except
bajo / under	*para* / for, in order to
con / with	*por* / by, for
contra / against	*salvo* / except, save
de / of, from	*según* / according to
desde / after, from, since	*sin* / without
durante / during	*sobre* / on, upon, over, above
en / in, on	
entre / among, between	*tras* / after, behind

acerca de / about	*detrás de* / in back of, behind
además de / in addition to, besides	
	en contra de / against
alrededor de / around	*en cuanto a* / as far as
antes de / before	*en lugar de* / in place of, instead of
antes de nada / before anything	
	en medio de / in the middle of
antes de nadie / before anyone	
	en vez de / instead of
cerca de / near	*encima de* / on top of, upon
con rumbo a / in the direction of	*enfrente de* / opposite
	frente a / in front of
debajo de / underneath	*fuera de* / outside of
delante de / in front of	*junto a* / next to
dentro de / within, inside (of)	*lejos de* / far from
después de / after	*por valor de* / worth

Many prepositional phrases, such as the ones given above, would not be prepositional if the preposition *de* were not included in the phrase; without the preposition *de,* most of them are adverbs.

además / furthermore; *además de* / in addition to
alrededor / around; *alrededor de* / around
debajo / under; *debajo de* / underneath
lejos / far, far off; *lejos de* / far from

The use of the preposition *de* with these adverbs, and others, changes the part of speech to a preposition, as in such prepositional phrases as:

lejos de la escuela / far from the school
alrededor de la casa / around the house

Generally speaking, prepositions require a noun or a pronoun right after them (sometimes an infinitive, as in *sin decir nada* / without saying anything).

§9.4
USES OF
PREPOSITIONS

Generally speaking, prepositions are used in the following categories:

---

preposition + a noun: *con María* / with Mary;
   con mi amigo / with my friend
preposition + a pronoun: *para ella* / for her;
   para usted / for you
preposition + infinitive: *sin hablar* / without talking
verb + preposition: *gozar de algo* / to enjoy something

---

§9.5
SPECIAL CASES
§9.5–1
Personal *a*

In Spanish, the preposition *a* is used in front of a noun direct object of a verb if the direct object is a person or something personified.

Conozco a su hermana Elena. / I know your sister Helen.
¿Conoce Ud. a Roberto? / Do you know Robert?
Llamo al médico. / I am calling the doctor.

The personal *a* is used in front of an indefinite pronoun when it is direct object of a verb and it refers to a person, for example: *nadie, ninguno (ninguna), alguien, alguno (alguna), quien:*

Mis padres están visitando a alguien en el hospital. / My
   parents are visiting someone in the hospital.
¿Ve Ud. a alguien? / Do you see anybody?
No veo a nadie. / I don't see anybody.

The personal *a* is used in front of a geographic name if it is used as direct object:

Este verano pensamos visitar a Colombia. / This summer we
   plan to visit Colombia.

But if the geographic place contains a definite article in front of it (which is part of its name), the personal *a* is not used:

¿Ha visitado Ud. la Argentina? / Have you visited Argentina?
*La familia Gómez en Guadalajara quiere visitar los Estados
Unidos.* / The Gómez family in Guadalajara wants to visit the
   United States.

The personal *a* is used in front of a noun which is a domestic animal when personified and when it is direct object:

Quiero a mi gatito. / I love my kitten.

The personal *a* is not generally used with the verb *tener* when it means "to have."

Tengos dos hermanas y dos hermanos. / I have two sisters and two brothers.

But when *tener* means "to hold," the personal *a* is generally used:

La enfermera tenía al niño en los brazos. / The nurse was holding the child in her arms.

§9.5–2
Para con

The prepositional expression *para con,* meaning "to" or "toward," in the sense of with respect to or as regards, is used to denote a mental attitude or feeling about a person:

Nuestra profesora de español es muy amable para con nosotros. / Our Spanish teacher is very kind to us.

§9.5–3
Para and *por*

These two prepositions are generally translated into English as "for."

Use *para* when you mean:

Destination:

Mañana salgo para Madrid. / Tomorrow I am leaving for Madrid.

Intended for:

Este vaso es para María y ese vaso es para José. / This glass is for Mary and that glass is for Joseph.
Esta taza es para café; es una taza para café. / This cup is for coffee; it is a coffee cup.

Purpose (in order to):

Estudio para llegar a ser médico. / I am studying in order to become a doctor.

A comparison of some sort:

Para ser norteamericano, habla español muy bien. / For an American, he speaks Spanish very well.

At some point in future time:

Esta lección es para mañana. / This lesson is for tomorrow.

Use *por* when you mean:

A length of time:
> *Me quedé en casa por tres días.* / I stayed at home for three days.

In exchange for:
> *¿Cuánto dinero me dará Ud. por mi trabajo?* / How much money will you give me for my work?

To send for:
> *Vamos a enviar por el médico.* / We are going to send for the doctor.

By:
> *Este libro fue escrito por dos autores.* / This book was written by two authors.
> *Quiero enviar esta carta por avión.* / I want to send this letter by air mail.

For the sake of, as an obligation, on someone's behalf:
> *Quiero hacerlo por usted.* / I want to do it for you.

Through:
> *Dimos un paseo por el parque.* / We took a walk through the park.

Along, by the edge of:
> *Anduvimos por la playa.* / We walked along the beach.

To fight for:
> *Luché por mi amigo.* / I fought for my friend.

Out of, because of + noun:
> *No quisieron hacerlo por miedo.* / They refused to do it out of (for) fear.

Per, when expressing frequency:
> *Los alumnos asisten a la escuela cinco días por semana.* Students attend school five days a (per) week.

To go for someone or something:
> *Mi madre fue por Carmen.* / My mother went for (went to get) Carmen.
> *Mi madre fue por pan.* / My mother went for (went to get) bread.

To ask about, to inquire about, using *preguntar por:*
> *Pregunto por el médico.* / I am asking for the doctor.

To indicate something that may or may not get done:
> *Me queda mucho trabajo por hacer.* / I have a lot of work remaining that may or may not get done.

§9.5–4
Por or *de*

The preposition *por* is sometimes translated into English as "by," although it has other meanings, such as "through," "for."

The preposition *de* is sometimes translated into English as "by" and it has other meanings, too, such as "of," "from," "in."

When using a passive meaning that expresses an action performed by someone or something, *por* is generally used.

Use the preposition *de* to express "by" when using a passive meaning if some emotion or feeling is expressed instead of an action.

> *La señora Gómez es respetada de todos los alumnos.* / Mrs. Gómez is respected by all the students.

§9.5–5
Special uses of *para* and *por*

¿Para qué . . . ? and *¿Por qué . . . ?*

Both of these interrogatives mean "why" but they are not used interchangeably. If by "why" you mean for what reason, use *¿por qué . . . ?* If by "why" you mean for what purpose (what for?), use *¿para qué . . . ?*

> *Juanita, ¿por qué lloras?* / Jeanie, why (for what reason) are you crying?
> *Mamá, ¿para qué tenemos uñas?* / Mom, why (what for, for what purpose) do we have fingernails?

EJERCICIOS/EXERCISES

The answers to these exercises begin right after the last question in each group.

I. **Educational Tour. Speaking and Writing proficiencies**

Situation: You have just arrived in Barcelona. You are on an educational tour in Spain with a group of students from your school or college. Your guide is **Señorita López** who is a graduate student at the university working for her doctorate degree. You have been asking her questions about Barcelona. Now she has a few questions to ask you because she is impressed with your ability and zeal to speak some Spanish.

Participate in this dialogue. You are playing the role of **Tú,** which is the second person, singular, subject pronoun meaning *you.* It is a familiar form that a teacher can use when talking to a student, a parent when talking to a member of a family, between close friends, and even when talking to a pet. The plural of **tú** is **vosotros** *(masculine)* or **vosotras** *(feminine).* The polite singular form for *you* is **Usted (Ud.),** as you well remember. The plural form of **Usted (usted, Ud.)** is **Ustedes (Uds.).**

Señorita López: Tú hablas español muy bien.

Tú:

_____

(Thank her.)

Señorita López: ¿Cuántos años hace que tú estudias español?

Tú:

_____

(Tell her you've been studying Spanish for three years.)

Señorita López: ¿Dónde vives?

Tú:

_____

(Tell her in what city and country you live.)

Señorita López: ¿Qué asignaturas estudias en la escuela o en el colegio?

Tú:

_____

(Tell her what subjects you are studying in school or college.)

Señorita López: ¿Te gusta mi país?

Tú:

_____

(Tell her you like the country, the Spanish people, the culture, music, and art.)

Señorita López: Gracias. Bueno. Ahora, vamos al Rastro. Es un mercado callejero de artículos baratos o de segunda mano.*

Tú:

_____

(Tell her, "Oh, the flea market!!")

Señorita López: Eso es. En español lo llamamos El Rastro.**

Tú:

_____

(Ask her what the word for "flea" is in Spanish: **¿Cómo se dice** *flea* **en español?**)

Señorita López: Se dice la pulga. Vamos. ¡Cuidado con las pulgas!***

***un mercado callejero** / street market; **los artículos baratos** / cheap articles; **o** / or; **de segunda mano** / secondhand.
****lo llamamos** / we call it.
*****¡Cuidado con las pulgas!** / Watch out for the fleas!

II. **Match the following commonly used Spanish idiomatic expressions with the English equivalents by writing the appropriate number on the line. Refer to the previous pages if you have to, the vocabulary at the end of the book, or a standard Spanish-English/English-Spanish dictionary.**

1. a caballo   ___ near
2. a menudo   ___ you're welcome
3. poco a poco   ___ to mail, post a letter
4. a la derecha   ___ from today on
5. a la izquierda   ___ often
6. echar al correo   ___ round-trip ticket
7. con los brazos abiertos   ___ kneeling, on one's knees
8. dar la mano con alguien   ___ from time to time
9. un billete de ida y vuelta   ___ on horseback
10. cerca de   ___ little by little
11. de hoy en adelante   ___ to go shopping
12. ir de compras   ___ to the right
13. de vez en cuando   ___ on the left
14. de rodillas   ___ with open arms
15. de nada   ___ to shake hands with someone

Answers to the preceding group of exercises.

I. Muchas gracias, señorita.

Hace tres años que estudio español.

Vivo en la ciudad de Nueva York en los Estados Unidos.

Estudio dos lenguas, el español y el francés, la historia, las matemáticas, la biología, la música, y el arte.

Me gusta mucho su país. Me gustan, también, la cultura española, la música, el arte, y los españoles.

¿Cómo se dice *flea* en español?

II. **Matching question answers:**

10, 15, 6, 11, 2, 9, 14, 13, 1, 3, 12, 4, 5, 7, 8

§10.

Conjunctions

DEFINITION

A conjunction is a word that connects words, phrases, clauses or sentences.

**§10.1
COMMON
CONJUNCTIONS**

These terms are the most frequently used:

a fin de que. / so that, in order that
a menos que / unless
antes (de) que / before
apenas . . . cuando / hardly, scarcely . . . when
así que / as soon as, after
aun / even, still
aunque / although
como / as, since, how
como si / as if
con tal (de) que / provided that
cuando / when
de manera que / so that
de modo que / so that, in such a way that
después (de) que / after
e / and
en cuanto / as soon as
hasta que / until
luego que / as soon as, after
mas / but
mas que / even if, however much
mientras / while
mientras que / while, so long as, as long as
ni / neither, nor (*ni . . . ni* / neither . . . nor)
ni siquiera / not even
a condición de que / on condition that
a pesar de que / in spite of
así . . . como / both . . . and
aun cuando / even if
caso que / in case that
como que / it seems that, apparently

como quiera que / although, since
con la condición de que / on condition that
dado caso que / supposing that
dado que / supposing that
de condición que / so as to
de suerte que / so that, in such a manner as
desde que / since
empero / yet, however, notwithstanding

These conjunctions may be less familiar to you:

y, pero, o, porque. / and, but, or, because.
ni sólo . . . (sino) también / not only . . . but also
o / or (*o . . . o* / either . . . or)
o sea . . . o sea / either . . . or
para que / in order that, so that
pero / but
por cuanto / inasmuch as
porque / because
pues que / since
puesto que / although, since, inasmuch as, as long as
que / that, because
según que / according as
si / if, whether
sin embargo / nevertheless, notwithstanding, however (in whatever way)
sin que / without
sino / but, but rather
sino que / but that, but rather that
siquiera / though, although, whether, or

tan pronto como / as soon as
u / or
y / and
ya . . . ya / now . . . now
ya que / since, seeing that
en caso de que / in case, in case that
en razón de que / for the reason that
entretanto que / meanwhile, while
más bien que / rather than
mientras tanto / meanwhile

no bien . . . cuando / no sooner . . . than
por más que / no matter how, however much
por razón de que / for the reason that
salvo que / unless
siempre que / whenever, provided that
tan luego como / therefore
tanto . . . como / as much . . . as

§10.2
OTHER
CONJUNCTIONS

§10.2–1
Pero and *sino*

These two words are conjunctions and they both mean "but." Note the uses:

Me gustaría venir a tu casa esta noche pero no puedo. / I would like to come to your house tonight but I can't.

Use *sino* to mean "but rather," "but on the contrary:"

Pedro no es pequeño sino alto. / Peter is not short but tall.
Mi automóvil no es amarillo sino blanco. / My car is not yellow but white.

Note that when you use *sino* the first part of the sentence is negative. Also note that *sino* may be followed by an infinitive:

Pablo no quiere alquilar el automóvil sino comprarlo. / Paul does not want to rent the car but to buy it.

If a clause follows *sino,* use *sino que:*

Pablo no alquiló el automóvil sino que lo compró. / Paul did not rent the car but bought it.

And note finally that *sino* is used instead of *pero* when you make a clear contrast between a negative thought in the first part of the sentence and a positive thought in the second part. If no contrast is made or intended, use *pero:*

María no conoce al niño pero le habla. / Mary does not know the child but talks to him.

§10.2–2
Pero and *mas*

These two words are conjunctions and they both mean "but." In plays and poems an author may sometimes use *mas* instead of *pero.* In conversation and informal writing, *pero* is used. Note that *mas* with no accent mark means "but" and *más* (with the accent mark) means "more."

§10.2–3
O and *U*

These two words, which are conjunctions, mean "or." Use *o* normally but when a word that is right after *o* begins with *o* or *ho,* use *u:*

> *muchachos u hombres* / boys or men; *septiembre u octubre* / September or October

§10.2–4
Y and *E*

These two words, which are conjunctions, mean "and." Use *y* normally but when a word that is right after *y* begins with *i* or *hi,* use *e:*

> *María es bonita e inteligente.* / Mary is pretty and intelligent.
> *Fernando e Isabel; padre e hijo* / father and son
> *madre e hija* / mother and daughter

However, if *y* is followed by a word that begins with *hie,* keep *y:*

> *flores y hierba* / flowers and grass

Special Topics

§11.

Exclamatory *¡Qué . . . !* and *¡Tal . . . !*

In English, when we exclaim What a class! What a student! What an idea! or Such an idea! we use the indefinite article a or an. In Spanish, however, we do not use the indefinite article.

¡Qué clase! ¡Qué alumno! ¡Qué alumna! ¡Qué idea! OR *¡Tal idea!*

If an adjective is used to describe the noun, we generally use *más* or *tan* in front of the adjective, in order to intensify the exclamation.

¡Qué chica tan bonita! / What a pretty girl!
¡Qué libro más interesante! / What an interesting book!

When we use *¡Qué!* + an adjective, the meaning in English is "How . . . !"

¡Qué difícil es! / How difficult it is!

§12.

Idioms

> *¿Cuánto tiempo hace que* + present tense . . . ?

¿Cuánto tiempo hace que Ud. estudia español? / How long have you been studying Spanish?
¿Cuánto tiempo hace que Ud. espera el autobús? / How long have you been waiting for the bus?

Use the present tense of the verb when the action of studying, waiting, etc. is still going on at the present.

> *¿Cuánto tiempo hacía que* + imperfect tense

If the action of the verb began in the past and ended in the past, use the imperfect tense.

¿Cuánto tiempo hacía que Ud. hablaba cuando yo entré en la sala de clase? / How long had you been talking when I entered into the classroom?

> *¿Desde cuándo* + present tense . . . ?

This is another way of asking: How long (since when) + the present perfect tense in English, as given above.

¿Desde cuándo estudia Ud. español? / How long have you been studying Spanish?

Present tense + *desde hace* + length of time

Estudio español desde hace tres años. / I have been studying Spanish for three years.

> *¿Desde cuándo* + imperfect tense . . . ?

¿Desde cuándo hablaba Ud. cuando yo entré en la sala de clase? / How long had you been talking when I entered into the classroom?

Imperfect tense + *desde hacía* + length of time

(Yo) hablaba desde hacía una hora cuando Ud. entró en la sala de clase / I had been talking for one hour when you entered into the classroom.

Hace + length of time + *que* + present tense

Hace tres años que estudio español. / I have been studying
Spanish for three years.
Hace veinte minutos que espero el autobús. / I have been
waiting for the bus for twenty minutes.
¿Cuántos años hace que Ud. estudia español? / How many
years have you been studying Spanish?
¿Cuántas horas hace que Ud. mira la televisión? / How many
hours have you been watching television?

Hacía + length of time + *que* + imperfect tense

---

*Hacía una hora que yo hablaba cuando Ud. entró en la sala de
clase.* / I had been talking for one hour when you
entered the classroom.

Hay and *hay que* + infinitive

The word *hay* is not a verb. Its English equivalent is:
There is . . . or There are. . . .

Hay muchos libros en la mesa. / There are many books on the
table.
Hay una mosca en la sopa. / There is a fly in the soup.

Hay que + infinitive is an impersonal expression that
denotes an obligation and it is commonly translated into
English as: One must . . . or it is necessary to . . .

Hay que estudiar para aprender. / It is necessary to study in
order to learn.

Medio and *mitad*

Both these words mean "half" but note the uses:
Medio is an adjective and it agrees with the noun it
modifies:

Necesito media docena de huevos. / I need half a dozen eggs.
Llegaremos en media hora. / We will arrive in a half hour (in
half an hour).

Medio is also used as an adverb:

*Los caballos corrieron rápidamente y ahora están medio
muertos.* / The horses ran fast and now they are half dead.

Mitad is a feminine noun:

El alumno estudió la mitad de la lección / The pupil studied half (of) the lesson.

§12.2 COMMON EXPRESSIONS

with *a*

a bordo / on board
a caballo / on horseback
a cada instante / at every moment, at every turn
a casa / home (Use with a verb of motion; use *a casa* if you are going to the house; use *en casa* if you are in the house.
a eso de / about, around

Llegaremos a Madrid a eso de las tres de la tarde. / We will arrive in Madrid at about 3 o'clock in the afternoon.

a fines de / about the end of, around the end of

Estaremos en Madrid a fines de la semana. / We will be in Madrid around the end of the week.

a mano / by hand
a mediados de / around the middle of

Estaremos en Málaga a mediados de julio. / We will be in Málaga around the middle of July.

a menudo / often, frequently
a mi parecer / in my opinion
a pesar de / in spite of
a pie / on foot
a principios de / around the beginning of

Estaremos en México a principios de la semana que viene.
We will be in Mexico around the beginning of next week.

a saltos / by leaps and bounds
a tiempo / on time
a través de / across, through
a veces / at times, sometimes
estar a punto de / to be about to

Estoy a punto de salir. / I am about to leave.

frente a / in front of
junto a / beside, next to
poco a poco / little by little
ser aficionado a / to be a fan of
uno a uno / one by one

with *a la*

a la derecha / to (on, at) the right
a la española / in the Spanish style
a la francesa / in the French style
a la italiana / in the Italian style
a la izquierda / to (on, at) the left
a la larga / in the long run
a la madrugada / at an early hour, at daybreak
a la semana / a week, per week
a la vez / at the same time

with *al*

al + infinitive / on, upon + present participle

> *Al entrar en la cocina, comenzó a comer.* / Upon entering into the kitchen, he began to eat.

al aire libre / outdoors, in the open air
al amanecer / at daybreak, at dawn
al anochecer / at nightfall, at dusk
al cabo / finally, at last
al cabo de / at the end of
al contrario / on the contrary
al día / current, up to date
al día siguiente / on the following day, on the next day
al fin / at last, finally
al lado de / next to, beside
al menos / at least
al mes / a month, per month
al parecer / apparently
al principio / at first
echar al correo / to mail, to post a letter

with *con*

con frecuencia / frequently
con los brazos abiertos / with open arms
con motivo de / on the occasion of
con mucho gusto / gladly, willingly, with much pleasure
con permiso / excuse me, with your permission
con rumbo a / in the direction of
ser amable con / to be kind to

---

with *cuanto, cuanta, cuantos, cuantas*

---

cuanto antes / as soon as possible

> *¿Cuánto cuesta?* / How much is it? How much does it cost?

cuanto más . . . tanto más . . . / the more . . . the more . . .

> *Cuanto más estudio tanto más aprendo.* / The more I study the
> more I learn.
> *¿Cuántos años tiene Ud.?* / How old are you?

unos cuantos libros / a few books; *unas cuantas flores* / a
few flowers

---

with *dar* and *darse*

---

dar a / to face

> *El comedor da al jardín.* / The dining room faces the garden.

dar con algo / to find something, to come upon something

> *Esta mañana di con dinero en la calle.* / This morning I found
> money in the street.

dar con alguien / to meet someone, to run into someone, to
come across someone, to find someone

> *Anoche, di con mi amiga Elena en el cine.* / Last night I met my
> friend Helen at
> the movies.

dar contra / to hit against
dar de beber a / to give something to drink to
dar de comer a / to feed, to give something to eat to

> *Me gusta dar de comer a los pájaros en el parque.* / I like to
> feed the
> birds in
> the
> park.

dar en / to hit against, to strike against
dar la bienvenida / to welcome
dar la hora / to strike the hour
dar la mano a alguien / to shake hands with someone
dar las gracias a alguien / to thank someone
dar los buenos días a alguien / to say good morning (hello)
    to someone
dar por + past participle / to consider

> *Lo doy por perdido.* / I consider it lost.

dar recuerdos a / to give one's regards (best wishes) to
dar un abrazo / to embrace
dar un paseo / to take a walk
dar un paseo a caballo / to go horsebacking riding
dar un paseo en automóvil (en coche) / to go for a drive
dar un paseo en bicicleta / to ride a bicycle
dar una vuelta / to go for a short walk, to go for a stroll
dar unas palmadas / to clap one's hands
dar voces / to shout
darse cuenta de / to realize, to be aware of, to take into account
darse la mano / to shake hands with each other
darse prisa / to hurry

---

with *de*

acabar de + infinitive / to have just + past participle

> *María acaba de llegar.* / Mary has just arrived.
> *María acababa de llegar.* / Mary had just arrived.

acerca de / about, concerning
alrededor de / around
alrededor de la casa / around the house
antes de / before
aparte de / aside from
billete de ida y vuelta / round-trip ticket
cerca de / near, close to
de abajo / down, below
de acuerdo / in agreement, in accord
de aquí en adelante / from now on
de arriba / upstairs
de arriba abajo / from top to bottom
de ayer en ocho días / a week from yesterday
de balde / free, gratis
de broma / jokingly
de buena gana / willingly
de cuando en cuando / from time to time
de día / by day, in the daytime
de día en día / from day to day
de esa manera / in that way
de ese modo / in that way
de esta manera / in this way
de este modo / in this way
de hoy en adelante / from today on, from now on
de hoy en ocho días / a week from today

de la mañana / in the morning (Use this when a specific time is mentioned)

> *Tomo el desayuno a las ocho de la mañana.* / I have breakfast at 8 o'clock in the morning.

de la noche / in the evening (Use this when a specific time is mentioned.)

> *Mi amigo llega a las neuve de la noche.* / My friend is arriving at 9 o'clock in the evening.

de la tarde / in the afternoon (Use this when a specific time is mentioned)

> *Regreso a casa a las cuatro de la tarde.* / I am returning home at 4 o'clock in the afternoon.

de madrugada / at dawn, at daybreak
de mal humor / in bad humor, in a bad mood
de mala gana / unwillingly
de memoria / by heart (memorized)
de moda / in fashion
de nada / you're welcome
de ningún modo / no way, in no way, by no means
de ninguna manera / no way, in no way, by no means
de noche / by night, at night, during the night
de nuevo / again
de otra manera / in another way
de otro modo / otherwise
de pie / standing
de prisa / in a hurry
de pronto / suddenly
de repente / all of a sudden
de rodillas / kneeling, on one's knees
de todos modos / anyway, in any case, at any rate
de uno en uno / one by one
de veras / really, truly
de vez en cuando / from time to time
ir de compras / to go shopping
no hay de qué / you're welcome, don't mention it
un poco de / a little (of)
un poco de azúcar / a little sugar

with *decir*

decirle al oído / to whisper in one's ears
dicho y hecho / no sooner said than done
Es decir . . . / That is to say . . .
querer decir / to mean

> *¿Qué quiere decir este muchacho?* / What does this boy mean?

with *día, días*

al día / current, up to date
al romper el día / at daybreak
algún día / someday
de día en día / day by day
día por día / day by day
estar al día / to be up to date
hoy día / nowadays
por día / by the day, per day
quince días / two weeks
un día de éstos / one of these days

with *en*

en bicicleta / by bicycle
en broma / jokingly, in fun
en cambio / on the other hand
en casa / at home (Use *en casa* if you are in the house; use a casa with a verb of motion, if you are going to the house)

> *Me quedo en casa esta noche.* / I am staying home tonight.
> *Salgo de la escuela y voy a casa.* / I'm leaving school and I'm going home.

en casa de / at the house of

> *María está en casa de Elena.* / Mary is at Helen's house.

en caso de / in case of
en coche / by car
en cuanto / as soon as
en cuanto a / as for, with regard to, in regard to
en efecto / as a matter of fact, in fact
en este momento / at this moment
en lo alto de / on top of it, at the top of, up
en lugar de / in place of, instead of
en medio de / in the middle of
en ninguna parte / nowhere

en punto / sharp, exactly (telling time)

> *Son las dos en punto.* / It is two o'clock sharp.

en seguida / immediately, at once
en todas partes / everywhere
en vano / in vain
en vez de / instead of
en voz alta / in a loud voice
en voz baja / in a low voice

with *estar*

está bien / all right, okay
estar a punto de + infinitive / to be about + infinitive

> *Estoy a punto de salir.* / I am about to go out.

estar conforme con / to be in agreement with
estar de acuerdo / to agree
estar de acuerdo con / to be in agreement with
estar de boga / to be in fashion, to be fashionable
estar de buenas / to be in a good mood
estar de pie / to be standing
estar de vuelta / to be back
estar para + infinitive / to be about to

> *Estoy para salir.* / I am about to go out.

estar por / to be in favor of
no estar para bromas / not to be in the mood for jokes

with *haber*

ha habido . . . / there has been . . . , there have been . . .
había . . . / there was . . . , there were . . .
habrá . . . / there will be . . .
habría . . . / there would be . . .
hubo . . . / there was . . . , there were . . .

with *hacer* and *hacerse*

hace poco / a little while ago
hace un año / a year ago

> *Hace un mes que partió el señor Molina.* / Mr. Molina left
> one month ago.

hace una hora / an hour ago
hacer daño a alguien / to harm someone

hacer el baúl / to pack one's trunk
hacer el favor de + infinitive / please

> *Haga Ud. el favor de entrar.* / Please come in.

hacer el papel de / to play the role of
hacer falta / to be wanting, lacking, needed
hacer la maleta / to pack one's suitcase
hacer pedazos / to smash, to break, to tear into pieces
hacer un viaje / to take a trip
hacer una broma / to play a joke
hacer una pregunta / to ask a question
hacer una visita / to pay a visit
hacerle falta / to need

> *A Juan le hace falta un lápiz.* / John needs a pencil.

hacerse / to become

> *Elena se hizo dentista.* / Helen became a dentist.

hacerse daño / to hurt oneself, to harm oneself
hacerse tarde / to be getting late

> *Vámonos; se hace tarde.* / Let's leave; it's getting late.

| with *hasta* |

hasta ahora / until now
hasta aquí / until now, up to here
hasta después / see you later, until later
hasta entonces / see you then, see you later, up to that
   time, until that time
hasta la vista / see you again
hasta luego / see you later, until later
hasta mañana / see you tomorrow, until tomorrow

| with *lo* |

a lo largo de / along
a lo lejos / in the distance
a lo menos / at least
lo bueno / what is good, the good part

> *¡Lo bueno que es!* / How good it is!
> *¡Lo bien que está escrito!* / How well it is written!

lo de + infinitive, adverb, or noun / "that matter of . . . ",
   "that business of . . . "
lo escrito / what is written
lo malo / what is bad, the bad part

lo más pronto posible / as soon as possible
lo mejor / what is best, the best part
lo primero que debo decir / the first thing I must say
lo simpático / whatever is kind
por lo contrario / on the contrary
por lo menos / at least
por lo pronto / in the meantime, for the time being
¡Ya lo creo! / I should certainly think so!

---

with *luego*

desde luego / naturally, of course, immediately
hasta luego / see you later, so long
luego luego / right away
luego que / as soon as, after

---

with *mañana*

ayer por la mañana / yesterday morning
de la mañana / in the morning (Use this when a specific
  time is mentioned):

  Voy a tomar el tren a las seis de la mañana. / I am going to
  take the train at six o'clock in the morning.

mañana por la mañana / tomorrow morning
mañana por la noche / tomorrow night
mañana por la tarde / tomorrow afternoon
pasado mañana / the day after tomorrow
por la mañana / in the morning (Use this when no exact
  time is mentioned):

  El señor Pardo llega por la mañana. / Mr. Pardo is arriving in
  the morning.

pro la mañana temprano / early in the morning

---

with *mismo*

ahora mismo / right now
al mismo tiempo / at the same time
allá mismo / right there
aquí mismo / right here
así mismo / the same, the same thing
el mismo de siempre / the same old thing
eso mismo / that very thing
hoy mismo / this very day
lo mismo / the same, the same thing

lo mismo da / it makes no difference, it amounts to the same thing
lo mismo de siempre / the same old story
lo mismo que / the same as, as well as
por lo mismo / for the same reason

---
with *no*

Creo que no. / I don't think so, I think not.
No es verdad. / It isn't so, It isn't true; *¿No es verdad?* / Isn't that so?
No hay de qué. / You're welcome.
No hay remedio. / There's no way. It cannot be helped.
No importa. / It doesn't matter.
No + verb + *más que* + amount of money

> *No tengo más que un dólar.* / I have only one dollar.

todavía no / not yet
ya no / no longer

---
with *para*
---

estar para + infinitive / to be about to, to be at the point of

> *El autobús está para salir.* / The bus is about to leave.

para con / to, toward

> *Nuestra profesora de español es muy amable para con nosotros.* / Our Spanish teacher is very kind to us.

para eso / for that matter
para mí / for my part
para que / in order that, so that
para ser / in spite of being

> *Para ser tan viejo, él es muy ágil.* / In spite of being so old, he is very agile.

para siempre / forever
un vaso para agua / a water glass; *una taza para café* / a coffee cup

---
with *poco*
---

a poco / in a short while, presently
dentro de poco / in short while, in a little while
en pocos días / in a few days
poco a poco / little by little

poco antes / shortly before
poco después / shortly after
por poco / nearly, almost
un poco de / a little (of)

> *Quisiera un poco de azúcar.* / I would like a little sugar.

---

with *por*

---

acabar por + infinitive / to end up by + present participle

> *Mi padre acabó por comprarlo.* / My father finally ended up by
> buying it.

al por mayor / wholesale
al por menor / retail (sales)
ayer por la mañana / yesterday morning
ayer por la noche / yesterday evening
ayer por la tarde / yesterday afternoon
estar por / to be in favor of
mañana por la mañana / tomorrow morning
mañana por la noche / tomorrow night, tomorrow evening
mañana por la tarde / tomorrow afternoon
por ahora / for just now, for the present
por aquí / this way, around here
por avión / by air mail
por consiguiente / consequently
por desgracia / unfortunately
por Dios / for God's sake
por ejemplo / for example
por el contrario OR *por lo contrario* / on the contrary
por escrito / in writing
por eso / for that reason, therefore
por favor / please

> *Entre, por favor.* / Come in, please.

por fin / at last, finally
por hora / by the hour, per hour
por la mañana / in the morning
por la noche / in the evening
por la noche temprano / early in the evening
por la tarde / in the afternoon
por lo común / commonly, generally, usually
por lo general / generally, usually
por lo menos / at least
por lo tanto / consequently, therefore
por lo visto / apparently

por mi parte / as for me, as far as I am concerned
por poco / nearly, almost
por semana / by the week, per week
por supuesto / of course
por teléfono / by phone
por todas partes / everywhere

with *pronto*

al pronto / at first
de pronto / suddenly
lo más pronto posible / as soon as possible
por de pronto / for the time being
por el pronto OR *por lo pronto* / in the meantime, for the
   time being
tan pronto como / as soon as

with *que*

Creo que no / I don't think so, I think not.
Creo que sí / I think so.
el año que viene / next year
la semana que viene / next week
¡Qué lástima¡ / What a pity!
¡Qué le vaya bien! / Good luck!
¡Qué lo pase Ud. bien! / Good luck! (I wish you a good
   outcome!)

with *ser*

Debe de ser . . . / It is probably . . .
Debe ser . . . / It ought to be . . .
Es de mi agrado / It's to my liking.
Es hora de . . . / It is time to . . .
Es lástima OR *Es una lástima* / It's a pity; It's too bad.
Es que . . . / The fact is . . .
para ser / in spite of being

   Para ser tan viejo, él es muy ágil. / In spite of being so old,
                                        he is very nimble.

sea lo que sea / whatever it may be
ser aficionado a / to be a fan of

   Soy aficionado al béisbol. / I'm a baseball fan.

ser amable con / to be kind to

> *Mi profesora de español es amable conmigo.* / My Spanish
> teacher is kind to me.

ser todo oídos / to be all ears

> *Te escucho; soy todo óidos.* / I'm listening to you; I'm all ears.

| with *sin* |

sin aliento / out of breath
sin cuidado / carelessly
sin duda / without a doubt, undoubtedly
sin ejemplo / unparalleled, nothing like it
sin embargo / nevertheless, however
sin falta / without fail
sin novedad / nothing new, same as usual

| with *tener* |

¿Cuántos años tienes?

> *¿Cuántos años tiene Ud.?* / How old are you?
> *Tengo diez y seis años.* / I am sixteen years old.

¿Qué tienes?

> *¿Qué tiene Ud.?* / What's the matter? What's the matter with
> you?
> *No tengo nada.* / There's nothing wrong; There's nothing the
> matter (with me).

tener algo que hacer / to have something to do
tener calor / to feel (to be) warm (persons)
tener cuidado / to be careful
tener dolor de cabeza / to have a headache
tener dolor de estómago / to have a stomach ache
tener éxito / to be successful
tener frío / to feel (to be) cold (persons)
tener ganas de + infinitive / to feel like + present participle

> *Tengo ganas de tomar un helado.* / I feel like having an ice
> cream.

tener gusto en + infinitive / to be glad + infinitive

> *Tengo mucho gusto en conocerle.* / I am very glad to meet you.

tener hambre / to feel (to be) hungry
tener la bondad de / please; please be good enough to . . .

> *Tenga la bondad de cerrar la puerta.* / Please close the door.

tener la culpa de algo / to take the blame for something, to be to blame for something

> *Tengo la culpa de eso.* / I am to blame for that.

tener lugar / to take place

> *El accidente tuvo lugar anoche.* / The accident took place last night.

tener miedo de / to be afraid of
tener mucha sed / to feel (to be) very thirsty (persons)
tener mucho calor / to feel (to be) very warm (persons)
tener mucho frío / to feel (to be) very cold (persons)
tener mucho que hacer / to have a lot to do
tener poco que hacer / to have little to do
tener prisa / to be in a hurry
tener que + infinitive / to have + infinitive

> *Tengo que estudiar.* / I have to study.

tener razón / to be right

> *Ud. tiene razón.* / You are right.

no tener razón / to be wrong

> *Ud. no tiene razón.* / You are wrong.

tener sed / to feel (to be) thirsty (persons)
tener sueño / to feel (to be) sleepy
tener suerte / to be lucky

| with *todo, toda, todos, todas* |

a todo / at most
a todo correr / at full speed
ante todo / first of all, in the first place
así y todo / in spite of everything
de todos modos / anyway, in any case, at any rate
en un todo / in all its parts
en todo y por todo / in each and every way
ir a todo correr / to run by leaps and bounds
por todo / throughout
sobre todo / above all, especially
toda la familia / the whole family
todas las noches / every night
todas las semanas / every week
todo el mundo / everybody
todos cuantos / all those that
todos los años / every year
todos los días / every day

| with *vez* and *veces* |

a la vez / at the same time
a veces / sometimes, at times
alguna vez / sometime
algunas veces / sometimes
cada vez / each time
cada vez más / more and more (each time)
de vez en cuando / from time to time
dos veces / twice, two times
en vez de / instead of
muchas veces / many times
otra vez / again, another time, once more
raras veces / few times, rarely
tal vez / perhaps
una vez / once, one time
una vez más / once more, one more time
unas veces / sometimes
varias veces / several times

| with *y* |

dicho y hecho / no sooner said than done
sano y salvo / safe and sound
un billete de ida y vuelta / round-trip ticket
¿Y bien? / And then? And so? So what?
y eso que / even though
y por si eso fuera poco . . . / and as if that were not
   enough . . .

| with *ya* |

¡Hazlo ya! ¡Hágalo ya! / Do it now!
no ya . . . sino / not only . . . but also
¡Pues ya! / Of course! Certainly!
si ya . . . / If only . . .
¡Ya lo creo! / I should certainly think so! Of course!
Ya lo veré. / I'll see to it.
ya no / no longer
Ya pasó. / It's all over now.
ya que / since, as long as, seeing that . . .
¡Ya se ve! / Yes, indeed!
¡Ya voy! / I'm coming! I'll be there in a second!

EJERCICIOS/EXERCISES

The answers to these exercises begin right after the last question in each group.

I. **Sopa de letras.**
   Alphabet soup.
   Busque cuatro sinónimos del adjetivo *contento*.
   Look for four synonyms of the adjective contento.
   Los cuatro sinónimos pueden aparecer de derecha a izquierda,
   The four synonyms can appear from right to left,
   de izquierda a derecha, de abajo arriba y viceversa.
   from left to right, from bottom to top, from top to bottom.

   Tip: The four Spanish synonyms of the adjective **contento**/*content* that you are looking for in the puzzle here below are: **feliz, encantado, plácido, satisfecho.** Look for them and when you find them draw a line around each one. One of them is printed backwards. After you find them, write each one three times, in Spanish of course, just for the practice.

G	A	C	S	E	X
C	O	N	A	N	O
I	Z	P	T	C	D
F	E	L	I	Z	A
K	L	Á	S	A	T
O	Q	C	F	N	N
R	I	I	E	T	A
J	M	D	C	O	C
N	P	O	H	P	N
D	E	L	O	X	E

II. **Providing, obtaining information. Speaking and Writing Proficiency**

   Situation: You and some of your friends are waiting on the corner for the yellow school bus. One of your friends is Juana Robles. She wants to obtain some information. Provide answers to her questions in this dialogue.

   You are playing the role of **Tú.** You may provide the Spanish words for the suggested English words or you may use your own words and ideas.

Juana: **¡Hola! ¿Cómo estás? ¿Qué tal?**
             (How are things?)

Tú: _____

             (Greet your friend and tell her how you feel.)

Juana: **Dime, ¿cuántos minutos hace que tú esperas el autobús?**
             Tell me, how many minutes have you been waiting for the bus?

Tú: _____

             (Say that you have been waiting for the bus for ten minutes.)

Juana: **¿Y ayer por la mañana? ¿Cuántos minutos hacía que tú esperabas el autobús cuando llegó?**
             And yesterday morning? How many minutes had you been waiting for the bus when it arrived?

Tú: _____

             _____

             (Tell her that yesterday morning you had been waiting for the bus twenty minutes when it arrived finally/**finalmente.**)

Juana: **¡Mira, mira! ¡El autobús llega!**

Tú: _____

             (Make an exclamation, such as, Finally!)

III. Escriba la forma correcta del adjetivo demostrativo según el modelo a continuación. (Write the correct form of the demonstrative adjective according to the following models.)

Modelos: libro   este libro/_this book_
               pluma   esta pluma/_this pen_
               chicos   estos chicos/_these boys_
               escuelas   estas escuelas/_these schools_

1. pluma _____   6. hombre _____

2. escuelas _____   7. mujer _____

3. lápiz _____   8. lápices _____

4. cuaderno _____   9. libros _____

5. muchacha _____   10. lección _____

IV. Escriba la forma correcta del adjetivo demostrativo según el modelo a continuación. *(Write the correct form of the demonstrative adjective according to the following models.)*

Modelos:	libro	ese libro/*that book*
	pluma	esa pluma/*that pen*
	chicos	esos chicos/*those boys*
	escuelas	esas escuelas/*those schools*

1. pluma _____
2. escuelas _____
3. lápiz _____
4. cuaderno _____
5. muchacha _____

6. hombre _____
7. mujer _____
8. lápices _____
9. libros _____
10. lección _____

Mnemonic Tip	**este, estos, esta, estas** have the t's; **ese, esos, esa, esas** don't have the t's.

Answers to the preceding group of exercises.

Sopa de letras / Alphabet soup.

I.

G	A	C	S	E	X
C	O	N	A	N	O
I	Z	P	T	C	D
F	E	L	I	Z	A
K	L	Á	S	A	T
O	Q	C	F	N	N
R	I	I	E	T	A
J	M	D	C	O	C
N	P	O	H	P	N
D	E	L	O	X	E

II. Providing, obtaining information.

¡Hola! Estoy bien, gracias.

Hace diez minutos que espero el autobús.

Ayer por la mañana, hacía veinte minutos que esperaba el autobús cuando llegó finalmente.

¡Ah! Finalmente!

III. 1. esta pluma
    2. estas escuelas
    3. este lápiz
    4. este cuaderno
    5. esta muchacha
    6. este hombre
    7. esta mujer
    8. estos lápices
    9. estos libros
    10. esta lección

IV. 1. esa pluma
    2. esas escuelas
    3. ese lápiz
    4. ese cuaderno
    5. esa muchacha
    6. ese hombre
    7. esa mujer
    8. esos lápices
    9. esos libros
    10. esa lección

§13.

Dates, Days, Months, Seasons

§13.1
DATES

¿Cuál es la fecha? / What's the date?
¿Cuál es la fecha de hoy? / What's the date today?
Es el primero de junio. / It is June first.
Es el dos de mayo. / It is May second.

Note that when stating the date, in Spanish we use *el primero,* which is an ordinal number, for the first day of any month. To state all other dates, use the cardinal numbers: *Hoy es el dos de enero, el tres de febrero, el cuatro de marzo,* etc.

¿A cuántos estamos hoy? / What's the date today?
Estamos a cinco de abril. / It's April 5th.

When stating a date, the English word "on" is expressed in Spanish by using the definite article *el* in front of the date:

María nació el cuatro de julio. / Mary was born on the fourth of July.

• When stating the year, in Spanish we use thousand and hundreds:

el año mil novecientos ochenta y seis / the year 1986
But: *el año dos mil siete* / the year 2007

This is very different from English, which is usually stated as nineteen eighty or nineteen hundred eighty. In Spanish we must state *mil* (one thousand) + *novecientos* (nine hundred): *mil novecientos setenta y nueve* (1979), *mil novecientos ochenta y uno* (1981).
• To sum up: *Hoy es domingo, el ocho de julio, de dos mil siete.* / Today is Sunday, July 8, 2007.

§13.2
DAYS

• The days of the week, which are all masculine, are:

domingo / Sunday; *lunes* / Monday; martes / Tuesday; *miércoles* / Wednesday; *jueves* / Thursday; *viernes* / Friday; *sábado* / Saturday.

• In Spanish, the days of the week are ordinarily not capitalized. In newspapers, magazines, business letters, and elsewhere, you sometimes see them capitalized.

• When stating the day of the week in English we may use "on," but in Spanish we use *el* or *los* in front of the day of the week.

> *el lunes* / on Monday; *los lunes* / on Mondays

Note that the days of the week whose last letter is *s* do not change in the plural: *el martes / los martes; el miércoles / los miércoles.* BUT: *el sábado / los sábados; el domingo / los domingos.*

> *¿Qué día es?* / What day is it?
> *¿Qué día es hoy?* / What day is it today?
> *Hoy es lunes.* / Today is Monday.

§13.3
MONTHS

• The months of the year, which are all masculine, are:

> *enero* / January; *febrero* / February; *marzo* / March; *abril* / April; *mayo* / May; *junio* / June; *julio* / July; *agosto* / August; *septiembre* / September; *octubre* / October; *noviembre* / November; *diciembre* / December.

• In Spanish, the months of the year are ordinarily not capitalized. In newspapers, magazines, business letters, and elsewhere, you sometimes see them capitalized.
• To say in + the name of the month, use *en: en enero* / in January; OR: *en el mes de enero* / in the month of January
• The plural of *el mes* is *los meses.*

§13.4
SEASONS

• The seasons of the year *(las estaciones del año)* are:

> *la primavera* / spring; *el verano* / summer; *el otoño* / autumn, fall; *el invierno* / winter.

• In Spanish, the seasons of the year are not capitalized.
• The definite article usually precedes a season of the year:

> *¿En qué estación hace frío?* / In what season is it cold?
> *Generalmente, hace frío en el invierno.* / Generally, it is cold in winter.

§14.

Telling Time

Son las tres de la tarde.
OR:
Son las tres de la mañana.

¿Qué hora es? / What time is it?
Es la una. / It is one o'clock.

Note that the 3rd person singular of *ser* is used because the time is one (o'clock), which is singular.

Son las dos. / It is two o'clock.

Note that the 3rd person plural of *ser* is used because the time is two (o'clock), which is more than one.

Son las tres, son las cuatro. / It is three o'clock, it is four o'clock.

When the time is a certain number of minutes after the hour, the hour is stated first *(Es la una)* + *y* + the number of minutes:

Es la una y cinco. / It is five minutes after one o'clock (It is 1:05).
Son las dos y diez. / It is ten minutes after two o'clock (It is 2:10).

When the hour is a quarter after, you can express it by using either *y cuarto* or *y quince (minutos)*:

Son las dos y cuarto OR *Son las dos y quince (minutos).* / It is 2:15.

When it is half past the hour, you can express it by using either *y media* or *y treinta (minutos)*:

Son las dos y media OR *Son las dos y treinta.* / It is 2:30.

When the time is a certain number of minutes of (to, toward, before) the hour, state the hour that it will be + *menos* + the number of minutes. If it is 15 minutes before the hour, use *menos cuarto* (a quarter of).

Son las cinco menos veinte. / It is twenty minutes to five OR It is 4:40.
Son las cuatro menos cuarto. / It is a quarter of (to) four OR It is 3:45.

When you are not telling what time it is and you want only to say at a certain time, merely say:

a la una, a las dos, a las tres / at one o'clock, at two o'clock, at three o'clock *a la una y cuarto* / at 1:15; *a las cuatro y media* / at 4:30

¿A qué hora va Ud. a la clase de español? / At what time do you go to Spanish class?

Voy a la clase a las dos y veinte. / I go to class at 2:20.

¿A qué hora toma Ud. el almuerzo? / At what time do you have lunch?

Tomo el almuerzo a las doce en punto. / I have lunch at exactly twelve o'clock.

¿A qué hora toma Ud. el autobús para ir a la escuela? / At what time do you take the bus to go to school?

Tomo el autobús a las ocho en punto. / I take the bus at eight o'clock sharp.

¿Llega Ud. a la escuela a tiempo? / Do you arrive at school on time?

Llego a la escuela a eso de las ocho y media. / I arrive at school at about 8:30.

When you state what time it is or at what time you are going to do something, sometimes you have to make it clear whether it is in the morning (A.M.), in the afternoon (P.M.), or in the evening (P.M.):

Tomo el tren a las ocho de la noche. / I am taking the train at 8:00 P.M. (at eight o'clock in the evening).

Tomo el tren a las ocho de la mañana. / I am taking the train at 8:00 A.M. (at eight o'clock in the morning).

Tomo el tren a las cuatro de la tarde. / I am taking the train at 4:00 P.M. (at four o'clock in the afternoon).

Tomo el tren a las tres de la madrugada. / I am taking the train at 3:00 A.M. (at three o'clock in the morning).

Note that in Spanish we say *de la madrugada* (before daylight hours) instead of *de la noche* if the time is between midnight and the break of dawn.

¿Qué hora es? / What time is it? *Es mediodía* / It is noon.

¿Qué hora es? / What time is it? *Es medianoche* / It is midnight.

¿A qué hora toma Ud. el almuerzo? / At what time do you have lunch? *Tomo el almuerzo a mediodía* (**OR** *al mediodía*).

¿A qué hora se acuesta Ud. por lo general? / At what time do you generally get to bed? *Generalmente, me acuesto a medianoche* (or *a la medianoche*).

When telling time in the past, use the imperfect indicative tense of the verb *ser:*

Eran las dos cuando tomé el almuerzo hoy. / It was two o'clock when I had lunch today.

Era la una cuando los vi. / It was one o'clock when I saw them.

¿Qué hora era cuando sus padres llegaron a casa? / What time was it when your parents arrived home?

Eran las dos de la madrugada. / It was two in the morning.

The future tense is used when telling time in the future or when you wonder what time it is at present or when you want to state what time it probably is:

> *En algunos minutos serán las tres* / In a few minutes it will be three o'clock.
> *¿Qué hora será?* / I wonder what time it is.
> *Serán las seis.* / It is probably six o'clock.

When wondering what time it was in the past or when stating what time it probably was in the past, use the conditional:

> *¿Qué hora sería?* / I wonder what time it was? *Serían las seis cuando llegaron.* / It was probably six o'clock when they arrived.

When no specific time is stated and you merely want to say in the morning, in the afternoon, or in the evening, use the preposition *por* instead of *de:*

> *Los sábados estudio mis lecciones por la mañana, juego por la tarde, y salgo por la noche.* / On Saturdays I study my lessons in the morning, I play in the afternoon, and I go out in the evening.

To express a little after the hour, state the hour + *y pico:*

> *Cuando salí eran las seis y pico.* / When I went out it was a little after six o'clock.

To say about or around a particular time, say *a eso de* + the hour:

> *Te veré a eso de la una.* / I will see you about one o'clock.
> *Te veré a eso de las tres.* / I will see you around three o'clock.

Instead of using *menos* (of, to, toward, before the hour), you may use the verb *faltar,* which means to be lacking: *Faltan cinco minutos para las tres* / It's five minutes to three (in other words, five minutes are lacking before it is three o'clock). In this construction, which is idiomatic, note the use of the preposition *para.*

§14.2 "OFFICIAL" TIME EXPRESSIONS

Finally, note another way to tell time, which is used on radio and TV, in railroad and bus stations, at airports, and at other places where many people gather. It is the 24-hour system around the clock.

When using the 24 hours around the clock, the stated time is perfectly clear and there is no need to say *de la madrugada, de la mañana, de la tarde,* or *de la noche.*

When using the 24-hour system around the clock, there is no need to use *cuarto, media, menos* or *y* (except when *y* is required in the cardinal number: *diez y seis*).

When you hear or see the stated time using this system, subtract 12 from the number that you hear or see. If the number is less than 12, it is A.M. time. Midnight is *veinticuatro horas.* This system uses the cardinal numbers.

---

trece horas / 1 P.M.
catorce horas / 2 P.M.
veinte horas / 8 P.M.
quince horas treinta / 15.30; 3:30 P.M.
veinte horas cuarenta y dos / 20.42; 8:42 P.M.
nueve horas diez / 09.10; 9:10 A.M.

---

§15.

Weather Expressions

¿Qué tiempo hace? / What is the weather like?
Hace buen tiempo. / The weather is good.
Hace calor. / It is warm (hot).
Hace fresco hoy. / It is cool today.
Hace frío. / It is cold.
Hace mal tiempo. / The weather is bad.
Hace sol. / It is sunny.
Hace viento. / It is windy.
¿Qué tiempo hacía cuando Ud. salió esta mañana? / What was the weather like when you went out this morning?
Hacía mucho frío ayer por la noche. / It was very cold yesterday evening.
Hacía mucho viento. / It was very windy.
¿Qué tiempo hará mañana? / What will the weather be like tomorrow?
Se dice que hará mucho calor. / They say it will be very hot.

with *haber*

Hay lodo. / It is muddy. *Había lodo.* / It was muddy.
Hay luna. / The moon is shining. OR There is moonlight.
Había luna ayer por la noche. / There was moonlight yesterday evening.
¿Hay mucha nieve aquí en el invierno? / Is there much snow here in winter?
Hay neblina. / It is foggy; *Había mucha neblina.* / It was very foggy.
Hay polvo. / It is dusty. *Había mucho polvo.* / It was very dusty.

Other weather expressions

Está lloviendo ahora. / It is raining now.
Está nevando. / It is snowing.
Esta mañana llovía cuando tomé el autobús. / This morning it was raining when I took the bus.
Estaba lloviendo cuando tomé el autobús. / It was raining when I took the bus.

Estaba nevando cuando me desperté. / It was snowing
     when I woke up.
¿Nieve mucho aquí en el invierno? / Does it snow much
     here in winter?
Las estrellas brillan. / The stars are shining.
¿Le gusta a usted la lluvia? / Do you like rain?
¿Le gusta a usted la nieve? / Do you like snow?

§16.

Numbers

§16.1
CARDINAL
NUMBERS:
ZERO TO
ONE
HUNDRED
MILLION

0	cero	50	cincuenta
1	uno, una	51	cincuenta y uno,
2	dos		cincuenta y una
3	tres	52	cincuenta y dos, etc.
4	cuatro	60	sesenta
5	cinco	61	sesenta y uno, sesenta
6	seis		y una
7	siete	62	sesenta y dos,
8	ocho		etc.
9	nueve		
10	diez	70	setenta
11	once	71	setenta y uno,
12	doce		setenta y una
13	trece	72	setenta y dos,
14	catorce		etc.
15	quince	80	ochenta
16	dieciséis	81	ochenta y uno,
17	diecisiete		ochenta y una
18	dieciocho	82	ochenta y dos,
19	dicinueve		etc.
20	veinte		
21	veintiuno	90	noventa
22	veintidós	91	noventa y uno,
23	veintitrés		noventa y una
24	veinticuatro	92	noventa y dos, etc.
25	veinticinco		
26	veintiséis	100	ciento (cien)
27	veintisiete	101	ciento uno,
28	veintiocho		ciento una
29	veintinueve	102	ciento dos, etc.
30	treinta		
31	treinta y uno, treinta y una	200	doscientos, doscientas
32	treinta y dos, etc.	300	trescientos, trescientas
40	cuarenta	400	cuatrocientos, cuatrocientas
41	cuarenta y uno,		
42	cuarenta y dos, etc.		

500	*quinientos, quinientas*	1,000,000	*un millón* (*de* + noun)
600	*seiscientos, seiscientas*	2,000,000	*dos millones* (*de* + noun)
700	*setecientos, setecientas*	3,000,000	*tres millones* (de + noun)
800	*ochocientos, ochocientas*	100,000,000	*cien millones* (*de* + noun)
900	*novecientos, novecientas*		
1,000	*mil*		**Approximate numbers**
2,000	*dos mil*		*unos veinte libros* / about (some) twenty books
3,000	*tres mil*, etc.		
100,000	*cien mil*		
200,000	*doscientos mil, doscientas mil*		*unas treinta personas* / about (some) thirty persons
300,000	*trescientos mil, trescientas mil,* etc.		

Simple arithmetical expressions

dos y dos son cuatro	$2 + 2 = 4$
diez menos cinco son cinco	$10 - 5 = 5$
tres por cinco son quince	$3 \times 5 = 15$
diez dividido por dos son cinco	$10 \div 2 = 5$

§16.2 ORDINAL NUMBERS: FIRST TO TENTH

primero, primer, primera	first	1st
segundo, segunda	second	2nd
tercero, tercer, tercera	third	3rd
cuarto, cuarta	fourth	4th
quinto, quinta	fifth	5th
sexto, sexta	sixth	6th
séptimo, séptima	seventh	7th
octavo, octava	eighth	8th
noveno, novena	ninth	9th
décimo, décima	tenth	10th

Note that beyond 10th the cardinal numbers are used instead of the ordinal numbers, but when there is a noun involved, the cardinal number is placed after the noun:

el día 15, el día quince / the fifteenth day

Note also that in titles of monarchs, etc., the definite article is not used between the person's name and the number, as it is in English:

Alfonso XIII, Alfonso Trece / Alfonso the Thirteenth

And note that *noveno* changes to *nono* in such titles:

Luis IX, Luis Nono / Louis the Ninth

EJERCICIOS/EXERCISES

The answers to these exercises begin right after the last question in each group.

I.   Reporting Activities. Proficiency in Speaking and Writing.

A. Situation: Your Spanish teacher wants to know what you and your friends are doing today. You have been asked to go to the front of the class and give a report of six activities that you are doing together.

You may use your own words and ideas or any of the following. Either way, state six activities that you are performing today with your friends, for example: **Nosotros buscamos un taxi** / *We are looking for a taxi;* **Nosotros cantamos canciones españolas** / *We are singing Spanish songs;* **Nosotros dibujamos varios dibujos** / *We are sketching several drawings;* **Nosotros escuchamos la música española** / *We are listening to Spanish music;* **¡Nosotros lavamos todas las pizarras en todas las salas de clase de esta escuela!** / *We are washing all the chalkboards in all the classrooms of this school!* **Trabajamos mucho** / *We are working a lot.*

B. After giving your oral report, you may want to write the six activities on a sheet of paper to give to your instructor. First, practice writing them on the following lines:

1. _____

2. _____

3. _____

4. _____

5. _____

6. _____

II. **Doing Things While Talking in Spanish. Proficiency in Speaking and Writing.**

Today is Friday! T.G.I.F.! This is the day in Spanish class when students use their imagination and talents to do things while talking in Spanish.

A. **Situation:** You are supposed to say what you are doing and at the same time perform the action. You may use your own words and ideas or any of the following: **Estoy bailando** / I am dancing. Keep saying it while you do a short tap dance, or waltz around the room while saying **estoy bailando.** Then go to one of the windows in your classroom, open it, and say **estoy abriendo la ventana** / I am opening the window. Close the window while you are saying **estoy cerrando la ventana** / I am closing the window. You can keep opening and closing the window as many times as you wish but you must be sure to say in Spanish what you are doing at the same time.

Don't forget to use these: **Estoy cantando** / I am singing; **estoy buscando mi libro** / I'm looking for my book; **estoy comiendo** / I'm eating; **estoy bebiendo** / I'm drinking. You can perform these actions by using gestures and bodily movements as if you were a mime.

Later, practice what you said by writing the Spanish statements on these lines:

_____

_____

_____

_____

_____

B. **Situation:** Tell us at least five things that you can throw. You may use your own words, any vocabulary from the preceding pages, or from the vocabularies in the back pages of the book. **Puedo lanzar una pelota** / I can throw a ball; **puedo lanzar un huevo** / I can throw an egg; **puedo lanzar una banana** I can throw a banana. How many more can you say? Write them all on the lines:

_____

_____

_____

_____

_____

C. **Situation:** Finally, you can tell your classmates at least five things that you can look at or watch. You may use your own words or any of the following: **Puedo mirar la televisión** / I can watch television; **puedo mirar el cielo** / I can look at the sky; **puedo mirar el pájaro amarillo en la jaula** / I can look at the yellow bird in the cage; **puedo mirar las estrellas durante la noche** / I can look at the stars during the night. How many more can you say and write?

_____

_____

_____

_____

_____

| Mnemonic Tip |

Saber is to know something, to know a fact.
Conocer is to know in the sense of to be acquainted with a person, a place, a thing.

Example: **Yo sé que tú conoces a José, mi mejor amigo** / I know that you know José, my best friend.

Answers to the preceding group of exercises.

I. **Reporting Activities.**

Note to student: After you write your sentences in Spanish or these examples that follow, translate them into English and then write them again in Spanish just for the practice so that you can increase your vocabulary and improve your skill in writing what you can say in Spanish.

1. Nosotros buscamos un taxi.
2. Nosotros cantamos canciones españolas.
3. Nosotros dibujamos varios dibujos.
4. Nosotros escuchamos la música española.
5. Nosotros lavamos todas las pizarras en todas las salas de clase de esta escuela.
6. Trabajamos mucho.

II. Doing Things While Talking in Spanish.

A. Estoy bailando. Estoy abriendo la ventana. Estoy cerrando la ventana. Estoy cantando. Estoy buscando mi libro. Estoy comiendo. Estoy bebiendo agua *(water)*.

B. Puedo lanzar una pelota. Puedo lanzar un huevo. Puedo lanzar una banana.

C. Puedo mirar la televisión. Puedo mirar el cielo. Puedo mirar el pájaro amarillo en la jaula. Puedo mirar las estrellas durante la noche.

§ 17.

Synonyms

There are many Spanish words that are approximate in meaning to another. A list of these synonyms follows, along with the English counterparts.

acercarse (a), aproximarse (a) / to approach, to come near
acordarse (de), recordar / to remember
alabar, elogiar / to praise, to glorify, to eulogize
alimento, comida / food, nourishment
alumno (alumna), estudiante / pupil, student
andar, caminar / to walk
anillo, sortija / ring (finger)
antiguo (antigua), viejo (vieja) / ancient, old
asustar, espantar / to frighten, to terrify, to scare
atreverse (a), osar / to dare, to venture
aún, todavía / still, yet, even
ayuda, socorro, auxilio / aid, succor, help, assistance
barco, buque, vapor / boat, ship
bastante, suficiente / enough, sufficient
batalla, combate, lucha / battle, combat, struggle, fight
bonito (bonita), lindo (linda) / pretty
breve, corto (corta) / brief, short
burlarse de, mofarse de / to make fun of, to mock
camarero, mozo / waiter
campesino, rústico, labrador / farmer, peasant
cara, rostro, semblante / face
cariño, amor / affection, love
cocinar, cocer, guisar / to cook
comenzar, empezar, principiar / to begin, to start, to commence
comprender, entender / to understand, to comprehend
conquistar, vencer / to conquer, to vanquish
contento (contenta), feliz, alegre / content, happy, glad
contestar, responder / to answer, to reply
continuar, seguir / to continue
cruzar, atravesar / to cross
cuarto, habitación / room
cura, sacerdote / priest
chiste, chanza, broma / jest, joke, fun
dar un paseo, pasearse / to take a walk, to go for a walk
dar voces, gritar / to shout, to cry out
delgado, esbelto, flaco / thin, slender, slim, svelte
desafortunado, desgraciado / unfortunate

desaparecer, desvanecerse / to disappear, to vanish
desear, querer / to desire, to want, to wish
desprecio, desdén / scorn, disdain, contempt
diablo, demonio / devil, demon
diferente, distinto (distinta) / different, distinct
diversión, pasatiempo / diversion, pastime
echar, lanzar, tirar, arrojar / to throw, to lance, to hurl
elevar, levantar, alzar / to elevate, to raise, to lift
empleado (empleada), dependiente / employee, clerk
enojarse, enfadarse / to become angry, to become annoyed
enviar, mandar / to send
error, falta / error, mistake, fault
escoger, elegir / to choose, to select, to elect
esperar, aguardar / to wait for
esposa, mujer / wife, spouse
estrecho (estrecha), angosto (angosta) / narrow
famoso (famosa), célebre, ilustre / famous, celebrated,
    renowned, illustrious
fiebre, calentura / fever
grave, serio (seria) / serious, grave
habilidad, destreza / ability, skill, dexterity
hablador (habladora), locuaz / talkative, loquacious
halagar, lisonjear, adular / to flatter
hallar, encontrar / to find
hermoso (hermosa), bello (bella) / beautiful, handsome
igual, semejante / equal, alike, similar
invitar, convidar / to invite
irse, marcharse / to leave, to go away
joya, alhaja / jewel, gem
lanzar, tirar, echar / to throw, to lance, to hurl
lengua, idioma / language, idiom
lentamente, despacio / slowly
luchar, combatir, pelear, pugnar / to fight, to battle, to
    combat, to struggle
lugar, sitio / place, site
llevar, conducir / to take, to lead
maestro (maestra), profesor (profesora) / teacher, professor
marido, esposo / husband, spouse
miedo, temor / fear, dread
morir, fallecer, fenecer / to die, to expire
mostrar, enseñar / to show
nobleza, hidalguez, hidalguía / nobility
nunca, jamás / never
obtener, conseguir / to obtain, to get
odiar, aborrecer / to hate, to abhor
onda, ola / wave

país, nación / country, nation
pájaro, ave / bird
pararse, detenerse / to stop (oneself)
parecido, semejante / like, similar
pasar un buen rato, divertirse / to have a good time
pena, dolor / pain, grief
perezoso (perezosa), flojo (floja) / lazy
periódico, diario / newspaper
permiso, licencia / permission, leave
permitir, dejar / to permit, to allow, to let
poner, colocar / to put, to place
posponer, diferir, aplazar / to postpone, to defer, to put off,
   to delay
premio, galardón / prize, reward
quedarse, permanecer / to remain, to stay
rapidez, prisa, velocidad / rapidly, haste, speed, velocity
regresar, volver / to return (to a place)
rezar, orar / to pray
rogar, suplicar / to beg, to implore, to entreat
romper, quebrar / to break
sin embargo, no obstante / nevertheless, however
solamente, sólo / only
sorprender, asombrar / to surprise, to astonish
suceso, acontecimiento / happening, event
sufrir, padecer / to suffer, to endure
susto, espanto / fright, scare, dread
tal vez, acaso, quizá, quizás / maybe, perhaps
terminar, acabar, concluir / to terminate, to finish, to end
tonto (tonta), necio (necia) / foolish, stupid, idiotic
trabajo, tarea, obra / work, task
tratar de, intentar / to try to, to attempt
ya que, puesto que / since, inasmuch as

§ 18.

Antonyms

Here is a list of antonyms in Spanish, with the English translation of each work.

aburrirse / to be bored; *divertirse* / to have a good time
aceptar / to accept; *ofrecer* / to offer
acordarse de / to remember; *olvidar, olvidarse de* / to forget
admitir / to admit; / to deny
agradecido, agradecida / thankful; *ingrato, ingrata* / thankless
alejarse de / to go away from; *acercarse a* / to approach
algo / something; *nada* / nothing
alguien / someone; *nadie* / no one
alguno (algún) / some; *ninguno (ningún)* / none
amar / to love; *odiar* / to hate
amigo, amiga / friend; *enemigo, enemiga* /enemy
ancho, ancha / wide; *estrecho, estrecha* / narrow
antes (de) / before; *después (de)* / after
antiguo, antigua / ancient, old; *moderno, moderna* / modern
antipático, antipática / unpleasant; *simpático, simpática* / nice (people)
aparecer / to appear; *desaparecer* / to disappear
aplicado, aplicada / industrious; *flojo, floja* / lazy
apresurarse a / to hasten, to hurry; *tardar en* / to delay
aprisa / quickly; *despacio* / slowly
aquí / here; *allí* / there
arriba / above, upstairs; *abajo* / below, downstairs
ausente / absent; *presente* / present
bajar / to go down; *subir* / to go up
bajo, baja / low, short; *alto, alta* / high, tall
bien / well; *mal* / badly, poorly
bueno (buen), buena / good; *malo (mal), mala* / bad
caballero / gentleman; *dama* / lady
caliente / hot; *frío* / cold
caro, cara / expensive; *barato, barata* / cheap
cerca (de) / near; *lejos (de)* / far
cerrar / to close; *abrir* / to open
claro, clara / light; *oscuro, oscura* / dark
cobarde / cowardly; *valiente* / valiant, brave
cómico, cómica / comic, funny; *trágico, trágica* / tragic
comprar / to buy; *vender* / to sell
común / common; *raro, rara* / rare
con / with; *sin* / without
contra / against; *con* / with

corto, corta / short; *largo, larga* / long
costoso, costosa / costly, expensive; *barato, barata* / cheap, inexpensive
culpable / guilty, culpable; *inocente* / innocent
dar / to give; *recibir* / to receive
débil / weak, debilitated; *fuerte* / strong
dejar caer / to drop; *recoger* / to pick up
delante de / in front of; *detrás de* / in back of
delgado, delgada / thin; *gordo, gorda* / stout, fat
dentro / inside; *fuera* / outside
derrota / defeat; *victoria* / victory
descansar / to rest; *cansar* / to tire; *cansarse* / to get tired
descubrir / to uncover; *cubrir* / to cover
descuido / carelessness; *esmero* / meticulousness
desgraciado, desgraciada / unfortunate; *afortunado, afortunada* / fortunate
despertarse / to wake up; *dormirse* / to fall asleep
destruir / to destroy; *crear* / to create
desvanecerse / to disappear; *aparecer* / to appear
distinto, distinta / different; *semejante* / similar
dulce / sweet; *amargo* / bitter
duro, dura / hard; *suave, blando, blanda* / soft
elogiar / to praise; *censurar* / to criticize
empezar / to begin, to start; *terminar, acabar* / to end
encender / to light; *apagar* / to extinguish
encima (de) / on top; *debajo (de)* / under
entrada / entrance; *salida* / exit
esta noche / tonight, this evening; *anoche* / last night, yesterday evening
este / east; *oeste* / west
estúpido, estúpida / stupid; *inteligente* / intelligent
éxito / success; *fracaso* / failure
fácil / easy; *difícil* / difficult
fatigado, fatigada / tired; *descansado, descansada* / rested
feliz / happy; *triste* / sad
feo,fea / ugly; *hermoso, hermosa* / beautiful; *bello, bella* / beautiful
fin / end; *principio* / beginning
flaco, flaca / thin; *gordo, gorda* / fat
gastar / to spend (money); *ahorrar* / to save (money)
gigante / giant; *enano* / dwarf
grande (gran) / large, big; *pequeño, pequeña* / small, little
guerra / war; *paz* / peace
hablador, habladora / talkative; *taciturno, taciturna* / silent, taciturn
hablar / to talk, to speak; *callarse* / to keep silent
hembra / female; *macho* / male

ida / departure; *vuelta* / return *(ida y vuelta* / round trip)
ignorar / not to know; *saber* / to know
interesante / interesting; *aburrido, aburrida* / boring
inútil / useless; *útil* / useful
ir / to go; *venir* / to come
joven / young; *viejo, vieja* / old
jugar / to play; *trabajar* / to work
juventud / youth; *vejez* / old age
lejano / distant; *cercano* / nearby
lentitud / slowness; *rapidez* / speed
levantarse / to get up; *sentarse* / to sit down
libertad / liberty; *esclavitud* / slavery
limpio, limpia / clean; *sucio, sucia* / dirty
luz / light *sombra* / shadow
llegada / arrival; *partida* / departure
llenar / to fill *vaciar* / to empty
lleno, llena / full; *vacío, vacía* / empty
llorar / to cry, to weep; *reír* / to laugh
maldecir / to curse; *bendecir* / to bless
mañana / tomorrow; *ayer* / yesterday
más / more; *menos* / less
mejor / better; *peor* / worse
menor / younger; *mayor* / older
mentir / to lie; *decir la verdad* / to tell the truth
mentira / lie, falsehood; *verdad* / truth
meter / to put in; *sacar* / to take out
mismo, misma / same; *diferente* / different
mucho, mucha / much; *poco, poca* / little
nacer / to be born; *morir* / to die
natural / natural; *innatural* / unnatural
necesario / necessary; *innecesario* / unnecessary
negar / to deny; *otorgar* / to grant
noche / night; *día* / day
obeso, obesa / obese, fat; *delgado, delgada* / thin
obscuro, obscura / dark; *claro, clara* / light
odio / hate, hatred; *amor* / love
orgulloso / proud; *humilde* / humble
oriental / eastern; *occidental* / western
peligro / danger; *seguridad* / safety
perder / to lose; *ganar* / to win; *hallar* / to find
perezoso, perezosa / lazy; *diligente* / diligent
permitir / to permit; *prohibir* / to prohibit
pesado, pesada / heavy; *ligero, ligera* / light
ponerse / to put on (clothing); *quitarse* / to take off (clothing)
porvenir / future; *pasado* / past
posible / possible; *imposible* / impossible
pregunta / question; *respuesta, contestación* / answer

preguntar / to ask; *contestar* / to answer
presente / present; *ausente* / absent
prestar / to lend *pedir prestado* / to borrow
primero (primer), primera / first; *último, última* / last
puesta del sol / sunset; *salida del sol* / sunrise
quedarse / to remain; *irse* / to leave, to go away
quizá(s) / maybe, perhaps; *seguro, cierto* / sure, certain
recto / straight; *tortuoso* / winding
rico, rica / rich; *pobre* / poor
riqueza / wealth; *pobreza* / poverty
rubio, rubia / blond; *moreno, morena* / brunette
ruido / noise; *silencio* / silence
sabio, sabia / wise; *tonto, tonta* / foolish
salir (de) / to leave (from); *entrar (en)* / to enter (in, into)
seco / dry; *mojado* / wet
separar / to separate; *juntar* / to join
sí / yes; *no* / no
siempre / always; *nunca* / never
subir / to go up; *bajar* / to go down
sucio / dirty; *limpio* / clean
sur / south; *norte* / north
temprano / early; *tarde* / late
tomar / to take; *dar* / to give
tonto / foolish; *listo* / clever
tranquilo / tranquil, peaceful; *turbulento* / restless, turbulent
unir / to unite; *desunir* / to disunite
usual / usual; *extraño, raro* / unusual
vida / life; *muerte* death
virtud / virtue; *vicio* / vice
y / and, plus; *menos* / minus, less

EJERCICIOS/EXERCISES

The answers to these exercises begin right after the last question in each group.

I. **Shopping. Speaking and Writing Proficiencies.**

Situation: After your conversation with Señorita López, the other students in the group stay at the hotel for a snack. You and Señorita López go to El Rastro, the flea market. You are still playing the role of yourself, **Tú.** If you have enthusiasm and zeal to increase your Spanish vocabulary, review the vocabularies in this book in each lesson, the vocabularies at the end of the book, and what you can find and use in a standardized English-Spanish, Spanish-English dictionary. You may use your own words and ideas.

Señorita López:	**¡Aquí estamos en El Rastro! ¿Quieres ir de compras?**
Tú:	_____
	(Tell her yes, you want to go shopping.)
Señorita López:	**¿Qué piensas comprar? ¿Tienes bastante dinero?**
Tú:	_____
	(Tell her you have enough money and you want to buy **una almohada** / a pillow.)
Señorita López:	**¡Una almohada! ¿Por qué?**
Tú:	_____
	(Tell her the pillow on your bed at the hotel is not good. Or, give another reason.)
Señorita López:	**Bueno, si tú insistes.**
Tú:	_____
	(Say there are **(hay)** many **inexpensive** articles here. Then ask her where the pillows are.)
Señorita López:	**Las almohadas están allá a la izquierda.**
Tú:	_____
	(Ask the saleslady **(la vendedora)** how much this pillow costs. Start with **Perdóneme, señora, con permiso** / Pardon me, madam, with your permission.)
La vendedora:	**Esta almohada es muy bonita. No tiene muchas pulgas. Cuesta solamente diez centavos.***
Tú:	_____
	(Tell her you'll take it / **La tomo.**)
La vendedora:	**¡Cuidado con las pulgas, señorita!**
Tú:	_____
	(Thank her and say good-bye. Say also, "Have a nice day!")**

***diez centavos** / ten cents
****Pase un buen día.**

II. Reading Proficiency.

Directions: In the following passage there are five blank spaces numbered 1 through 5. Each blank space represents a missing word. For each blank space, four possible completions are provided. Only one of them makes sense in the context of the passage and is grammatically correct.

First, read the passage in its entirety to determine its general meaning. Then read it a second time. For each blank space choose the completion that makes the best sense and is grammatically correct. Write its letter or the Spanish word in the space provided.

Ahora voy a distribuir los regalos de Navidad.

_____ regalo no es para _____ Es para

1. A. **Esto**
   B. **Este**
   C. **Esta**
   D. **Estos**

2. A. **me**
   B. **mi**
   C. **mí**
   D. **yo**

_____ y _____ son para los niños.

3. A. **ti**
   B. **tu**
   C. **tú**
   D. **yo**

4. A. **éstos**
   B. **éstas**
   C. **éste**
   D. **ésta**

Entre tú y yo, querido mío, ¡San Nicolás no nos

_____ nada este año!

5. A. **trajo**
   B. **traje**
   C. **traerías**
   D. **traeríamos**

Answers to the preceding group of exercises.

I. Shopping. Speaking and Writing Proficiencies.

Sí, quiero ir de compras.

Tengo bastante dinero y deseo (quiero) comprar una almohada.

La almohada de mi cama en el hotel no es buena.

Hay muchas cosas aquí que no cuestan mucho.

¿Dónde están las almohadas?

Perdóneme, señora, con permiso. ¿Cuánto cuesta (cuánto vale) esta almohada?

La tomo.

Muchas gracias, señora. Adiós. Pase un buen día *or* Pase muy buenos días.

II. Reading Proficiency.

1. **B**   2. **C**   3. **A**   4. **A**   5. **A**

§ 19.

Cognates

Another good way to increase your vocabulary is to become aware of cognates. A cognate is a word whose origin is the same as another word in other languages. There are many cognates in Spanish and English. Their spelling is sometimes identical or very similar in both languages. Most of the time, the meaning is the same or similar; sometimes they appear to be related because of the similar or identical spelling but they are not true cognates. Those are described as "false cognates"—for example, the Spanish word *actual* means present-day, not actual; the English word actual is expressed in Spanish as *real, verdadero, efectivo,* or *existente.* Also, the Spanish word *pan* means bread, not pan. The English word pan is *cacerola, cazuela,* or *sartén* in Spanish.

Generally speaking, Spanish words that have certain endings have equivalent endings in English.

SPANISH ENDING OF A WORD	EQUIVALENT ENGLISH ENDING OF A WORD
-ario	-ary
-ción	-tion
-dad	-ty
-fía	-phy
-ia	-y
-ía	-y
-io	-y
-ista	-ist
-mente	-ly
-orio	-ory
-oso	-ous

There are others, but the above seem to be the most common. Also note that Spanish words that begin with *es* are generally equivalent to an English word that begins with s. Just drop the *e* in the beginning of the Spanish word and you have a close equivalent to the spelling of an English word.

especial / special; *estudiante* / student

Here are examples to illustrate true cognates whose spellings are identical or similar:

actor / actor	*historia* / history
admiración / admiration	*hotel* / hotel
atención / attention	*idea* / idea
autoridad / authority	*invitación* / invitation
central / central	*manual* / manual
civilización / civilization	*nación* / nation
color / color	*naturalmente* / naturally
correctamente / correctly	*necesario* / necessary
chocolate / chocolate	*necesidad* / necessity
dentista / dentist	*novelista* / novelist
doctor / doctor	*piano* / piano
dormitorio / dormitory, bedroom	*posibilidad* / possibility
escena / scene	*radio* / radio
estúpido / stupid	*realidad* / reality
famoso / famous	*remedio* / remedy
farmacia / pharmacy	*sección* / section
finalmente / finally	*sociedad* / society
fotografía / photography	*universidad* / university
generoso / generous	*violín* / violin
geografía geography	*vocabulario* / vocabulary

§20.

"Tricky Words," "False Cognates," and "False Friends"

The Spanish words on this list and on the following page do not always mean in English what they mean in Spanish. **¡Cuidado!** Be careful! Think twice about each one when using them.

actual / present, of the present time, of the present day
el anciano, la anciana / old (man or woman)
antiguo, antigua / former, old, ancient
la apología / eulogy, defense
la arena / sand
asistir a / to attend, to be present at
atender / to attend to, to take care of
el auditorio / audience
el bachiller, la bachillera / graduate of a secondary school; also means babbler
el bagaje / beast of burden, military equipment
la bala / bullet, shot, bale, ball
bizarro, bizarra / brave, gallant, generous
el campo / field, country(side), military camp
el carbón / coal, charcoal, carbon
el cargo / duty, post, responsibility, burden, load
la carta / letter (to mail)
el collar / necklace
colorado, colorada / red, ruddy
la complexión / temperament, constitution
la conferencia / lecture
la confianza / confidence, trust
la confidencia / secret, trust
constipado, constipada / head cold or common cold
la consulta / conference
convenir / to agree, to fit, to suit, to be suitable
la chanza / joke, fun
de / from, of
dé / give
la decepción / disappointment
el delito / crime
la desgracia / misfortune
el desmayo / fainting

diario, diaria / daily
el diario / diary, journal, daily newspaper
disfrutar / to enjoy
divisar / to perceive indistinctly
el dormitorio / bedroom, dormitory
el editor / publisher
embarazada / pregnant
emocionante / touching (causing an emotion)
esperar / to hope, to expect, to wait for
el éxito / success, outcome
la fábrica / factory
hay / there is, there are (idiomatic)
el idioma / language
ignorar / not to know, to be unaware
intoxicar / to poison, to intoxicate
el labrador / farmer
largo, larga / long
la lectura / reading
la librería / bookstore
la maleta / valise, suitcase
el mantel / tablecloth
mayor / greater, older
la mesura / moderation
la pala / shovel
el palo / stick, pole
el pan / bread
pasar / to happen, to pass
el pastel pie; *la pintura al pastel* / pastel painting
pinchar / to puncture, to prick, to pierce
realizar / to achieve (to realize, in the sense of achieving
    something: He realized his dreams, his dreams came
    true)
recordar / to remember
el resfriado / common cold (illness)
restar / to deduct, to subtract
sano, sana / healthy
soportar / to tolerate, to bear, to endure, to support
suceder / to happen, to come about, to succeed (follow)
el suceso / event, happening
la tabla / board, plank, table of contents
la tinta / ink, tint
la trampa / trap, snare, cheat, trick
tu / your
tú / you
el vaso / drinking glass

EJERCICIOS/EXERCISES

The answers to these exercises begin right after the last question in each group.

I. **Preferring and Insisting. Proficiency in Speaking and Writing.**

Situation: You and your friend Juan are trying to convince each other about adopting a course of action. Your role is **Tú**.

You may vary and extend this dialogue with your own words and ideas, using as many verbs in the present subjunctive as you can. Consult the Table of Contents and the Index for the location of the present subjunctive in the book and review the verb forms and the vocabulary used there.

Juan: **¿Quién va a hacer el trabajo para nosotros?**

Tú: _____

(Tell Juan that you want María to do it.)

Juan: **Pero yo prefiero que José lo haga.**

Tú: _____

(And I'm telling you that I want María to do it.)

Juan: **¿Por qué insistes?**

Tú: _____

(I am insisting because María knows how to do the work.)

Juan: **¿Y José no sabe hacerlo?**

Tú: _____

(José doesn't know anything.)

Juan: **¿Tu dices que José no sabe nada?**

Tú: _____

(That's right. / **Eso es.**) José doesn't know how to do the work.)

Juan: **Pide a Elena que escriba los ejercicios para nosotros.**

Tú: _____

(Good idea! I'm going to ask Elena to write the exercises for us.)

II. Dining Out. More Proficiency in Speaking and Writing.

Situation: You are in a restaurant in a small town in Spain. You are listening to a conversation between a waiter and a customer near your table. She is telling him something about the bowl of soup he just served her.

Read the following conversation once from beginning to end. Then, review it again. When you are ready, make your selection of answers as given by numbers in parentheses that match the blank lines. They are all verb forms. They are at the end of this selection.

La cliente: Camarero, por favor, quiero __(1)__ algo. Para mí, __(2)__ una cosa muy importante y __(3)__ muy enfadada con usted.

El camarero: ¿Qué __(4)__, señora? ¿Le __(5)__ a Ud. la sopa? ¿__(6)__ yo darle algo más?

La cliente: Quisiera __(7)__ que hay una mosca en esta sopa.

El camarero: ¿En el bol de sopa que yo le __(8)__?

La cliente: Sí, sí. No __(9)__ duda. Es seguro.

El camarero: Ud. me dice que hay una mosca en la sopa que yo le __(10)__? ¿No le gustan a Ud. las moscas?

La cliente: Para responder a su pregunta, no me gustan las moscas, especialmente en mi sopa y no __(11)__ comer este bol de sopa. Es repugnante.

El camarero: Lo siento, señora. Voy a llevarlo inmediatamente. __(12)__.

Now, select your answers as given by numbers in parentheses in the above dialogue that match the numbers on the blank lines above.

(1)   A. digo   B. decirle   C. decía   D. dígame

(2)   A. sea   B. está   C. es   D. soy

(3)   A. estoy   B. soy   C. está   D. estamos

(4)   A. desean   B. desea   C. deseamos
      D. deseas

(5)   A. gustan   B. gustaron   C. gusta   D. gustado

(6)   A. Puede   B. Puedes   C. Puedo   D. Podamos

(7)   A. tomar   B. decimos   C. comer   D. informarle

(8)   A. serví   B. sirvió   C. pedir   D. sofoqué

(9)   A. haber   B. tiene   C. hay   D. conozco

(10) A. sirvió   B. serví   C. servir   D. comió

(11) A. poder   B. puedo   C. soy   D. estoy

(12) A. Dígame   B. Pregúntame   C. Escríbame
      D. Perdóneme

III. Read the following newspaper advertisement and answer the question under it.

¡Ponga su anuncio

en este periódico!

Llámenos

al 1-800-por-amor

o

Llene y envíenos este cupón.

Nombre _____

Dirección (address) _____

Ciudad _____ Estado _____ Zona postal_____

Teléfono (   ) _____

Escriba su anuncio aquí. _____

Envíenos este cupón a: **El Mundo Hoy,** 8 Lancaster Street, Albany, New York 12204

Who would be interested in this newspaper advertisement?

    A. Sports fans.

    B. People who love to read newspapers.

    C. Someone who wants to place an advertisement.

    D. Anyone who wants to give an opinion about **El Mundo Hoy**.

IV. Patience / *Paciencia.* **More Proficiency in Speaking and Writing.**

Situation: You and Sofía have been waiting and waiting for Rosa to arrive so the three of you can go to the Cine 10. You are both getting impatient. You are playing the role of **Tú.** Write the Spanish on the lines for the English suggested under the lines. You may use your own words and ideas. Review the use of the present subjunctive of verb forms.

Sofía: Hace una hora que esperamos a Rosa. ¡Qué muchacha!

Tú: _____

(Let's have patience, Sofía. I think she will come.)

Sofía: ¡¿Tengamos paciencia?! Yo no tengo mucha paciencia. Le hablaré a Rosa cuando venga.

Tú: _____

(Me, too/**Yo, también.** I will talk to Rosa when she comes.)

Sofía: En cuanto *(As soon as)* **yo la vea, le hablaré francamente** *(frankly).*

Tú: _____

(Me, too. As soon as I see her, I will talk to her frankly.)

Sofía: Quedémonos *(Let's stay)* **aquí hasta que llegue.**

Tú: _____

_____

(You can stay/ **Tú puedes quedarte** here until she arrives. I'm leaving/**Yo me voy** before it rains.)

Answers to the preceding group of exercises.

I. **Preferring and Insisting. Proficiency in Speaking and Writing.**

Quiero que María lo haga.

Y yo te digo que quiero que María lo haga.

Yo insisto porque María sabe hacer el trabajo.

José no sabe nada.

Eso es. José no sabe hacer el trabajo.

¡Buena idea! Voy a pedir a Elena que escriba los ejercicios para nosotros.

II. **Dining out. More Proficiency in Speaking and Writing.**

1. decirle **B**		7. informarle **D**	
2. es **C**		8. serví **A**	
3. estoy **A**		9. hay **C**	
4. desea **B**		10. serví **B**	
5. gusta **C**		11. puedo **B**	
6. puedo **C**		12. perdóneme **D**	

III. **Newspaper advertisement.**

The answer to the multiple-choice question is **C**.

IV. **Patience /** *Paciencia.* **More Proficiency in Speaking and Writing.**

Tengamos paciencia, Sofía. Creo (Pienso) que vendrá.

Yo, también. Le hablaré a Rosa cuando venga.

Yo, también. En cuanto yo la vea, le hablaré francamente.

Tú puedes quedarte aquí hasta que llegue. Yo me voy antes (de) que llueva.

LET'S REVIEW

§21.

Test Yourself—20 Minitests, Based on the First 20 Chapters

The Answers section for this Test Yourself review starts on page 236. Consult the Table of Contents and the Index for topics in other sections of the book.

§1. PRONOUNC- ING SPANISH SOUNDS

Choose the correct answer by circling the letter.

1. The vowel *a* in the Spanish word *la* is pronounced similarly as in the English word
   A. ate   B. father   C. way   D. April

2. The vowel *e* in the Spanish word *le* is pronounced similarly as in the English word
   A. week   B. let   C. see   D. father

3. The vowel *u* in the Spanish word *tu* is pronounced similarly as in the English word
   A. cup   B. cute   C. too   D. pudding

4. In Spanish, the letter *g* in front of the vowels *e* or *i* is pronounced as the underlined letter in the English word
   A. help   B. jet   C. go   D. argue

5. In Spanish, the letter *g* in front of the vowels *a, o,* or *u* is pronounced as the underlined letter in the English word
   A. game   B. garage   C. juice   D. gem

6. The letter *h* in a Spanish word, as in *hermano,* is
   A. always pronounced   B. sometimes pronounced
   C. rarely pronounced   D. not pronounced

7. Two vowels together, as in the Spanish word *Europa,* are pronounced separately and they are considered to be a
   A. pure vowel   B. diphthong
   C. triphthong   D. consonant

8. The letter *ñ* in a Spanish word, as in *niño*, is pronounced similarly as in the English word

    A. no   B. canon   C. onion   D. knowledge

9. The double *ll* in a Spanish word, as in *llamo*, is pronounced similarly as in the English word
    A. hello   B. lame   C. yes   D. million

10. The letter *d* in a Spanish word, as in *dar*, is pronounced similarly as in the English word
    A. dare   B. thin   C. dad   D. the

§2.
CAPITALIZA-
TION,
PUNCTUATION,
SYLLABLES

I. Divide the following Spanish words into syllables.

   EXAMPLE: *hermano her - ma - no*

   1. *eso* _____   6. *aprendo* _____
   2. *mucho* _____   7. *instituto* _____
   3. *caballo* _____   8. *comprender* _____
   4. *perro* _____   9. *aeroplano* _____
   5. *hermana* _____   10. *huevo* _____

II. In English, state the simple rule regarding stress when pronouncing a Spanish word. _____

   _____

   _____

   _____

   _____

III. In pronouncing a Spanish word, if the word ends in a vowel, *n* or *s*, raise your voice on the vowel in the _____ syllable of the word.

IV. Stressing a vowel means _____ your voice on that vowel.

V. Match the Spanish words designating punctuation marks with the English equivalent.

   1. *apóstrofo*   ____ period
   2. *comillas*   ____ colon
   3. *paréntesis*   ____ comma
   4. *principio de*   ____ apostrophe
      interrogación   ____ ellipses
   5. *fin de interrogación*   ____ quotation marks
   6. *punto*   ____ semicolon
   7. *coma*   ____ parentheses
   8. *punto y coma*   ____ beginning question
   9. *dos puntos*   mark
   10. *puntos suspensivos*   ____ final question mark

§3.
NOUNS

I. On the line in front of each of the following nouns, indicate the gender of the noun by writing *el* if masculine or *la* if feminine.

EXAMPLE: _la_ madre

1. __ chico	8. __ ciudad	15. __ coche
2. __ chica	9. __ costumbre	16. __ mano
3. __ tío	10. __ alumno	17. __ foto
4. __ tía	11. __ alumna	18. __ día
5. __ vaca	12. __ estudiante	19. __ clima
6. __ toro	13. __ leche	20. __ aire
7. __ lección	14. __ gente	21. __ paraguas

II. Write the Spanish for each of the following.

1. a history class _____
2. a gold watch _____
3. a little drinking glass _____
4. a darling little dog _____
5. a dear old granny _____
6. a coffee cup _____

III. Write the Spanish word with its definite article for what is requested; for example, *el campo.*

1. The Spanish word for country where you find farmlands as opposed to life in a city is _____.
2. The Spanish word for country which is a synonym of nation is _____.
3. The Spanish word for country in the same sense as native land is _____.
4. The Spanish word for time referring to the hour on a clock or watch is _____.
5. The Spanish word for time referring to a vague or indefinite duration of time is _____.
6. The Spanish noun used to express the weather is

_____.

7. The Spanish noun for time in the sense of occasions or different times (the first time, the last time) is

_____.

IV. Write in Spanish, the plural for each of the following nouns.

EXAMPLE: *el chico los chicos*

1. *la chica* _____   3. *la dentista* _____
2. *el dentista* _____   4. *el profesor* _____

5. *la profesora* _____   13. *el tocadiscos* _____
6. *la flor* _____   14. *el sacapuntas* _____
7. *el lápiz* _____   15. *el paraguas* _____
8. *la luz* _____   16. *el lunes* _____
9. *la lección* _____   17. *el martes* _____
10. *la ilusíon* _____   18. *el mes* _____
11. *el francés* _____   19. *el abrelatas* _____
12. *el país* _____   20. *el joven* _____

§4.
ARTICLES

1. Write the four forms in Spanish for the definite article masculine singular and plural and for the feminine singular and plural. _____

2. Write the four forms in Spanish for the indefinite article masculine singular and plural and for the feminine singular and plural. _____

3. On the blank line, write the Spanish word for the indefinite article.

   EXAMPLE: _un_ *libro.*

   A. _____ *naranja* C. _____ *platos*
   B. _____ *libro*   D. _____ *casas*

4. On the blank line, write the Spanish word for the definite article.

   EXAMPLE: _el_ *libro.*

   A. _____ *cuaderno* C. _____ *profesoras*
   B. _____ *señores*   D. _____ *ciudad*

5. When the preposition *a* is in front of the definite article *el*, it contracts to ____, as in *Voy ____ cine* / I'm going to the movies.

6. When the preposition *de* is in front of the definite article *el*, it contracts to ____, as in *Vengo ____ cine*, / I'm coming from the movies.

7. Write the Spanish for each of the following.
   A. John's book _____
   B. John's and Mary's books _____
   C. the United States _____
   D. the women's children _____
   E. It's one o'clock. No! It's two o'clock. _____
   _____

F. the girl's notebooks _____

G. the boy's little dog _____

H. What a book! _____

I. I like coffee. _____

J. I speak Spanish. _____

K. El Greco's paintings _____

L. The little girl's doll _____

M. Seeing is believing. _____

N. I am writing in Spanish. _____

O. I see how easy it is. _____

§5.
ADJECTIVES

I. Complete the following statements or questions by selecting the correct missing adjective and circle the letter of your choice.

1. *¿Es _____ la profesora de español?*
    A. *inteligente*   B. *alto*   C. *español*   D. *gran*

2. *Esta pregunta es*
    A. *difícil*   B. *trabajadora*   C. *fáciles*   D. *cada*

3. *Roberto, Felipe y Marta están*
    A. *cansados* B. *cansado* C. *cansadas* D. *cansada*

4. *¿Le gusta a usted _____ bicicleta?*
    A. *este*   B. *esto*   C. *esta*   D. *ésta*

5. *¿ _____ día es hoy?*
    A. *cuál*   B. *qué*   C. *cuáles*   D. *este*

II. Several words in one word. Using the letters in the word *ESPAÑA*, how many Spanish words can you write? Write four words at least.

E S P A Ñ A

1. _____   3._____

2. _____   4._____

III. Write the Spanish for each of the following.

1. a tall, handsome man _____

2. a tall, beautiful and intelligent woman _____

    _____

3. one house, _____; some boys _____;
    many times _____

IV. Match the following.
    1. this book   ___ *esos libros*
    2. these books   ___ *aquel libro*
    3. that book   ___ *estos libros*
    4. those books   ___ *ese libro*
    5. that book (farther away   ___ *aquellos libros*
       or out of sight)   ___ *este libro*
    6. those books (farther
       away or out of sight)

V. Each of the following sentences contains a blank. From the four choices given, select the one that can be inserted in the blank to form a grammatically correct sentence and circle the letter of your choice.

1. *¿Conoce Ud. a _____ amigas?*
   A. *mía*   B. *mías*   C. *mi*   D. *mis*

2. *_____ alumno no oye nada porque es sordo.*
   A. *Esta*   B. *Ésta*   C. *Aquel*   D. *Esto*

3. *María es tan _____ como Roberto.*
   A. *alto*   B. *alta*   C. *altos*   D. *altas*

4. *¡Hola, amigo _____! ¿Qué tal?*
   A. *mi*   B. *mío*   C. *mis*   D. *mía*

5. *Estos libros son _____.*
   A. *las mías*   B. *míos*   C. *mías*   D. *mis*

§6.
PRONOUNS

I. Several words in one word. Using the letters in the word *PRONOMBRE*, how many Spanish words can you write? Write six words at least.

P R O N O M B R E

1. _____
2. _____
3. _____
4. _____
5. _____
6. _____

II. Underline the subject pronouns in the following paragraph.

> *Pablo, José y yo somos amigos. Cuando nosotros vamos a la escuela, tomamos el autobus y hablamos con las chicas y los chicos. Ellas son muy bonitas e inteligentes.*

III. Underline the direct object pronouns in the following paragraph.

> Anoche María y yo fuimos a una fiesta en casa de Ricardo. El padre de Ricardo dijo: "Yo te conozco, María. ¿Me conoces tú?"
>
> "Sí, sí. Yo le conozco, señor", contestó María. "Mis padres le conocen también. ¿Conoce Ud. a mi amigo José?"
>
> "Sí, sí. Lo conozco muy bien porque es amigo de mi hijo Ricardo".

IV. Read again the short selection in Spanish in III above. Here, write in Spanish the subject pronouns that you can find in it. _____

_____

V. Each of the following sentences contains a blank. From the four choices given, select the one that can be inserted in the blank to form a grammatically correct sentence and circle the letter of your choice.

1. ¿Está Ud. enfermo?—Sí, ___ estoy.
   A. le   B. la   C. lo   D. los

2. A mí, ___ gusta el helado.
   A. me   B. mi   C. yo   D. le

3. A Ricardo, ___ bastan cien dólares.
   A. le   B. les   C. me   D. lo

4. Juan está ___.
   A. lo escribiendo   B. escribiéndolo
   C. lo escribir   D. escribirlo

5. María no ___.
   A. me lo da   B. lo me da   C. da me lo   D. me da lo

6. Juan quiere ___.
   A. me lo dar   B. dármelo   C. darmelo   D. dar me lo

7. Todas las mañanas yo ___ lavo con agua y jabón.
   A. se   B. me   C. nos   D. os

8. Este regalito es para ___.
   A. tí   B. ti   C. te   D. tú

9. Me gustan estos guantes y ___.
   A. estos   B. éstas   C. aquello   D. ésos

10. ¿De quién es este lápiz?—Es ___.
    A. el mío   B. lo mío   C. mío   D. mi

VI. Complete this crossword puzzle in Spanish.

HORIZONTAL:

1. Demonstrative pronoun, feminine, singular
2. Personal pronoun as subject, 1st person, singular
5. Indirect object pronoun, 3d person plural
6. Reflexive pronoun, 3d person, singular and plural
7. Subject pronoun, 2d person, singular
8. Direct and indirect object pronoun, 1st person, singular
10. Direct object pronoun, 3d person, singular, masculine

VERTICAL:

3. Personal pronoun as subject, 3d person, singular
4. Direct object pronoun, 3d person, singular, feminine
5. Indirect object pronoun, 3d person, singular
9. Personal pronoun as subject, 3d person, singular, masculine

§7.
VERBS

I. In the following paragraph, underline the verb forms that are in the preterit tense.

Antes de regresar a su asiento, Juanita vio a un hombre. Cuando Juanita vio al hombre, ella le dijo: "Buenos días, señor". Juanita le dio al hombre su programa y su pluma para escribir su autógrafo. El hombre lo escribió en el programa que Juanita tenía a la mano.

II. The words in the following sentences are scrambled. Unscramble them to find a meaningful sentence and write it on the line provided.

1. *leyendo / está / Pablo / la cocina / en / el periódico.*

   _____

2. *será / Ud. / años / en / diez / rico.* _____

   _____

3. *de Lola / al fin / acepta / Pedro / invitación / la* ___

   _____

III. Complete this acrostic word game in Spanish.

1.	D							
2.	I							
3.	S							
4.	C							
5.	O							
6.	S							

1. Spanish infinitive meaning to return something to someone or to some place.
2. Imperfect indicative of *ir*, 1st and 3d person, singular
3. Preterit tense of *saber*, 1st person, singular
4. Imperfect indicative of *cantar*, 1st and 3d person, singular
5. Present indicative of *oír*, 1st person, singular
6. I gave them *(m.)* to her.

IV. In this acrostic complete each word in Spanish by writing the past participle of the infinitive given for each row.

1.	E								
2.	N								
3.	A								
4.	M								
5.	O								
6.	R								
7.	A								
8.	D								
9.	O								

1. *escribir*   4. *morir*   7. *aprender*
2. *nacer*   5. *oír*   8. *decir*
3. *abrir*   6. *reír*   9. *obtener*

§8. ADVERBS

I. Change the following adjectives into adverbs using the *mente* ending in Spanish.

1. *lento* _____   3. *rápido* _____

2. *fácil* _____   4. *feliz* _____

II. Write at least ten common adverbs in Spanish that do not end in *mente*.

1. _____   6. _____

2. _____   7. _____

3. _____   8. _____

4. _____   9. _____

5. _____   10. _____

III. In this dialogue, you and Juanita are talking about the exams in June and summer vacation. Complete the conversation by writing on the blank line an appropriate Spanish adverb from those given here.

bien rápidamente recientemente siempre también

Juanita: ¿Estás preparado para tus exámenes?

Usted: Sí, estoy _____ preparado para mis exámenes.

Juanita: Mañana tengo un examen más y luego empiezan las vacacioines.

Usted: Los días de vacaciones van a pasar _____.

Juanita: El verano pasado lo pasamos en las montañas.

Usted: Mi familia y yo _____ vamos a las montañas.

Juanita: En julio hacemos un viaje a Puerto Rico.

Usted: Y mi familia y yo _____.

Juanita: Voy a mandarte una tarjeta postal desde San Juan si me das tu dirección.

Usted: ¡Pero yo te di _____ mi dirección! ¿La perdiste?

IV. Unscramble the following letters to find an adverb in Spanish. Then write the adverb on the line provided.

| N A C N U | _____ |

§9.
PREPOSITIONS

I. Match the following.

1. *contra* ____ among, between
2. *hacia* ____ against
3. *entre* ____ during
4. *durante* ____ with
5. *con* ____ toward

II. And match these.

1. *según* ____ without
2. *sin* ____ on, upon
3. *salvo* ____ after, behind
4. *sobre* ____ according to
5. *tras* ____ except

III. Each of the following sentences contains a blank. From the four choices given, select the preposition that can be inserted in the blank to form a grammatically correct sentence and circle the letter of your choice.

1. *Conozco* _____ *su hermana Elena.*

   A. *a*   B. *con*   C. *de*   D. *no preposition needed*

2. *Nuestra profesora de español es muy amable* _____ *nosotros.*
   A. *para*   B. *con*   C. *para con*   D. *por*

3. *Usted habla español muy bien* _____ *ser norteamericano.*
   A. *por*   B. *para*   C. *con*   D. *de*

4. *Esta taza es* _____ *café.*
   A. *por*   B. *a*   C. *para*   D. *al*

5. *Estudio* _____ *llegar a ser médico.*
   A. *por*   B. *para*   C. *a*   D. *con*

§10.
CONJUNCTIONS

I. In the following paragraph underline all the conjunctions that you find and write them on the lines provided.

Yo no puedo ir a la fiesta en casa de Elena esta noche porque tengo muchas tareas y, como mi madre está enferma, debo quedarme en casa; pero mañana es posible o dentro de tres días.

_____

_____

II. Complete the following conjunctions by writing on the blank line the Spanish word that is missing.

1. *A fin* _____ *que* / so that, in order that

2. *a menos* _____ / unless

3. *como* _____ / as if

4. *para* _____ / in order that, so that

5. *sin* _____ / nevertheless, however (in whatever way)

III. On the blank line write either *pero, sino,* or *sino que,* whichever is appropriate to mean "but" or "but rather."

1. *Me gustaría venir a tu casa esta noche* _____ *no puedo.*

2. *Pedro no es pequeño* _____ *alto.*

3. *Mi coche no es amarillo* _____ *blanco.*

4. *Pablo no alquiló el automóvil* _____ *lo compró.*

5. *María no conoce al niño* _____ *le habla.*

IV. Five conjunctions in Spanish are hidden in this clock: one conjunction from 12 to 6; one at 3; one at 6; another from 7 to 10; and one at 11. Note that the same letter can be common to the one that follows. This clock has no hands. It's a word clock! Write the missing letters on the lines.

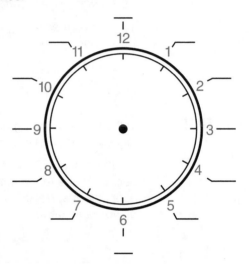

From 12 to 6 write the Spanish for the conjunction "but rather that."

At 3 write the Spanish for the conjunction "or."

At 6 write the Spanish for the conjunction "and" when *y* cannot be used.

From 7 to 10, write the Spanish for the conjunction "but."

At 11, write the Spanish for the conjunction "and" when *e* cannot be used.

§11. EXCLAMATORY STATEMENTS

I. Match the following.

1. *¡Qué clase!*
2. *¡Qué alumno!*
3. *¡Qué idea!*
4. *¡Tal idea!*
5. *¡Qué chica tan bonita!*
6. *¡Qué libro más interesante!*
7. *¡Qué difícil es!*
8. *¡Qué fácil es!*
9. *¡Qué día!*
10. *¡Qué prueba!*

___ What a day!
___ What a pupil!
___ What an idea!
___ What a test!
___ Such an idea!
___ What a pretty girl!
___ What a class!
___ How difficult it is!
___ How easy it is!
___ What an interesting book!

§12.
IDIOMS

I. Each of the following sentences contains a blank. From the four choices given, select the one that can be inserted in the blank to form a grammatically correct sentence and circle the letter of your choice.

1. ¿Cuánto tiempo _____ que Ud. estudia español?
    A. hay   B. hace   C. cuando   D. es

2. Hace un año _____ estudio español.
    A. yo   B. como   C. ese   D. que

3. ¿Cuánto tiempo _____ que Ud. hablaba cuando yo entré en la sala de clase?
    A. hace   B. hacía   C. hay   D. es

4. Hacía una hora que yo _____ cuando Ud. entró en la sala de clase.
    A. hablo   B. estoy hablando   C. hablaba
    D. hablé

5. ¿Cuántas moscas _____ en la sopa?
    A. hace   B. hacen   C. hay   D. hacía

II. For each of the following common idiomatic expressions, write in Spanish on the blank line the missing word or words in order to complete them. Choose from among the following: a, a la, al, con, dar, darse, de, en, estar, hacer, hacerse, hasta, para, poco, por, ser, tener, una, unas, y.

1. _____ menudo
2. _____ izquierda
3. _____ día siguiente
4. _____ rumbo a
5. _____ la hora
6. _____ prisa
7. acabar _____ + infinitive
8. de hoy _____ ocho días
9. _____ a punto de + infinitive
10. _____ un viaje
11. _____ daño
12. _____ luego
13. _____ mí
14. por _____
15. _____ avión
16. _____ aficionado a
17. _____ dolor de cabeza
18. _____ vez
19. _____ veces
20. un billete de ida _____ vuelta

§13.
DATES,
DAYS,
MONTHS,
SEASONS

I. Each of the following sentences contains a blank. From the four choices given, select the one that can be inserted in the blank to form a sensible and grammatically correct sentence and circle the letter of your choice.

1. ¿Cuál es la fecha?—Hoy es el _____ de enero.
   A. un   B. uno   C. primer   D. primero

2. ¿A cuántos estamos hoy?—Estamos _____ cinco de abril.
   A. por   B. a   C. el   D. la

3. Los días de la semana son domingo, lunes, martes, miércoles, jueves, viernes, y _____.
   A. sabado   B. sábado   C. enero   D. marzo

4. Hay _____ estaciones en el año.
   A. cinco   B. cuatro   C. cuarto   D. tres

5. Generalmente, en Nueva York hace frío en _____.
   A. el verano   B. el invierno   C. la primavera
   D. el otoño

§14.
TELLING TIME

I. Study the clocks and underneath each clock write on the blank line in Spanish words the time that is given.

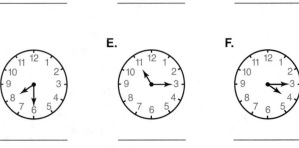

A.   B.   C.

_____   _____   _____

D.   E.   F.

_____   _____   _____

II. Answer the following questions in Spanish.

1. *¿A qué hora va Ud. a la clase de español?* _____

_____

2. *¿A qué hora toma Ud. el almuerzo?* _____

_____

3. *¿A qué hora toma Ud. el autobús para ir a la escuela?* _____

_____

4. *¿A qué hora se acuesta Ud. por lo general?* _____

_____

5. *¿Qué hora era cuando sus padres llegaron a casa?*

_____

§15. WEATHER EXPRESSIONS

I. Read the statement in English and select the correct equivalent in Spanish by drawing a circle around the letter of your choice.

1. What's the weather like today?
   A. *¿Hace buen tiempo hoy?*   B. *¿Hace calor hoy?*
   C. *¿Qué tiempo hace hoy?*   D. *¿Qué hora es?*

2. It's very warm today.
   A. *Hace calor hoy.*   B. *Hace mucho frío hoy.*
   C. *Hace fresco hoy.*   D. *Hace mucho calor hoy.*

3. It's foggy this morning.
   A. *Hay polvo esta mañana.*
   B. *Hay neblina esta noche.*
   C. *Hay neblina esta mañana.*
   D. *Está nevando esta mañana.*

4. Do you like rain?
   A. *¿Le gusta a usted el helado?*
   B. *¿Le gusta a usted la nieve?*
   C. *¿Le gustan a usted la nieve y la lluvia?*
   D. *¿Le gusta a usted la lluvia?*

5. Is there much snow here in winter?
   A. *¿Hay mucha lluvia aquí en la primavera?*
   B. *¿Hay lodo aquí en el verano?*
   C. *¿Hay mucha nieve aquí en el invierno?*
   D. *¿Hace mucho sol aquí en el verano?*

6. The stars are shining.
   A. *Hay neblina y polvo.*   B. *Hace mucho viento.*
   C. *Hace mal tiempo hoy.*   D. *Las estrellas brillan.*

7. It's raining now.
   A. *Está nevando ahora.*   B. *Está lloviendo ahora.*
   C. *Esta mañana llovía.*   D. *No está lloviendo.*

8. It was very foggy this morning.
   A. *Había mucho polvo esta mañana.*
   B. *Había neblina esta mañana.*
   C. *Hay mucha neblina esta mañana.*
   D. *Había mucha neblina esta mañana.*

9. There was moonlight yesterday evening.
   A. *Hay luna esta noche.*
   B. *Había mucho polvo ayer por la noche.*
   C. *Hay polvo esta noche.*
   D. *Había luna ayer por la noche.*

10. It was snowing when I woke up.
   A. *Estaba lloviendo cuando me desperté.*
   B. *Estaba nevando cuando usted se despertó.*
   C. *Estaba lloviendo cuando usted se despertó.*
   D. *Estaba nevando cuando me desperté.*

§16.
NUMBERS

I. Each of the following sentences contains a blank. From the four choices given, select the one that can be inserted in the blank to form a sensible and grammatically correct sentence and circle the letter of your choice.

1. *Dos _____ tres son cinco.*
   A. *menos*   B. *por*   C. *y*   D. *dividido por*

2. *Diez _____ cuatro son seis.*
   A. *por*   B. *y*   C. *dividido por*   D. *menos*

3. *Cinco _____ seis son treinta.*
   A. *y*   B. *por*   C. *dividido por*   D. *menos*

4. *Veinte _____ diez son dos.*
   A. *menos*   B. *por*   C. *y*   D. *dividido por*

II. Match the following ordinal numbers.

1. *décimo*   _____ fifth
2. *cuarto*   _____ ninth
3. *sexto*   _____ eighth
4. *quinto*   _____ fourth
5. *noveno*   _____ sixth
6. *octavo*   _____ tenth

§17.
SYNONYMS

I. Match the following synonyms.

1. *acercarse (a)*   _____ *viejo*
2. *acordarse (de)*   _____ *mozo*
3. *alabar*   _____ *caminar*
4. *alimento*   _____ *elogiar*
5. *alumno*   _____ *cocer, guisar*
6. *antiguo*   _____ *estudiante*
7. *andar*   _____ *comida*
8. *camarero*   _____ *recordar*
9. *cocinar*   _____ *aproximarse (a)*
10. *feliz*   _____ *alegre*

II. Read the synonyms in English and select the correct equivalent in Spanish by drawing a circle around the letter of your choice.

1. to cross
   A. *cruzar, atravesar*   B. *comenzar, empezar*
   C. *comprender, entender*   D. *contestar, responder*

2. jest, joke, fun
   A. *camarero, mozo*   B. *chiste, chanza, broma*
   C. *aún, todavía*   D. *anillo, sortija*

3. to shout, to cry out
   A. *dar voces, gritar*   B. *dar un paseo, pasearse*
   C. *burlarse de, mofarse de* D. *esperar, aguardar*

4. to break
   A. *romper, quebrar*   B. *rogar, suplicar*
   C. *asombrar, sorprender*   D. *acabar, concluir*

5. to suffer, to endure
   A. *padecer, sufrir*   B. *romper, quebrar*
   C. *luchar, pelear*   D. *mostrar, enseñar*

§18.
ANTONYMS

I. Read the words in English that are antonyms in each of the following and select the correct equivalent in Spanish by drawing a circle around the letter of your choice.

1. to be bored / to have a good time
   A. *aburrirse / divertirse*
   B. *apresurarse a / tardar en*
   C. *aparecer / desaparecer*
   D. *olvidarse de / acordarse de*

2. friend / enemy
   A. *bajo, baja / alto, alta*
   B. *amigo, amiga / enemigo, enemiga*
   C. *caro, cara / barato, barata*
   D. *feo, fea / hermoso, hermosa*

3. quickly / slowly
   A. *barato / caro*
   B. *arriba / abajo*
   C. *aquí / allí*
   D. *aprisa / despacio*

4. someone / no one
   A. *algo / nada*
   B. *alguien / nadie*
   C. *alguno / ninguno*
   D. *dentro / fuera*

5. to talk, to speak / to keep silent
   A. *ignorar / saber*
   B. *hablar / callarse*
   C. *maldecir / bendecir*
   D. *negar / otorgar*

II. Match the following antonyms.

1. *llorar* _____ *vaciar*
2. *limpio* _____ *nacer*
3. *llenar* _____ *sucio*
4. *morir* _____ *reír*
5. *amor* _____ *odio*

§19.
COGNATES

I. Alphabet soup. In this word puzzle, find the Spanish words for the English words given below. As you find each one, circle it and check it off the list. The Spanish words are written horizontally, vertically, diagonally.

dormitory, bedroom	correctly
reality	necessary
vocabulary	dentist
photography	city
generous	diary

G	E	N	E	C	I	U	D	A	D	C	O	R	R	E
U	B	C	V	O	A	A	C	L	A	R	I	O	H	L
S	E	C	E	N	D	O	O	V	O	C	A	B	R	Y
D	O	R	M	I	I	T	R	O	M	E	N	T	E	K
C	B	A	L	R	A	L	R	C	A	T	I	C	A	L
Y	X	A	A	Z	O	G	E	N	E	R	O	S	O	U
B	E	I	C	M	N	E	C	E	S	A	R	I	O	E
R	D	E	G	D	E	N	T	I	S	T	A	F	O	T
V	O	C	A	B	U	L	A	R	I	O	F	O	T	O
G	R	U	P	D	O	R	M	I	T	O	R	I	O	P
S	O	L	I	E	L	G	E	N	E	R	A	L	Y	L
I	M	A	G	I	N	A	N	C	I	A	O	E	I	L
D	O	R	M	I	F	O	T	O	G	R	A	F	Í	A
V	O	C	A	B	U	L	E	I	R	O	D	E	A	L

§20 "TRICKY WORDS," "FALSE COGNATES," AND "FALSE FRIENDS"

I. Several words in one word. Using the letters in the word CONSTIPADO, how many Spanish words can you write? Write at least ten.

> C O N S T I P A D O

1. _____   3. _____   5. _____   7. _____   9. _____

2. _____   4. _____   6. _____   8. _____   10. _____

II. Match the following tricky Spanish words with their English equivalents.

1. *actual* _____ letter (to mail, post)
2. *la anciana* _____ joke, fun
3. *el bagaje* _____ pregnant
4. *la carta* _____ sand
5. *embarazada* _____ present, of the present time
6. *el éxito* _____ beast of burden
7. *el suceso* _____ drinking glass
8. *la chanza* _____ the old woman
9. *el vaso* _____ success, outcome
10. *la arena* _____ event, happening

Answers

§1.
**PRONOUNC-
ING SPANISH
SOUNDS**

1. B.	3. C.	5. A.	7. B.	9. C
2. B.	4. A.	6. D.	8. C.	10. D.

1–10—*see* **§1.**

§2.
**CAPITALIZA-
TION, PUNC-
TUATION,
SYLLABLES**

I. 1. *e–so.*
2. *mu–cho.*
3. *ca–ba–llo*
4. *pe–rro.*
5. *her–ma–na.*
6. *a–pren–do.*
7. *ins–ti–tu–to.*
8. *com–pren–der.*
9. *a–e–ro–pla–no.*
10. *hue–vo.*

II. If a Spanish word ends in a vowel, the letter *n* or *s*, emphasize the second-to-last syllable of the word.

III. second-to-last.

IV. raising; emphasizing.

V. 6, 9, 7, 1, 10, 2, 8, 3, 4, 5.

I–V—see **§2.**

§3.
NOUNS

I. 1. *el*	8. *la*	15. *el*
2. *la*	9. *la*	16. *la*
3. el	10. *el*	17. *la*
4. *la*	11. *la*	18. *el*
5. *la*	12. *el, la*	19. *el*
6. *el*	13. *la*	20. *el*
7. *la*	14. *la*	21. *el*

1–21—see **§3.–3.2.**

II. 1. *una clase de historia*   4. *un perrito*
2. *un reloj de oro*   5. *una abuelita*
3. *un vasito*   6. *una taza para café*

1–6—see **§3.3, §3.3–1, 3.3–2.**

III. 1. *el campo*   3. *la patria*   5. *el tiempo*   7. *la vez*
2. *la nación*   4. *la hora*   6. *el tiempo*

1–7—see **§3.3–4** and **§3.3–5.**

IV. 1. *las chicas*   11. *los franceses*
     2. *los dentistas*   12. *los países*
     3. *las dentistas*   13. *los tocadiscos*
     4. *los profesores*   14. *los sacapuntas*
     5. *las profesoras*   15. *los paraguas*
     6. *las flores*   16. *los lunes*
     7. *los lápices*   17. *los martes*
     8. *las luces*   18. *los meses*
     9. *las lecciones*   19. *los abrelatas*
    10. *las ilusiones*   20. *los jóvenes*

1–20—see **§3.**, **§3.1**, **§3.2.**

§4.
ARTICLES

1. *el, los, la, las*—see **§4.1.**
2. *un, unos, una, unas*—see **§4.2.**
3. A. *una*   B. *un*   C. *unos*   D. *unas*
   see **§4.2 – §4.2–2.**
4. A. *el*   B. *los*   C. *las*   D. *la*—see **§4.1 – §4.1–2.**
5. *al; al*—see **§4.1.**
6. *del; del*—see **§4.1.**
7. A. *el libro de Juan*—see **§4.1–1.**
   B. *los libros de Juan y de María*—see **§4.1–1.**
   C. *los Estados Unidos*—see **§4.1–1.**
   D. *los niños de las mujeres*—see **§4.1–1.**
   E. *Es la una. ¡No! Son las dos.*—see **§4.1–1.**
   F. *los cuadermos de la chica (de la muchacha)*—see
      §4.1–1.
   G. *el perrito del chico (del muchacho)*—see **§4.1–1.**
   H. *¡Qué libro!*—see **§4.2–2.**
   I. *Me gusta el café.*—see **§4.1–1.**
   J. *Hablo español.*—see **§4.1–2.**
   K. *Los cuadros de El Greco*—see **§4.1.**
   L. *la muñeca de la chiquita*—see **§4.1–1.**
   M. *Ver es creer.*—see **§4.1–1.**
   N. *Estoy escribiendo en español.*—see **§4.1–2.**
   O. *Veo lo fácil que es.*—see **§4.3.**

§5.
ADJECTIVES

I. 1. A—*see* **§5.1.**
    2. A—*see* **§5.1.**
    3. A—*see* **§5.3.**
    4. C—*see* **§5.4–3.**
    5. B—*see* **§5.4–5.**

II. 1. *es*   2. *se*   3. *esa*   4. *ésa*

III. 1. *un hombre alto y hermoso*—see **§5.4–1.**

2. *una mujer alta, hermosa e intelligente—see* **§5.4–1** and **§10.2–4** to find out when to use *y* or *e*, either of which means and.
3. *una casa; algunos muchachos (chicos); muchas veces—see* **§5.4–2.**

IV. 4, 5, 2, 3, 6, 1—*see* **§5.4–3.**

V. 1. D—*see* **§5.4–4.**
   2. C—*see* **§5.4–3.**
   3. B—*see* **§5.6–1.**
   4. B—*see* **§5.4–4.**
   5. B—*see* **§5.4–4.**

§6. PRONOUNS

I. 1. *no*   3. *me*   5. *pone*
  2. *nombre*   4. *por*   6. *poner*

II. *yo, nosotros, ellas—see* **§6.1–1.**

III. *te, me, le, lo—see* **§6.1–2.**

IV. *yo, tú, Ud.—see* **§6.1–1.**

V. 1. C—*see* **§6.1–2.**   6. B—*see* **6.1–5.**
  2. A—*see* **§6.1–3.**   7. B—*see* **§6.1–6.**
  3. A—*see* **§6.1–3.**   8. B—*see* **§6.2.**
  4. B—*see* **§6.1–4.**   9. D—*see* **§6.3.**
  5. A—*see* **§6.1–5.**   10. C—*see* **§6.4–1.**

VI.

§7. VERBS

I. *vio, dijo, dio, escribió. see* **§7.5–3** and **§7.7–3.**

II. 1. *Pablo está leyendo el periódico en la cocina. see* **§7.3–2** and **§7.5–15.**
  2. *En diez años Ud. será rico. see* **§7.5–4, §7.7–8,** and **§7.9.**

3. *Al fin, Pedro acepta la invitación de Lola. see*
§7.5–1, §7.7–1, and **§12.2** expressions with *al.*

III.

1.	D	E	V	O	L	V	E	R
2.	I	B	A					
3.	S	U	P	E				
4.	C	A	N	T	A	B	A	
5.	O	I	G	O				
6.	S	E	L	O	S	D	I	

see **§7.5–1, §7.7–1, §7.5–2, §7.7–2, §7.5–3, §7.6–18, §7.7–3, §7.7–8, §7.9,** and **§6.1–5.**

IV.

1.	E	S	C	R	I	T	O	
2.	N	A	C	I	D	O		
3.	A	B	I	E	R	T	O	
4.	M	U	E	R	T	O		
5.	O	Í	D	O				
6.	R	E	Í	D	O			
7.	A	P	R	E	N	D	I	D	O
8.	D	I	C	H	O			
9.	O	B	T	E	N	I	D	O

see **§7.3–1.**

§8.
ADVERBS

I. 1. *lentamente*　2. *fácilmente*　　3. *rápidamente*
4. *felizmente—see* **§8.1.**

II. 1. *abajo, arriba, bien, mal, hoy, mañana, siempre, nunca, aquí, allí—see* **§8.1.**

III. *bien, rápidamente, siempre, también, racientemente— see* **§8.–§8.5.**

IV. *NUNCA—see* **§8.1.**

§9.
PREPOSITIONS
I. 3, 1, 4, 5, 2   II.   2, 4, 5, 1, 3

I and II—*see* **§9.1.**

III. 1. A—*see* **§9.5–1.**
2. C—*see* **§9.5–2.**
3. B—*see* **§9.5–3.**
4. C—*see* **§9.5–3.**
5. B—*see* **§9.5–3.**

§10.
CONJUNCTIONS
I. *porque, y, como, pero, o*—*see* **§10.1.**

II. 1. *de*   2. *que*   3. *si*   4. *que*
5. *embargo*—*see* **§10.1.**

III. 1. *pero*   2. *sino*   3. *sino*   4. *sino que*
5. *pero*—*see* **§10.2–1.**

IV.

see **§10.2–1 —§10.2–4.**

§11.
EXCLAMATORY STATEMENTS
I. 9, 2, 3, 10, 4, 5, 1, 7, 8, 5—*see* **§11.**

§12.
IDIOMS
I. 1. B—*see* **§12.1.**
2. D—*see* **§12.1.**
3. B—*see* **§12.1.**
4. C—*see* **§12.1.**
5. C—*see* **§12.1.**

II. 1. *a*   2. *a la*   3. *al*   4. *con*   5. *dar*
6. *darse*   7. *de*   8. *en*   9. *estar*   10. *hacer*
11. *hacerse*   12. *hasta*   13. *para*   14. *poco*
15. *por*   16. *ser*   17. *tener*   18. *una*
19. *unas (muchas, varias)*   20. *y—see* **§12.2,**
common expressions using certain key words.

§13.
DATES, DAYS, MONTHS, SEASONS

I. 1. D—*see* **§13.1.**
2. B—*see* **§13.1.**
3. B—*see* **§13.2.**
4. B—*see* **§13.4** and **§16.1** and **§16.2.**
5. B—*see* **§13.4.**

§14.
TELLING TIME

I. **A.**

Son las cinco
y diez.

B.

Es la una.

C.

Son las seis
menos cuarto.

D.

Son las siete
y media.

E.

Son las once
y cuarto.

F.

Son las cuarto
y cuarto.

see **§14.1 – §14.2.**

II. 1. *Voy a la clase de español a las dos y veinte.—see*
   §14.1.
2. *Tomo el almuerzo a las doce en punto.—see* **§14.1.**
3. *Tomo el autobús a las ocho en punto.—see* **§14.1.**
4. *Generalmente (Por lo general), me acuesto a*
   medianoche.—see **§14.1.**
5. *Eran las dos de la madrugada cuando mis padres*
   llegaron a casa.—see **§14.1.**

§15.
WEATHER EXPRESSIONS

I. 1. C   2. D   3. C   4. D   5. C
6. D   7. B   8. D   9. D   10. D

§16. NUMBERS

I.   1. C   2. D   3. B   4. D

II. 4, 5, 6, 2, 3, 1

§17. SYNONYMS

I.   6, 8, 7, 3, 9, 5, 4, 2, 1, 10

II. 1. A   2. B   3. A   4. A   5. A

§18. ANTONYMS

I.   1. A   2. B   3. D   4. B   5. B

II. 3, 4, 2, 1, 5

§19. COGNATES

G	E	N	E	C	I	U	D	A	D	C	O	R	R	E
U	B	C	V	O	A	A	C	L	A	R	I	O	H	L
S	E	C	E	N	D	O	O	V	O	C	A	B	R	Y
D	O	R	M	I	I	T	R	O	M	E	N	T	E	K
C	B	A	L	R	A	L	R	C	A	T	I	C	A	L
Y	X	A	A	Z	O	G	E	N	E	R	O	S	O	U
B	E	I	C	M	N	E	C	E	S	A	R	I	O	E
R	D	E	G	D	E	N	T	I	S	T	A	F	O	T
V	O	C	A	B	U	L	A	R	I	O	F	O	T	O
G	R	U	P	D	O	R	M	I	T	O	R	I	O	P
S	O	L	I	E	L	G	E	N	E	R	A	L	Y	L
I	M	A	G	I	N	A	N	C	I	A	O	E	I	L
D	O	R	M	I	F	O	T	O	G	R	A	F	Í	A
V	O	C	A	B	U	L	E	E	I	R	O	D	E	A	L

§20. "TRICKY WORDS," "FALSE COGNATES," AND "FALSE FRIENDS"

I.   1. *con*   2. *ti*   3. *pan*   4. *no*   5. *da*
    6. *si*   7. *son*   8. *sopa*   9. *dan*   10. *poco*

II. 4, 8, 5, 10, 1, 3, 9, 2, 6, 7

PART TWO

GRAMMAR PRACTICE

§22.

Reading Comprehension

A. Paragraphs

Directions. Read each of the following paragraphs at least twice before selecting an answer to the question. The answers to these exercises are on page 258. After checking your answers, consult the vocabulary list beginning on page 349 so you can strengthen your knowledge of basic Spanish vocabulary.

1. Son las once y cincuenta y cinco de la noche. Miles de personas están reunidas en la Puerta del Sol para ver caer la bola que anunciará la llegada de la medianoche y el comienzo de un nuevo año. Ahora faltan solamente cinco minutos para que se termine este año. Deseamos que el año entrante sea mejor que el año anterior.

   1. ¿Cuál es la fecha de hoy?
      A. el 2 de mayo
      B. el 16 de septiembre
      C. el 12 de octubre
      D. el 31 de diciembre

2. Según un estudio realizado en Europa sobre los precios de alimentos, transportes, espectáculos y alojamientos, en seis países claves para el turismo internacional, se ha establecido la creencia de que España es un país relativamente barato para el turismo.

   2. ¿Por qué conviene viajar a España?
      A. Los precios son bajos.
      B. La gente es muy amable.
      C. Las comidas son excelentes.
      D. El clima es agradable.

3. En la nueva estructura del Museo del Prado en Madrid, parece que Goya va a sufrir, una vez más, los rigores del exilio. Esta vez no será un exilio elegido, sino forzado. No será en su persona, sino en su obra. Se van a exhibir sus pinturas en un edificio especial y aparte.

3. ¿Qué diferencia podrá notar un visitante al Museo del Prado?
   A. El sistema de visitas será mejorado.
   B. Habrá una exposición de obras antiguas.
   C. Las pinturas de Goya estarán en otro lugar.
   D. Se dedicará mucho más espacio a los pintores modernos.

4. La feria anual de Peñuelas, al norte de Santiago de Chile, fue cancelada porque los únicos animales presentados a la exposición fueron: doce cabras, seis pollos, nueve vacas y una pareja de conejos.

   4. ¿Por qué no tuvo lugar esta feria?
      A. por falta de dinero
      B. por falta de animales
      C. por falta de espacio
      D. por falta de transporte

5. El único festival de música clásica de América Latina, el Festival Casals de Puerto Rico, todavía tiene grandes esperanzas de continuar a pesar de un clima económico difícil. El evento, aunque ayudado por el gobierno, ha recibido menos dinero. Además, tuvieron que subir los precios de la entrada.

   5. ¿En qué peligro está el Festival Casals de Puerto Rico?
      A. Hay músicos que no quieren participar en el Festival.
      B. Hay otros festivales clásicos que son más populares.
      C. Se encuentra bajo una crítica desfavorable.
      D. Puede sufrir un colapso por razones económicas.

6. El embajador argentino en Asunción recibió al equipo argentino en el aeropuerto, y esa noche los alojó en la embajada. De esta manera, los jugadores pudieron escapar del entusiasmo de los fanáticos paraguayos que no los querían dejar dormir. Así pasaron la noche tranquilos. El próximo día Paraguay y Argentina jugaron.

6. ¿Por qué pasó el equipo argentino la noche en la embajada?
   A. para dormir bien
   B. para participar en una fiesta
   C. para elegir un capitán
   D. para practicar más

7. Margarita, una muchacha inteligente que sabe algo de higiene y de medicina casera, está en "un mar de dudas." Ella quisiera tener una idea clara sobre la forma de combatir los resfriados. Por una parte, ha oído que los antibióticos no tienen ningún efecto sobre la gripe, y, por otra, ha visto que los médicos dan antibióticos para el resfriado.

   7. ¿Qué quiere saber Margarita?
      A. cómo hacerse enfermera
      B. cuál es el antibiótico preferido por los médicos
      C. cuál es el mejor tratamiento para un resfrío
      D. cómo reducir el uso de las medicinas

8. Se anunció hoy que el aniversario de la rebelión militar que puso fin a la República española dejará de ser fiesta nacional de España. Esto ocurrirá siete meses después de la muerte del General Franco. Los periódicos y las revistas de Madrid declararon esta tarde que el 24 de junio, fiesta del santo del rey Juan Carlos, será en adelante la fiesta del país.

   8. ¿Qué celebración se va a cambiar en España?
      A. el casamiento del rey
      B. la fiesta nacional
      C. la muerte del General Franco
      D. la libertad de prensa

9. El dueño de un famoso restaurante mexicano puso en la entrada un pequeño y seductor anuncio: "Entre, descanse, y coma aquí en paz. Nuestro televisor y nuestro tocadiscos están en reparación." En el espacio de una semana la clientela se había duplicado.

   9. ¿Por qué aumentó la clientela en este restaurante?
      A. Habían rebajado los precios.
      B. Habían cambiado el menú.
      C. Se podía comer con tranquilidad.
      D. Se gozaba de mejor servicio.

10. La obra del gran músico español Manuel de Falla es muy conocida y apreciada en Rusia. Un editorial de Moscú ha publicado una selección de piezas famosas de este compositor. Los cantantes rusos podrán interpretarlas en ruso o en español, porque la letra de las canciones se publica en los dos idiomas.

10. ¿Cómo muestran los rusos su afición a la música española?
    A. Muchos cantantes españoles reciben invitaciones a Rusia.
    B. Se compra un gran número de discos españoles.
    C. Se oye tocar frecuentemente el himno nacional español.
    D. Varias obras se editan en español y en ruso.

11. Cierto joven que está tratando de abandonar el cigarrillo asegura que para él esto no representa gran problema. "Cuando siento ganas de fumar," explica, "me calmo los nervios gritándoles a mis chicos."

11. ¿Cómo resuelve este señor su problema de fumar?
    A. Piensa en los peligros.
    B. Come dulces todo el día.
    C. Toma un tranquilizante todos los días.
    D. Levanta mucho la voz cuando habla con sus hijos.

12. Se celebró recientemente un homenaje a Manuel Zeno Gandía por haber tratado de mejorar la vida de los puertorriqueños. El doctor Zeno Gandía es uno de los hombres más ilustres de la historia de Puerto Rico. Es político liberal, médico eminente, periodista distinguido, escritor conocido.

12. ¿Por qué fue honrado Zeno Gandía?
    A. por sus esfuerzos humanitarios
    B. por sus estudios históricos
    C. por su poesía romántica
    D. por su interés en la independencia

13. En los primeros meses de este año, más de cien mil mensajes en cápsulas serán lanzados al mar. La intención del plan es conseguir datos sobre los corrientes y el movimiento de las aguas contaminadas en los mares. El problema es grave porque barcos petroleros pierden toneladas de petróleo todos los días. Resultado: playas contaminadas, flora y fauna destruidas.

13. ¿Para qué sirve este plan?
    A. para determinar el volumen del petróleo importado
    B. para obtener información sobre la polución de las aguas
    C. para saber la rapidez de los barcos
    D. para mejorar las comunicaciones por mar

14. El candidato dice en su discurso: "¿Quieren ustedes pagar menos impuestos? ¿Desean ustedes más y mejores servicios públicos? ¿Necesitan más ayuda estatal nuestras escuelas? ¿Desean mejores parques de recreo? Si todos ustedes están de acuerdo, deben votar por mí."

14. ¿Qué clase de reunión es?
    A. religiosa
    B. atlética
    C. escolar
    D. política

15. La hija de la Baronesa, una niña de unos doce años, nunca se presentaba ni en el comedor ni en el pasillo. Su madre le prohibía toda comunicación con los huéspedes. La chica se llamaba Elizabeth. Era una muchacha rubia, pálida y muy bonita. Sólo el estudiante Roberto hablaba con ella algunas veces en inglés.

15. ¿Qué se le prohibe a esta chica?
    A. comer mucho
    B. caminar por la calle
    C. hablar con los huéspedes
    D. conversar por teléfono

B. Long Selections

Directions. In the following passages, each blank space represents a missing word or expression. For each blank space, four possible completions are provided. Only one of them makes sense in the context of the passage. First, read the passage in its entirety to determine its general meaning. Then read it a second time. For each blank space choose the completion that makes the best sense. The answers to these exercises appear on page 258. After checking your answers, consult the vocabulary list beginning on page 349 so you can strengthen your knowledge of basic Spanish vocabulary.

Selection Number 1

Cada vez que llego a México siento muchísima alegría. Es que tengo la esperanza de ver al _____ por quien

    1. A. escritor
         B. médico
         C. músico
         D. pintor

siento la admiración más grande.

    Recién llegada, llamé a su casa. Mercedes, su inteligente mujer, me contestó que Gabriel estaba a punto de volver de Europa y que, en estas fechas, paseaba por Madrid. Nunca nos encontramos. ¡Qué mala suerte! Cada vez que él llega a aquella _____ yo estoy en México.

    2. A. calle
         B. montaña
         C. ciudad
         D. aldea

    Hace años conocí a Gabriel García Márquez en Barcelona. Acababa de estallar el "boom" de su novela, *Cien años de soledad*, y nuestra máxima ilusión era conocer el autor, hablar con él, entrevistarle. Todo resultaba imposible. Se negaba a hablarnos y su horror hacia las cámaras y los micrófonos era ya famoso.

    En aquella época hacía yo un programa de televisión llamado "Nuevas gentes" y tuve que quedarme en Barcelona con todo mi _____ para trabajar allí

    3. A. dinero
         B. alimento
         C. perfume
         D. equipo

durante un mes. Un buen día, por obra y gracia de amigos comunes, yo estaba _____ junto a García Márquez

    4. A. aburrida
       B. sentada
       C. enojada
       D. perdida

en la mesa de un pequeño restaurante.

Conversación agradable. Allí, nació una amistad que habría de continuar en México, adonde regresó el escritor después de ocho años de residencia en Barcelona.

Pocas veces he conocido a una familia tan _____ como la suya.

5. A. unida
   B. grande
   C. ignorante
   D. desagradable

Esto es lo que más me impresionó la primera vez que fui a su casa. Existe una auténtica amistad entre los cuatro. Padres e hijos se adoran y se necesitan, se divierten juntos, se ríen. ¡Ay, la importancia de la risa!

Selection Number 2

Cada país tiene distinta manera de disfrutar del arte de cocinar. En Madrid se _____ a todas horas. Por eso,

    6. A. descansa
       B. viaja
       C. come
       D. pesca

hay tabernas y bares con una gran variedad de platos sobre el mostrador, por ejemplo, jamón, queso, pescados, callos a la madrileña, mariscos. ¡Qué ricas son las tapas! A los madrileños y a los turistas, en general, les gusta ir a estos _____ y pedir distintas cosas.

   7. A. cines
     B. lugares
     C. museos
     D. jardines

Las tapas son pequeñas porciones de comida que se
acompañan con vino, con cerveza u otra _____.

8. A. bebida
    B. carne
    C. ensalada
    D. fruta

Estas tapas se toman especialmente como aperitivo.

Los bares están llenos alrededor de las dos de la tarde
antes del _____ y a eso de las nueve de la noche

9. A. trabajo
    B. almuerzo
    C. teatro
    D. desayuno

antes de la cena. Se dice que hay personas
que van de bar en bar para probar las diferentes
especialidades. Si una persona _____ esto

10. A. ve
     B. dice
     C. vende
     D. hace

diariamente, entonces existe el peligro de que aumente
mucho de peso.

Selection Number 3

Miguel Ríos tenía quince años. Era un chico normal
y corriente, y _____ poco dinero al mes trabajando

11. A. encontraba
     B. gastaba
     C. ganaba
     D. robaba

en una tienda de tejidos.

Todo iba bien hasta el día en que al dueño se le ocurrió abrir una pequeña sección de discos. Y ahí empezó todo. El joven dependiente vio, oyó y se convenció: Elvis Presley, Roy Orbison, discos hechos en América, rock y roll, ritmo, movimiento. A partir de aquel día, Miguel Ríos quiso ser _____.

  12. A. cantante
     B. cómico
     C. dueño
     D. bailarín

Pasaron más de diez años y Miguel Ríos, que se había llamado "Mike" durante un tiempo para acomodarse mejor a su estilo _____, estaba ahora sentado

  13. A. formal
     B. tradicional
     C. literario
     D. musical

junto al célebre presentador Johnny Carson, en el Tonight Show. No por nada, sino porque había llegado al número cuatro de las listas de discos más vendidos en los Estados Unidos con la versión en inglés de su Himno a la alegría.

Miguel _____ en todo el mundo unos siete

  14. A. pidió
     B. vendió
     C. perdió
     D. rompió

millones de discos del Himno.

Ningún otro cantante español lo había hecho hasta entonces, y ninguno lo ha hecho después con una sola _____ .

15. A. llamada
   B. canción
   C. visita
   D. palabra

C. Pictures

Directions: In this section there are seven pictures. Under each picture there is either an incomplete statement or a question. Look at the picture carefully, read the question or incomplete statement, and select the best answer from choices A, B, C, D. Answers appear on page 258.

Picture Number 1

1. Estas personas son . . .
   A. tejidos
   B. viajeros
   C. viajes
   D. viejos

Picture Number 2

2. ¿Qué está flotando sobre el agua?
   A. un velero de juguete
   B. una velita
   C. un zapato blanco
   D. un chico

Picture Number 3

3. ¿Qué ve usted en este escaparate de tienda?
   A. zapateros
   B. zapaterías
   C. zapatos
   D. tapicerías

Picture Number 4

4. Estas personas tienen los brazos . . .
   A. levantados
   B. bajados
   C. cortos
   D. anchos

Picture Number 5

5. ¿Qué se vende en esta tienda?
   A. teletas
   B. telas
   C. telefonemas
   D. televisores

Picture Number 6

6. ¿Qué está haciendo este hombre en el parque?
   A. Está llorando.
   B. Está comiendo.
   C. Está corriendo.
   D. Está leyendo.

Picture Number 7

7. Y estas personas, ¿qué están haciendo?
   A. Están bebiendo.
   B. Están bailando.
   C. Están cocinando.
   D. Están cenando.

Answers

A. Paragraphs

1. **D**	4. **B**	7. **C**	10. **D**	13. **B**
2. **A**	5. **D**	8. **B**	11. **D**	14. **D**
3. **C**	6. **A**	9. **C**	12. **A**	15. **C**

B. Long Selections

1. **A**	4. **B**	7. **B**	10. **D**	13. **D**
2. **C**	5. **A**	8. **A**	11. **C**	14. **B**
3. **D**	6. **C**	9. **B**	12. **A**	15. **B**

C. Pictures

1. **B**	3. **C**	5. **D**	7. **B**
2. **A**	4. **A**	6. **C**	

§23.

Writing

A. Lists of Words to Write on Given Topics

Directions. In this section, various topics are presented to encourage you to write lists of words and expressions in Spanish to enrich your vocabulary. If you need any help, consult Part One of this book and the vocabularies throughout the book and at the end of the book. If the word or expression you would like to write in Spanish is not in Part One or the vocabulary lists, consult a standard dictionary.

The answers to these tests begin right after the last question.

I. You have been invited to a wedding. You are planning to give the bride and groom a present. Write a list of four things you are considering.

1. _____ 3. _____
2. _____ 4. _____

II. Your friend is making plans to go to the circus with you. You prefer to go to the movies. Write four words or expressions you would use in the conversation to persuade your friend to go to the movies instead of the circus.

1. _____ 3. _____
2. _____ 4. _____

III. You are in a stationery shop **(una papelería)** because you want to buy a pen. Write four words or expressions you would use in this conversation.

1. _____ 3. _____
2. _____ 4. _____

IV. Write six words in Spanish that are things you like to eat or drink for breakfast.

1. _____ 4. _____
2. _____ 5. _____
3. _____ 6. _____

259

V. You are in a Spanish restaurant. Write the words for four vegetables that are on the menu.

1. _____   3. _____
2. _____   4. _____

VI. Now you are looking at the list of fish. Write four that are on the menu.

1. _____   3. _____
2. _____   4. _____

VII. Write the words for two kinds of cheese on the menu.

1. _____   2. _____

VIII. Write four words in Spanish for things in your house that sometimes need to be repaired.

1. _____   3. _____
2. _____   4. _____

IX. You are in a hospital visiting a friend who broke an arm and a leg. Write four words or expressions you would use in your conversation.

1. _____   3. _____
2. _____   4. _____

X. Write four words or expressions you would use while talking to a desk clerk at the airport.

1. _____   3. _____
2. _____   4. _____

B. Simple Guided Composition for Expression

Directions. Various situations are presented here to encourage you to write simple sentences in Spanish. If you need any help, consult Part One of this book, in particular §12.2, the formation of verb forms in §7., and the vocabulary list beginning on page 349. Sample sentences begin on page 267.

1. You are talking to the desk clerk in a hotel. Make the following three statements: Tell the clerk your name, say that you have a reservation, and present your passport.

_____
_____
_____

2. You are in a bookstore. Write three sentences saying that you want to buy a book on modern art, that you don't want to pay much, and that it is a present for a friend.

_____

_____

_____

3. You are talking to a friend. Write two sentences saying that you are going to the movies this evening. Ask your friend to come with you.

_____

_____

_____

4. You are in a restaurant. Tell the waiter that you would like two fried eggs, mashed potatoes, and peas. Then ask him to bring you a cup of coffee with cream.

_____

_____

_____

5. You don't feel well today. Tell the doctor you are sick, that you have a headache, a stomachache, and a pain in the neck.

_____

_____

6. You are on a tourist bus in Madrid. Tell the person next to you that you're going to El Parque del Retiro, that you're going to take a walk in the gardens, and that you're going to have dinner with some friends.

_____

_____

_____

7. Tell your Spanish teacher where you are going to spend the summer, with whom, and how many weeks you will be there.

_____

_____

_____

8. Your friends gave you a surprise birthday party. Write that you received many presents, that you ate a lot and you danced and sang.

_____

_____

_____

9. Your best friend asked you where you went yesterday. Say that you went to the pool and you swam.

_____

_____

_____

10. Another friend wants to know what you did last night. Say that you watched television, that you saw a good Spanish movie, and that you liked it a lot.

_____

_____

_____

C. Word Games to Increase Your Vocabulary

Directions. In this section there are ten word games. Follow the directions for each game. If you need any help, consult Part One of this book and the vocabulary lists beginning on page 349. Check your answers and solutions in the answers section beginning on page 267.

I. Parts of the body

la mano (hand)

el pelo (hair)

la cabeza (head)

la oreja (ear)

el brazo (arm)

el cuello (neck)

la boca (mouth)

el hombro (shoulder)

el pie (foot)

la rodilla (knee)

la pierna (leg)

These two dancers posed for a moment to give you a chance to learn some of the parts of the body. In the grid, find five of the words in the picture and draw a line around each of them. They are written horizontally, vertically, diagonally, and backwards.

M	A	N	O	O	D	O	L	A
R	O	D	I	Z	E	R	P	I
P	I	A	R	A	B	E	B	O
A	C	O	B	R	C	J	C	A
H	O	M	O	B	R	A	D	E
C	U	E	R	N	Z	E	I	P
R	N	A	C	E	L	P	O	A
P	E	L	B	O	D	I	L	L
E	H	A	M	R	B	A	O	U
R	C	O	B	O	R	J	E	A

II. Drop one letter in each of the following words to find new words. Write the new word on the line.
   1. la **cerveza**/beer   > la _____ /cherry
   2. el **perro**/dog   > _____ /but
   3. **fino**/thin   > el _____ /end
   4. el **clima**/climate   > la _____ /top
   5. la **cola**/tail   > la _____ /cabbage
   6. el **carro**/car   > _____ /expensive
   7. el **juego**/game   > el _____ /juice

III. The letters of the following words are scrambled. Put them in the correct order to find the word. Then write it on the line. The clues will help you.

   1. | E P I Ó R I D O C | _____

   Clue: It's something you read.

   2. | D E C P S A O | _____

   Clue: It's something you eat, usually on Fridays.

3. | P O S A | _____

Clue: It's something you eat in a bowl or cup.

4. | L U M A P | _____

Clue: You write with it.

5. | O S C A B E | _____

Clue: You sweep the floor with it.

IV. Choose a word in column B to complete the statement in column A. The English meanings of the Spanish words are given below.

	A	B
1.	Puedo escribir con _____ .	una bola de nieve
2.	Puedo lanzar _____ .	una persona
3.	Puedo mirar _____ .	una piscina
4.	Puedo leer _____	la música
5.	Puedo nadar en _____ .	una pelota
6.	Puedo aceptar_____ .	un regalo
7.	Puedo escuchar _____ .	la televisión
8.	Puedo comprar _____ .	una invitación
9.	Puedo ayudar a _____ .	un libro
10.	Puedo hacer _____ .	una pluma

aceptar to accept
ayudar to help
bola de nieve snowball
comprar to buy, to purchase
con with
en in
escribir to write
escuchar to listen (to)
hacer to make
invitación invitation
lanzar to throw
leer to read

libro book
mirar to watch, to look at
música music
nadar to swim
pelota ball
persona person
piscina swimming pool
pluma pen
puedo I can
regalo gift, present
televisión television

V. Add the accent mark (´) on the vowel in each of the following words to get another word, another meaning.

1. de/of, from   > _____ /give (*see* **dar** in **§7.7–6**)
2. se/yourself, *etc.* > yo _____ /I know
    (*see* **§6.1–6**)   (*see* **saber** in **§7.7–1**)
3. si/if   > _____ /yes
4. mi/my   > para/for _____ /me
    (*see* **§5.4–4**)   (*see* **§6.2**)
5. tu/your   > _____ /you
    (*see* **§5.4–4**)   (*see* **§6.1–1**)
6. el/the (*see* **§4.1**) > _____ /he (*see* **§6.1–1**)

VI. Match the articles of clothing with the parts of the body where the articles are worn by writing the corresponding number on the line. You learned these parts of the body above in game I.

La Ropa/Clothing   **Las Partes del cuerpo humano**/Parts of the human body

1. el **zapato**/shoe   _____ la **pierna**
2. el **guante**/glove   _____ la **cabeza**
3. la **bufanda**/scarf   _____ el **pie**
4. el **sombrero**/hat   _____ los **hombros**
5. la **media**/stocking   _____ el **cuello**
6. el **chal**/shawl   _____ la **mano**

VII. Change one letter to another letter in a Spanish word and get another word, another meaning.

1. **hay**/there is, there are _____ /today
2. el **hermano**/brother   la _____ /sister
3. el **cabello**/hair   el _____ /horse
4. la **madre**/mother   el _____ /father
5. la **casa**/house   la _____ /thing
6. **caro**/expensive   la _____ /face
7. **hecho**/done   el _____ /chest
8. el **hombro**/shoulder   el _____ /man
9. la **banana**/banana   el _____ /banana tree
10. la **banqueta**/footstool el _____ /banquet

VIII. Arrange these money bags **(las bolsas de dinero)** according to the letter on each bag to find the amount of Spanish pesetas they contain. Then write the Spanish word on the line below them.

IX. **¿Qué tiempo hace hoy?**/What's the weather like today? Well, if you really want to know, arrange these blocks of letters so they spell out today's weather announcement. Then write the two Spanish words on the line below.

X. Have you ever played a word game in English combining two words to get a new word with a new meaning? For example, extra + ordinary = extraordinary. Here are a few in Spanish for you to combine. Write the new Spanish word on the line.

1. **de**/of, from + **bajo**/down, under =
   _____ /underneath
2. **por**/by + **que**/what =
   _____ /because
3. **de**/of, from + **caer**/to fall =
   _____ /to decay
4. **de**/of, from + **tener**/to have, to hold =
   _____ /to detain
5. **a**/at, to + **Dios**/God =
   _____ /good-bye
6. **extra**/extra + **ordinario**/ordinary =
   _____ /extraordinary
7. **en**/in + **frente**/front =
   _____ /opposite
8. **sobre**/on, over, above + **todo**/all =
   _____ /overcoat
9. **sobre**/on, over, above + **humano**/human =
   _____ /superhuman
10. **para**/for + **sol**/sun =
    _____ /parasol

Answers

A. Lists of Words to Write on Given Topics

Note: The Spanish words and expressions given here are not the only answers. They are samples. If you do not know their meanings, consult the vocabulary beginning on page 349.

I.   1. un jarrón   3. una manta de cama
     2. una lámpara   4. cien dólares

II. 1. Prefiero   3. una película interesante
     2. al cine   4. una historia de amor

III. 1. Deseo   3. una pluma
     2. comprar   4. barato

IV. 1. el café   4. el huevo
     2. con leche   5. el pan tostado
     3. el jugo de naranja   6. la mantequilla

V.   1. las zanahorias   3. las habichuelas verdes
     2. las espinacas   4. las patatas

VI. 1. el salmón   3. la trucha
     2. el lenguado   4. el atún

VII. 1. el queso suizo   2. el roquefort

VIII. 1. el refrigerador   3. el aspirador
      2. el televisor   4. la lavadora

IX. 1. romperse el brazo   3. ¿cuándo?
     2. la pierna   4. ¿cómo?

X.   1. ¿a qué hora?   3. salir
     2. ¿cuánto cuesta?   4. llegar

B. Simple Guided Composition for Expression

1. Mi nombre es ... Tengo una reservación. Aquí tiene usted mi pasaporte.
2. Deseo comprar un libro sobre el arte moderno. No quiero pagar mucho. Es un regalo para un amigo.
3. Voy al cine esta noche. ¿Quieres venir conmigo?
4. Quisiera dos huevos fritos, puré de patatas, y guisantes. Tráigame una taza de café con crema, por favor.
5. Estoy enfermo (enferma). Tengo dolor de cabeza, dolor de estómago, y me duele el cuello.

6. Voy al Parque del Retiro. Voy a pasearme en los jardines. Voy a cenar con algunos amigos.
7. Voy a pasar el verano en las montañas con mi familia. Nos quedaremos allí tres semanas.
8. (Yo) recibí muchos regalos. En la fiesta (yo) comí mucho, bailé, y canté.
9. Ayer (yo) fui a la piscina y nadé.
10. Anoche (yo) miré la televisión. Vi una buena película española y me gustó mucho.

C. Word Games to Increase Your Vocabulary

I. Parts of the body

M	A	N	O	O	D	O	L	A
R	O	D	I	Z	E	R	P	I
P	I	A	R	A	B	E	B	O
A	C	O	B	R	C	J	C	A
H	O	M	O	B	R	A	D	E
C	U	E	R	N	Z	E	I	P
R	N	A	C	E	L	P	O	A
P	E	L	B	O	D	I	L	L
E	H	A	M	R	B	A	O	U
R	C	O	B	O	R	J	E	A

II.
1. cereza
2. pero
3. fin
4. cima
5. col
6. caro
7. jugo

III.
1. PERIÓDICO
2. PESCADO
3. SOPA
4. PLUMA
5. ESCOBA

IV.
1. una pluma
2. una pelota
3. la televisión
4. un libro
5. una piscina
6. una invitación
7. la música
8. un regalo
9. una persona
10. una bola de nieve

V. 1. dé 3. sí 5. tú
2. sé 4. mí 6. él

VI. 5, 4, 1, 6, 3, 2

VII. 1. hoy 5. cosa 9. banano
2. hermana 6. cara 10. banquete
3. caballo 7. pecho
4. padre 8. hombre

VIII. CIEN (one hundred)

IX. Hace sol. (It's sunny.)

X. 1. debajo 5. adiós 9. superhumano
2. porque 6. extraordinario 10. parasol
3. decaer 7. enfrente
4. detener 8. sobretodo

VERB REVIEW

§24.

Spanish Verb Conjugation Tables for Reference

Review the section on verbs in **§7.** in this book, in particular, **§7.5–19.** For an in-depth and extensive presentation of Spanish verb tenses and their uses, consult my Barron's book, *501 Spanish Verbs Fully Conjugated in All the Tenses*.

In Spanish there are fourteen major verb tenses. There are seven simple tenses identified below as tense numbers 1-7. A simple tense contains one verb form. There are seven compound tenses identified as tense numbers 8-14. A compound tense contains one verb form and a past participle. There is also the Imperative, which is not a tense but a mood.

FORMATION OF THE SEVEN SIMPLE TENSES
NUMBERS 1 TO 7 FOR REGULAR VERBS

There are three major types of regular verbs. In the infinitive form, they end in either **-ar, -er,** or **-ir.** For example, **hablar, beber, recibir.**

TENSE NO. 1 *PRESENTE DE INDICATIVO* (Present Indicative)

In the verb forms that follow on these pages, the subject pronouns are not stated. As you know, they are:

Singular: **yo, tú, Ud. (él, ella)**
Plural: **nosotros (nosotras), vosotros (vosotras), Uds. (ellos, ellas)**

For **-ar** type verbs, drop **ar** from the infinitive form. What is left is called the stem. Then add the following endings to the stem:

Singular: **o, as, a**
Plural: **amos, áis, an**

hablar to talk, to speak
Singular: **hablo, hablas, habla**
Plural: **hablamos, habláis, hablan**

For **-er** type verbs, drop **er** from the infinitive form. What is left is called the stem. Then add the following endings to the stem:

Singular: **o, es, e**
Plural: **emos, éis, en**

beber to drink
Singular: **bebo, bebes, bebe**
Plural: **bebemos, bebéis, beben**

For **-ir** type verbs, drop **ir** from the infinitive form. What is left is called the stem. Then add the following endings to the stem:

Singular: **o, es, e**
Plural: **imos, ís, en**

recibir to receive
Singular: **recibo, recibes, recibe**
Plural: **recibimos, recibís, reciben**

Refer to the above patterns of formation for the following regular **-ar, -er, -ir** verbs in the present indicative tense.

Note that at times some verb forms contain spelling changes in the stem. They are called orthographical changing verbs. See **§7.7** in this book.

---

abrir to open
Singular: **abro, abres, abre**
Plural: **abrimos, abrís, abren**

---

acabar to finish, to end, to complete
Singular: **acabo, acabas, acaba**
Plural: **acabamos, acabáis, acaban**

---

aceptar to accept
Singular: **acepto, aceptas, acepta**
Plural: **aceptamos, aceptáis, aceptan**

---

admitir to admit, to grant, to permit
Singular: **admito, admites, admite**
Plural: **admitimos, admitís, admiten**

---

afeitarse to shave oneself
Singular: **me afeito, te afeitas, se afeita**
Plural: **nos afeitamos, os afeitáis, se afeitan**

This is a reflexive verb because it contains the reflexive pronouns **me, te, se, nos, os, se**, as you can see. Review **§6.1—6** and **§7.1—2** in this book.

---

amar to love
Singular: **amo, amas, ama**
Plural: **amamos, amáis, aman**

---

aprender to learn
Singular: **aprendo, aprendes, aprende**
Plural: **aprendemos, aprendéis, aprenden**

---

ayudar to help, to aid, to assist
Singular: **ayudo, ayudas, ayuda**
Plural: **ayudamos, ayudáis, ayudan**

---

bailar to dance
Singular: **bailo, bailas, baila**
Plural: **bailamos, bailáis, bailan**

---

bajar to go down, to come down, to descend
Singular: **bajo, bajas, baja**
Plural: **bajamos, bajáis, bajan**

---

bañarse to bathe oneself, to take a bath
Singular: **me baño, te bañas, se baña**
Plural: **nos bañamos, os bañáis, se bañan**

This is a reflexive verb because it contains the reflexive pronouns **me, te, se, nos, os, se,** as you can see. Review **§6.1—6** and **§7.1—2** in this book.

cantar to sing
Singular: **canto, cantas, canta**
Plural: **cantamos, cantáis, cantan**

casarse to get married
Singular: **me caso, te casas, se casa**
Plural: **nos casamos, os casáis, se casan**

Review the reflexive pronouns in **§6.1—6** and **§7.1—2.**

cenar to dine, to have supper
Singular: **ceno, cenas, cena**
Plural: **cenamos, cenáis, cenan**

comer to eat
Singular: **como, comes, come**
Plural: **comemos, coméis, comen**

comprar to buy, to purchase
Singular: **compro, compras, compra**
Plural: **compramos, compráis, compran**

comprender to understand
Singular: **comprendo, comprendes, comprende**
Plural: **comprendemos, comprendéis, comprenden**

correr to run, to race, to flow
Singular: **corro, corres, corre**
Plural: **corremos, corréis, corren**

cubrir to cover
Singular: **cubro, cubres, cubre**
Plural: **cubrimos, cubrís, cubren**

deber to owe, must, ought
Singular: **debo, debes, debe**
Plural: **debemos, debéis, deben**

decidir to decide
Singular: **decido, decides, decide**
Plural: **decidimos, decidís, deciden**

desear to desire
Singular: **deseo, deseas, desea**
Plural: **deseamos, deseáis, desean**

escribir to write
Singular: **escribo, escribes, escribe**
Plural: **escribimos, escribís, escriben**

estudiar to study
Singular: **estudio, estudias, estudia**
Plural: **estudiamos, estudiáis, estudian**

insistir to insist
Singular: **insisto, insistes, insiste**
Plural: **insistimos, insistís, insisten**

llamarse to be named, to be called
Singular: **me llamo, te llamas, se llama**
Plural: **nos llamamos, os llamáis, se llaman**

Review the reflexive pronouns in **§6.1—6** and **§7.1—2** in this book.

partir to leave, to depart, to divide, to split
Singular: **parto, partes, parte**
Plural: **partimos, partís, parten**

permitir to permit, to allow
Singular: **permito, permites, permite**
Plural: **permitimos, permitís, permiten**

prohibir to prohibit, to forbid
Singular: **prohibo, prohibes, prohibe**
Plural: **prohibimos, prohibís, prohiben**

subir to go up, to get on (a train, bus)
Singular: **subo, subes, sube**
Plural: **subimos, subís, suben**

sufrir to suffer, to endure
Singular: **sufro, sufres, sufre**
Plural: **sufrimos, sufrís, sufren**

temer to fear, to dread
Singular: **temo, temes, teme**
Plural: **tememos, teméis, temen**

tomar to take, to have (something to eat or drink)
Singular: **tomo, tomas, toma**
Plural: **tomamos, tomáis, toman**

trabajar to work
Singular: **trabajo, trabajas, trabaja**
Plural: **trabajamos, trabajáis, trabajan**

unir to unite, to join
Singular: **uno, unes, une**
Plural: **unimos, unís, unen**

vender to sell
Singular: **vendo, vendes, vende**
Plural: **vendemos, vendéis, venden**

viajar to travel
Singular: **viajo, viajas, viaja**
Plural: **viajamos, viajáis, viajan**

vivir to live
Singular: **vivo, vives, vive**
Plural: **vivimos, vivís, viven**

For the uses of the present indicative tense with English translations, review **§7.5—1.**

There is also the ***progressive present tense***, when you say, *e.g.*, **estoy hablando**/I am talking, **Elena está estudiando**/Helen is studying. For the formation and use of that tense, review **§7.5—15.**

TENSE NO. 2   *IMPERFECTO DE INDICATIVO* (Imperfect Indicative)

For **-ar** type verbs, drop **ar** from the infinitive form. What is left is called the stem. Then add the following endings to the stem:

Singular: **aba, abas, aba**
Plural: **ábamos, abais, aban**

hablar to talk, to speak
Singular: **hablaba, hablabas, hablaba**
Plural: **hablábamos, hablabais, hablaban**

For **-er** and **-ir** verbs, drop **er** or **ir** from the infinitive form and add these endings:

Singular: **ía, ías, ía**
Plural: **íamos, íais, ían**

beber to drink   recibir to receive
Singular: **bebía, bebías, bebía**   **recibía, recibías, recibía**
Plural: **bebíamos, bebíais, bebían**   **recibíamos, recibíais, recibían**

cantar to sing
Singular: **cantaba, cantabas, cantaba**
Plural: **cantábamos, cantabais, cantaban**

comer to eat
Singular: **comía, comías, comía**
Plural: **comíamos, comíais, comían**

escribir to write
Singular: **escribía, escribías, escribía**
Plural: **escribíamos, escribíais, escribían**

> For the uses of the imperfect indicative tense with English translations, review **§7.5—2.**
>
> There is also the ***progressive past tense***, when you say, *e.g,* **(yo) estaba durmiendo**/ I was sleeping, **José estaba comiendo**/Joseph was eating. For the formation and use of that tense, review **§7.5—15.**

TENSE NO. 3   *PRETÉRITO* (Preterit)

For **-ar** type verbs, drop **ar** and add these endings:

Singular: **é, aste, ó**
Plural: **amos, asteis, aron**

---

hablar to talk, to speak
Singular: **hablé, hablaste, habló**
Plural: **hablamos, hablasteis, hablaron**

For **-er** and **-ir** verbs, drop **er** or **ir** and add these endings:

Singular: **í, iste, ió**
Plural: **imos, isteis, ieron**

---

beber to drink   **recibir** to receive
Singular: **bebí, bebiste, bebió**   **recibí, recibiste, recibió**
Plural: **bebimos, bebisteis, bebieron**   **recibimos, recibisteis, recibieron**

---

cantar to sing
Singular: **canté, cantaste, cantó**
Plural: **cantamos, cantasteis, cantaron**

---

comer to eat
Singular: **comí, comiste, comió**
Plural: **comimos, comisteis, comieron**

---

escribir to write
Singular: **escribí, escribiste, escribió**
Plural: **escribimos, escribisteis, escribieron**

For the uses of the preterit tense with English translations, review **§7.5—3.**

TENSE NO. 4 *FUTURO* (Future)

For **-ar, -er, -ir** verbs, add the following endings to the whole infinitive:

Singular: **é, ás, á**
Plural: **emos, éis, án**

Note the accent marks on the future endings except for **emos.**

---

hablar to talk, to speak
Singular: **hablaré, hablarás, hablará**
Plural: **hablaremos, hablaréis, hablarán**

---

beber to drink
Singular: **beberé, beberás, beberá**
Plural: **beberemos, beberéis, beberán**

recibir to receive
recibiré, recibirás, recibirá
recibiremos, recibiréis, recibirán

---

aceptar to accept
Singular: **aceptaré, aceptarás, aceptará**
Plural: **aceptaremos, aceptaréis, aceptarán**

---

aprender to learn
Singular: **aprenderé, aprenderás, aprenderá**
Plural: **aprenderemos, aprenderéis, aprenderán**

---

subir to go up, to get on (a train, bus)
Singular: **subiré, subirás, subirá**
Plural: **subiremos, subiréis, subirán**

For the uses of the future tense with English translations, review **§7.5—4.**

TENSE NO. 5 *POTENCIAL SIMPLE* (Conditional)

For **-ar, -er, -ir** verbs, add the following endings to the whole infinitive:

Singular: **ía, ías, ía**
Plural: **íamos, íais, ían**

Note that these endings are the same for the imperfect indicative (Tense No. 2) for **-er** and **-ir** verbs, added to the stem of the infinitive, but for the conditional they are added to the whole infinitive.

---

hablar to talk, to speak
Singular: **hablaría, hablarías, hablaría**
Plural: **hablaríamos, hablaríais, hablarían**

---

beber to drink
Singular: **bebería, beberías, bebería**
Plural: **beberíamos, beberíais, beberían**

vivir to live
viviría, vivirías, viviría
viviríamos, viviríais, vivirían

---

bailar to dance
Singular: **bailaría, bailarías, bailaría**
Plural: **bailaríamos, bailaríais, bailarían**

---

comer to eat
Singular: **comería, comerías, comería**
Plural: **comeríamos, comeríais, comerían**

---

partir to leave
Singular: **partiría, partirías, partiría**
Plural: **partiríamos, partiríais, partirían**

For the uses of the conditional with English translations, review **§7.5—5.**

TENSE NO. 6 *PRESENTE DE SUBJUNTIVO* (Present Subjunctive)

To form this tense regularly, go to the present indicative (Tense No. 1), 1st person singular of the verb you have in mind to use, drop the ending **o** and...

for **-ar** verbs, add these endings:
Singular: **e, es, e**
Plural: **emos, éis, en**

for **-er** and **-ir** verbs, add these endings:
Singular: **a, as, a**
Plural: **amos, áis, an**

As you can see, the characteristic vowel in the present subjunctive endings for **-ar** verbs is **e** in the six persons.

hablar to talk, to speak
Singular: **hable, hables, hable**
Plural: **hablemos, habléis, hablen**

The characteristic vowel in the present subjunctive endings for **-er** and **-ir** verbs is **a** in the six persons. To know when to use the subjunctive, review **§7.5—18.**

beber to drink
Singular: **beba, bebas, beba**
Plural: **bebamos, bebáis, beban**

vivir to live
viva, vivas, viva
vivamos, viváis, vivan

cenar to dine, to have supper
Singular: **que yo cene, que tú cenes, que Ud. (él, ella) cene**
Plural: **que nosotros cenemos, que vosotros cenéis, que Uds. (ellos, ellas) cenen**

deber to owe, must, ought
Singular: **que yo deba, que tú debas, que Ud. (él, ella) deba**
Plural: **que nosotros debamos, que vosotros debáis, que Uds. (ellos, ellas) deban**

subir to go up, to get on (a train, bus)
Singular: **que yo suba, que tú subas, que Ud. (él, ella) suba**
Plural: **que nosotros subamos, que vosotros subáis, que Uds. (ellos, ellas) suban**

For the uses of the present subjunctive with English translations, review **§7.5—6.**

TENSE NO. 7   *IMPERFECTO DE SUBJUNTIVO* (Imperfect Subjunctive)

For all verbs, drop the **ron** ending of the 3d person plural of the preterit tense (No. 3) and add these endings:

Singular:	**ra, ras, ra**	or **se, ses, se**
Plural:	**ramos, rais, ran**	**semos, seis, sen**

---

hablar to talk, to speak
Singular: **hablara, hablaras, hablara**   or   **hablase, hablases, hablase**
Plural: **habláramos, hablarais, hablaran**   **hablásemos, hablaseis, hablasen**

---

beber to drink
Singular: **bebiera, bebieras, bebiera**   or   **bebiese, bebieses, bebiese**
Plural: **bebiéramos, bebierais, bebieran**   **bebiésemos, bebieseis, bebiesen**

---

vivir to live
Singular: **viviera, vivieras, viviera**   or   **viviese, vivieses, viviese**
Plural: **viviéramos, vivierais, vivieran**   **viviésemos, vivieseis, viviesen**

---

amar to love
Singular: **amara, amaras, amara**   or   **amase, amases, amase**
Plural: **amáramos, amarais, amaran**   **amásemos, amaseis, amasen**

---

comer to eat
Singular: **comiera, comieras, comiera**   or   **comiese, comieses, comiese**
Plural: **comiéramos, comierais,**   **comiésemos, comieseis,**
          comieran   **comiesen**

---

subir to go up, to get on (a train, bus)
Singular: **subiera, subieras, subiera**   or   **subiese, subieses, subiese**
Plural: **subiéramos, subierais, subieran**   **subiésemos, subieseis, subiesen**

Note that the only accent mark on the forms of the imperfect subjunctive is on the 1st person plural form and it is placed on the vowel that is *right in front* of the ending **ramos** or **semos**.

For the uses of the imperfect subjunctive with English translations, review **§7.5—7** and **§7.5—18**.

FORMATION OF THE SEVEN COMPOUND TENSES NUMBERS 8 TO 14

TENSE NO. 8 *PERFECTO DE INDICATIVO* (Present Perfect Ind.)

This commonly used compound past tense is based on Tense No. 1 of **haber**. In other words, you form this tense by using the auxiliary verb **haber** in the present indicative plus the past participle of the verb you have in mind to use.

To be able to form the seven compound tenses in Spanish, you must know the seven simple tenses of **haber**. For the complete conjugation of **haber** in the seven simple tenses, review **§7.5—19** where the forms are translated into English.

To learn how to form a past participle regularly and to learn the common irregular past participles, review **§7.3—1**.

For the uses of this tense with English translations, review **§7.5—8**.

---

abrir to open
Singular: **he abierto, has abierto, ha abierto**
Plural: **hemos abierto, habéis abierto, han abierto**

---

aceptar to accept
Singular: **he aceptado, has aceptado, ha aceptado**
Plural: **hemos aceptado, habéis aceptado, han aceptado**

---

acostarse to go to bed, to lie down
Singular: **me he acostado, te has acostado, se ha acostado**
Plural: **nos hemos acostado, os habéis acostado, se han acostado**

---

aprender to learn
Singular: **he aprendido, has aprendido, ha aprendido**
Plural: **hemos aprendido, habéis aprendido, han aprendido**

---

escribir to write
Singular: **he escrito, has escrito, ha escrito**
Plural: **hemos escrito, habéis escrito, han escrito**

TENSE NO. 9 *PLUSCUAMPERFECTO DE INDICATIVO* (Pluperfect Ind.)

This tense is based on Tense No. 2 of **haber**. In other words, you form this tense by using the auxiliary verb **haber** in the imperfect indicative plus the past participle of the verb you have in mind to use.

To be able to form the seven compound tenses in Spanish, you must know the seven simple tenses of **haber**. For the complete conjugation of **haber** in the seven simple tenses, review **§7.5—19** where the forms are translated into English.

To learn how to form a past participle regularly and to learn the common irregular past participles, review **§7.3—1**.

For the uses of this tense with English translations, review **§7.5—9**.

---

abrir to open
Singular: **había abierto, habías abierto, había abierto**
Plural: **habíamos abierto, habíais abierto, habían abierto**

---

aceptar to accept
Singular: **había aceptado, habías aceptado, había aceptado**
Plural: **habíamos aceptado, habíais aceptado, habían aceptado**

---

acostarse to go to bed, to lie down
Singular: **me había acostado, te habías acostado, se había acostado**
Plural: **nos habíamos acostado, os habíais acostado, se habían acostado**

---

aprender to learn
Singular: **había aprendido, habías aprendido, había aprendido**
Plural: **habíamos aprendido, habíais aprendido, habían aprendido**

---

bailar to dance
Singular: **había bailado, habías bailado, había bailado**
Plural: **habíamos bailado, habíais bailado, habían bailado**

---

dar to give
Singular: **había dado, habías dado, había dado**
Plural: **habíamos dado, habíais dado, habían dado**

---

escribir to write
Singular: **había escrito, habías escrito, había escrito**
Plural: **habíamos escrito, habíais escrito, habían escrito**

---

ir to go
Singular: **había ido, habías ido, había ido**
Plural: **habíamos ido, habíais ido, habían ido**

---

lavarse to wash oneself
Singular: **me había lavado, te habías lavado, se había lavado**
Plural: **nos habíamos lavado, os habíais lavado, se habían lavado**

---

salir to go out
Singular: **había salido, habías salido, había salido**
Plural: **habíamos salido, habíais salido, habían salido**

TENSE NO. 10　*PRETÉRITO ANTERIOR* (Preterit Perfect)

This tense is based on Tense No. 3 of **haber**. In other words, you form this tense by using the auxiliary verb **haber** in the preterit tense plus the past participle of the verb you have in mind to use.

To be able to form the seven compound tenses in Spanish, you must know the seven simple tenses of **haber**. For the complete conjugation of **haber** in the seven simple tenses, review **§7.5—19** where the forms are translated into English.

To learn how to form a past participle regularly and to learn the common irregular past participles, review **§7.3—1**.

> For the uses of this tense with English translations, review **§7.5—10.**

decir to say, to tell
Singular: **hube dicho, hubiste dicho, hubo dicho**
Plural:　　**hubimos dicho, hubisteis dicho, hubieron dicho**

estar to be
Singular: **hube estado, hubiste estado, hubo estado**
Plural:　　**hubimos estado, hubisteis estado, hubieron estado**

For the complete conjugation of **estar** in all 14 tenses plus the imperative, review **§7.7—8.**

hablar to talk, to speak
Singular: **hube hablado, hubiste hablado, hubo hablado**
Plural:　　**hubimos hablado, hubisteis hablado, hubieron hablado**

hacer to do, to make
Singular: **hube hecho, hubiste hecho, hubo hecho**
Plural:　　**hubimos hecho, hubisteis hecho, hubieron hecho**

For the complete conjugation of **hacer** in all 14 tenses plus the imperative, review **§7.7—8.**

ir to go
Singular: **hube ido, hubiste ido, hubo ido**
Plural:　　**hubimos ido, hubisteis ido, hubieron ido**

For the complete conjugation of **ir** in all 14 tenses plus the imperative, review **§7.7—8.**

salir to go out
Singular: **hube salido, hubiste salido, hubo salido**
Plural:　　**hubimos salido, hubisteis salido, hubieron salido**

ser to be
Singular: **hube sido, hubiste sido, hubo sido**
Plural: **hubimos sido, hubisteis sido, hubieron sido**

> For the complete conjugation of **ser** in all 14 tenses plus the imperative, review **§7.7—8.**

TENSE NO. 11 *FUTURO PERFECTO* (Future Perfect)

This tense is based on Tense No. 4 of **haber.** In other words, you form this tense by using the auxiliary verb **haber** in the future tense plus the past participle of the verb you have in mind to use.

To be able to form the seven compound tenses in Spanish, you must know the seven simple tenses of **haber.** For the complete conjugation of **haber** in the seven simple tenses, review §7.5—19 where the forms are translated into English.

To learn how to form a past participle regularly and to learn the common irregular past participles, review §7.3—1.

For the uses of this tense with English translations, review §7.5—11.

---

acostarse to go to bed, to lie down
Singular: **me habré acostado, te habrás acostado, se habrá acostado**
Plural: **nos habremos acostado, os habréis acostado, se habrán acostado**

---

leer to read
Singular: **habré leído, habrás leído, habrá leído**
Plural: **habremos leído, habréis leído, habrán leído**

---

levantarse to get up
Singular: **me habré levantado, te habrás levantado, se habrá levantado**
Plural: **nos habremos levantado, os habréis levantado, se habrán levantado**

---

llegar to arrive
Singular: **habré llegado, habrás llegado, habrá llegado**
Plural: **habremos llegado, habréis llegado, habrán llegado**

---

morir to die
Singular: **habré muerto, habrás muerto, habrá muerto**
Plural: **habremos muerto, habréis muerto, habrán muerto**

---

oír to hear
Singular: **habré oído, habrás oído, habrá oído**
Plural: **habremos oído, habréis oído, habrán oído**

---

poner to put
Singular: **habré puesto, habrás puesto, habrá puesto**
Plural: **habremos puesto, habréis puesto, habrán puesto**

---

terminar to finish
Singular: **habré terminado, habrás terminado, habrá terminado**
Plural: **habremos terminado, habréis terminado, habrán terminado**

---

ver to see
Singular: **habré visto, habrás visto, habrá visto**
Plural: **habremos visto, habréis visto, habrán visto**

---

volver to return
Singular: **habré vuelto, habrás vuelto, habrá vuelto**
Plural: **habremos vuelto, habréis vuelto, habrán vuelto**

TENSE NO. 12 *POTENCIAL COMPUESTO* (Conditional Perfect)

This tense is based on Tense No. 5 of **haber.** In other words, you form this tense by using the auxiliary verb **haber** in the conditional plus the past participle of the verb you have in mind to use.

To be able to form the seven compound tenses in Spanish, you must know the seven simple tenses of **haber.** For the complete conjugation of **haber** in the seven simple tenses, review **§7.5—19** where the forms are translated into English.

To learn how to form a past participle regularly and to learn the common irregular past participles, review **§7.3—1.**

For the uses of this tense with English translations, review **§7.5—12.**

---

andar to walk
Singular: **habría andado, habrías andado, habría andado**
Plural: **habríamos andado, habríais andado, habrían andado**

---

comer to eat
Singular: **habría comido, habrías comido, habría comido**
Plural: **habríamos comido, habríais comido, habrían comido**

---

creer to believe
Singular: **habría creído, habrías creído, habría creído**
Plural: **habríamos creído, habríais creído, habrían creído**

---

dormir to sleep
Singular: **habría dormido, habrías dormido, habría dormido**
Plural: **habríamos dormido, habríais dormido, habrían dormido**

---

ir to go
Singular: **habría ido, habrías ido, habría ido**
Plural: **habríamos ido, habríais ido, habrían ido**

---

pensar to think
Singular: **habría pensado, habrías pensado, habría pensado**
Plural: **habríamos pensado, habríais pensado, habrían pensado**

---

réir to laugh
Singular: **habría reído, habrías reído, habría reído**
Plural: **habríamos reído, habríais reído, habrían reído**

---

romper to break
Singular: **habría roto, habrías roto, habría roto**
Plural: **habríamos roto, habríais roto, habrían roto**

---

sentir to feel sorry, to regret, to feel
Singular: **habría sentido, habrías sentido, habría sentido**
Plural: **habríamos sentido, habríais sentido, habrían sentido**

ser to be
Singular: **habría sido, habrías sido, habría sido**
Plural: **habríamos sido, habríais sido, habrían sido**

TENSE NO. 13 *PERFECTO DE SUBJUNTIVO* (Present Perfect Sbj.)

This tense is based on Tense No. 6 of **haber.** In other words, you form this tense by using the auxiliary verb **haber** in the present subjunctive plus the past participle of the verb you have in mind to use.

To be able to form the seven compound tenses in Spanish, you must know the seven simple tenses of **haber.** For the complete conjugation of **haber** in the seven simple tenses, review **§7.5—19** where the forms are translated into English.

To learn how to form a past participle regularly and to learn the common irregular past participles, review **§7.3—1.**

For the uses of this tense with English translations, review **§7.5—13** and **§7.5—18.**

---

abrir to open
Singular: **haya abierto, hayas abierto, haya abierto**
Plural: **hayamos abierto, hayáis abierto, hayan abierto**

---

contestar to answer, to reply
Singular: **haya contestado, hayas contestado, haya contestado**
Plural: **hayamos contestado, hayáis contestado, hayan contestado**

---

cubrir to cover
Singular: **haya cubierto, hayas cubierto, haya cubierto**
Plural: **hayamos cubierto, hayáis cubierto, hayan cubierto**

---

dar to give
Singular: **haya dado, hayas dado, haya dado**
Plural: **hayamos dado, hayáis dado, hayan dado**

---

decir to say, to tell
Singular: **haya dicho, hayas dicho, haya dicho**
Plural: **hayamos dicho, hayáis dicho, hayan dicho**

---

estar to be
Singular: **haya estado, hayas estado, haya estado**
Plural: **hayamos estado, hayáis estado, hayan estado**

For the complete conjugation of **estar** in all 14 tenses plus the imperative, review **§7.7—8.**

---

pedir to ask for, to request
Singular: **haya pedido, hayas pedido, haya pedido**
Plural: **hayamos pedido, hayáis pedido, hayan pedido**

servir to serve
Singular: **haya servido, hayas servido, haya servido**
Plural: **hayamos servido, hayáis servido, hayan servido**

telefonear to telephone
Singular: **haya telefoneado, hayas telefoneado, haya telefoneado**
Plural: **hayamos telefoneado, hayáis telefoneado, hayan telefoneado**

vestirse to dress oneself, to get dressed
Singular: **me haya vestido, te hayas vestido, se haya vestido**
Plural: **nos hayamos vestido, os hayáis vestido, se hayan vestido**

TENSE NO. 14   *PLUSCUAMPERFECTO DE SUBJUNTIVO* (Pluperfect Sbj.)

This tense is based on Tense No. 7 of **haber.** In other words, you form this tense by using the auxiliary verb **haber** in the imperfect subjunctive plus the past participle of the verb you have in mind to use.

   To be able to form the seven compound tenses in Spanish, you must know the seven simple tenses of **haber.** For the complete conjugation of **haber** in the seven simple tenses, review **§7.5—19** where the forms are translated into English.

   To learn how to form a past participle regularly and to learn the common irregular past participles, review **§7.3—1.**

> For the uses of this tense with English translations, review **§7.5—14** and **§7.5—18.**

dar to give
Singular: **hubiera dado, hubieras dado, hubiera dado**
Plural: **hubiéramos dado, hubierais dado, hubieran dado**

or: **hubiese dado, hubieses dado, hubiese dado**
           hubiésemos dado, hubieseis dado, hubiesen dado

decir to say, to tell
Singular: **hubiera dicho, hubieras dicho, hubiera dicho**
Plural: **hubiéramos dicho, hubierais dicho, hubieran dicho**

or: **hubiese dicho, hubieses dicho, hubiese dicho**
           hubiésemos dicho, hubieseis dicho, hubiesen dicho

ir to go
Singular: **hubiera ido, hubieras ido, hubiera ido**
Plural: **hubiéramos ido, hubierais ido, hubieran ido**

or: **hubiese ido, hubieses ido, hubiese ido**
           hubiésemos ido, hubieseis ido, hubiesen ido

oír to hear
Singular: **hubiera oído, hubieras oído, hubiera oído**
Plural: **hubiéramos oído, hubierais oído, hubieran oído**

or: **hubiese oído, hubieses oído, hubiese oído**
           hubiésemos oído, hubieseis oído, hubiesen oído

saber to know, to know how
Singular: **hubiera sabido, hubieras sabido, hubiera sabido**
Plural: **hubiéramos sabido, hubierais sabido, hubieran sabido**

or: **hubiese sabido, hubieses sabido, hubiese sabido**
           hubiésemos sabido, hubieseis sabido, hubiesen sabido

tomar to take
Singular: **hubiera tomado, hubieras tomado, hubiera tomado**
Plural: **hubiéramos tomado, hubierais tomado, hubieran tomado**

or: **hubiese tomado, hubieses tomado, hubiese tomado**
              hubiésemos tomado, hubieseis tomado, hubiesen tomado

§25.

Commonly Used Irregular Verbs, Including Orthographical Changing Verbs and Stem-Changing Verbs, in the Seven Simple Tenses and the Imperative

Note that the verb tables in this section also contain some commonly used verbs that change in spelling. They are called orthographic changing verbs. Review **§7.7.**

The names of the seven simple tenses for the seven tense numbers are given below. In the tables that follow, the tense number is used instead of the tense name. Refer to this list when you have to.

You must get into the habit of using the section called **Definitions of Basic Grammatical Terms with Examples** in the back pages of this book. Consult the Table of Contents for the page numbers.

Tense Number	
1	*Presente de Indicativo* (Present Indicative)
2	*Imperfecto de Indicativo* (Imperfect Indicative)
3	*Pretérito* (Preterit)
4	*Futuro* (Future)
5	*Potencial Simple* (Conditional)
6	*Presente de Subjuntivo* (Present Subjunctive)
7	*Imperfecto de Subjuntivo* (Imperfect Subjunctive)

The Imperative (Command) mood is used when telling someone to do or not to do something, *e.g.,* get up, don't get up; go, don't go. For the uses of the Imperative mood, review **§7.5—17.** The forms of the Imperative given in the tables below are in the following order:

> 2d pers. s. **(tú)**, 3d pers. s. **(Ud.)**
> 1st pers. pl. **(nosotros)**, 2d pers. pl. **(vosotros)**, 3d pers. pl. **(Uds.)**

For the formation of the *gerundio* (present participle) and for irregular present participles, review **§7.3—2.**

For the formation of the past participle and for irregular past participles, review **§7.3—1.**

For the meanings of the seven simple tenses and the imperative, review **§7.5—1** through **§7.5—7** and **§7.5—17.**

Review **§7.7—8** for the complete forms of the irregular verbs **estar**/to be; **hacer**/to do, to make; **ir**/to go; **ser**/to be.

In the following tables, the first line is the 1st, 2d, 3d persons of the singular. The second line is the 1st, 2d, 3d persons of the plural.

Verb forms that are irregular in certain tenses, including those with spelling changes (orthographic), are given only in those tenses. They are printed in boldface type. All the forms in the Imperative are printed in boldface type.

---

almorzar to lunch *gerundio* **almorzando** *past part.* **almorzado**

1 **almuerzo, almuerzas, almuerza**
   almorzamos, almorzáis, **almuerzan**

3 **almorcé**, almorzaste, almorzó
   almorzamos, almorzasteis, almorzaron

6 **almuerce, almuerces, almuerce**
   almorcemos, almorcéis, almuercen

Imperativo: **almuerza (no almuerces), almuerce**
            almorcemos, almorzad (no almorcéis), almuercen
Note: **zar** verbs change **z** to **c** before **e**. The stem vowel **o** changes to **ue** because it is stressed.

---

andar to walk   *gerundio* **andando**   *past part.* **andado**

**3   anduve, anduviste, anduvo
       anduvimos, anduvisteis, anduvieron**

**7   anduviera, anduvieras, anduviera
       anduviéramos, anduvierais, anduvieran**

or: **anduviese, anduvieses, anduviese
       anduviésemos, anduvieseis, anduviesen**

Imperativo: **anda (no andes), ande
             andemos, andad (no andéis), anden**

---

buscar to look for, to seek   *gerundio* **buscando**   *past part.* **buscado**

3   busqué, buscaste, buscó
       buscamos, buscasteis, buscaron

**6   busque, busques, busque
       busquemos, busquéis, busquen**

Imperativo: **busca (no busques), busque
             busquemos, buscad (no busquéis), busquen**
Note: **car** verbs change **c** to **qu** before **e**.

---

caber to be contained, to fit into   *gerundio* **cabiendo**   *past part.* **cabido**

1   quepo, cabes, cabe
       cabemos, cabéis, caben

**3   cupe, cupiste, cupo
       cupimos, cupisteis, cupieron**

**4   cabré, cabrás, cabrá
       cabremos, cabréis, cabrán**

**5   cabría, cabrías, cabría
       cabríamos, cabríais, cabrían**

**6   quepa, quepas, quepa
       quepamos, quepáis, quepan**

**7   cupiera, cupieras, cupiera
       cupiéramos, cupierais, cupieran**

or: **cupiese, cupieses, cupiese
       cupiésemos, cupieseis, cupiesen**

Imperativo: **cabe (no quepas), quepa
             quepamos, cabed (no quepáis), quepan**

---

caer to fall   *gerundio* **cayendo**   *past part.* **caído**

1   **caigo,** caes, cae
     caemos, caéis, caen

3   caí, caíste, **cayó**
     caímos, caísteis, **cayeron**

6   **caiga, caigas, caiga
     caigamos, caigáis, caigan**

7   **cayera, cayeras, cayera
     cayéramos, cayerais, cayeran**

or: **cayese, cayeses, cayese
     cayésemos, cayeseis, cayesen**

Imperativo: **cae (no caigas), caiga
             caigamos, caed (no caigáis), caigan**

---

coger to catch   *gerundio* **cogiendo**   *past part.* **cogido**

1   **cojo,** coges, coge
     cogemos, cogéis, cogen

6   **coja, cojas, coja
     cojamos, cojáis, cojan**

Imperativo: **coge (no cojas), coja
             cojamos, coged (no cojáis), cojan**
Note: **ger** verbs change **g** to **j** before **a** and **o.**

---

conducir to conduct, to drive   *gerundio* **conduciendo**   *past part.* **conducido**

1   **conduzco,** conduces, conduce
     conducimos, conducís, conducen

3   **conduje, condujiste, condujo
     condujimos, condujisteis, condujeron**

6   **conduzca, conduzcas, conduzca
     conduzcamos, conduzcáis, conduzcan**

7   **condujera, condujeras, condujera
     condujéramos, condujerais, condujeran**

or: **condujese, condujeses, condujese
     condujésemos, condujeseis, condujesen**

Imperativo: **conduce (no conduzcas), conduzca
             conduzcamos, conducid (no conduzcáis), conduzcan**
Note: **ducir** verbs, like **traducir** (to translate), have the same irregular forms
       as **conducir.**

---

conocer   to know, to be acquainted with   *gerundio* **conociendo**   *past part.* **conocido**

1   **conozco,** conoces, conoce
     conocemos, conocéis, conocen

6   **conozca, conozcas, conozca**
     conozcamos, conozcáis, conozcan

Imperativo: **conoce (no conozcas), conozca**
               conozcamos, conoced (no conozcáis), conozcan
Note: When preceded by a vowel, **cer** verbs insert **z** before **c** if **c** is followed by
       a or **o.**

---

contar   to count, to relate   *gerundio* **contando**   *past part.* **contado**

1   **cuento, cuentas, cuenta**
     contamos, contáis, **cuentan**

6   **cuente, cuentes, cuente**
     contemos, contéis, **cuenten**

Imperativo: **cuenta (no cuentes), cuente**
               contemos, contad (no contéis), cuenten
Note: The stem vowel **o** changes to **ue** because it is stressed.

---

creer   to believe   *gerundio* **creyendo**   *past part.* **creído**

3   creí, creíste, **creyó**
     creímos, creísteis, **creyeron**

7   **creyera, creyeras, creyera**
     creyéramos, creyerais, creyeran

or: **creyese, creyeses, creyese**
     creyésemos, creyeseis, creyesen

Note: When between vowels, unstressed **i** changes to **y.**

---

dar to give   *gerundio* **dando**   *past part.* **dado**

1   **doy,** das, da
     damos, dais, dan

3   **di, diste, dio**
     dimos, disteis, dieron

6   **dé,** des, **dé,**
     demos, deis, den

7   **diera, dieras, diera**
     diéramos, dierais, dieran

or: **diese, dieses, diese**
     diésemos, dieseis, diesen

Imperativo: **da (no des), dé**
             demos, dad (no deis), den

> Note: In Spanish novels, newspapers, and magazines the trend is to drop the
> accent mark on **di** and **dio** in the preterit (tense number 3) because it is
> not needed. One would pronounce **di** the same way with or without an
> accent mark. As for **dio**, the vowel **i** is a weak vowel and the vowel **o** is a
> strong vowel; therefore, a person naturally places the stress on **o**. As for
> the accent mark on **dé** in the present subjunctive (tense number 6), and in
> the imperative, it is used in order to distinguish it from the Spanish
> preposition **de.**

---

decir to say, to tell   *gerundio* **diciendo**   *past part.* **dicho**

1   **digo, dices, dice**
     decimos, decís, **dicen**

3   **dije, dijiste, dijo**
     dijimos, dijisteis, dijeron

4   **diré, dirás, dirá**
     diremos, diréis, dirán

5   **diría, dirías, diría**
     diríamos, diríais, dirían

6   **diga, digas, diga**
     digamos, digáis, digan

7   **dijera, dijeras, dijera**
     dijéramos, dijerais, dijeran

or: **dijese, dijeses, dijese
dijésemos, dijeseis, dijesen**

Imperativo: **di (no digas), diga
digamos, decid (no digáis), digan**

---

delinquir to be guilty, to offend   *gerundio* **delinquiendo**   *past part.* **delinquido**

1   **delinco,** delinques, delinque
delinquimos, delinquís, delinquen

6   **delinca, delincas, delinca
delincamos, delincáis, delincan**

Imperativo: **delinque (no delincas), delinca
delincamos, delinquid (no delincáis), delincan**
Note: **quir** verbs change **qu** to **c** before **a** and **o.**

---

dirigir to direct   *gerundio* **dirigiendo**   *past part.* **dirigido**

1   **dirijo,** diriges, dirige
dirigimos, dirigís, dirigen

6   **dirija, dirijas, dirija
dirijamos, dirijáis, dirijan**

Imperativo: **dirige (no dirijas), dirija
dirijamos, dirigid (no dirijáis), dirijan**
Note: **gir** verbs change **g** to **j** before **a** and **o.**

---

distinguir to distinguish   *gerundio* **distinguiendo**   *past part.* **distinguido**

1   **distingo,** distingues, distingue
distinguimos, distinguís, distinguen

6   **distinga, distingas, distinga
distingamos, distingáis, distingan**

Imperativo: **distingue (no distingas), distinga
distingamos, distinguid (no distingáis), distingan**
Note: **guir** verbs drop **u** before **o** and **a.**

dormir to sleep   *gerundio* **durmiendo**   *past part.* **dormido**

1   **duermo, duermes, duerme**
    dormimos, dormís, **duermen**

3   dormí, dormiste, **durmió**
    dormimos, dormisteis, **durmieron**

6   **duerma, duermas, duerma**
    durmamos, durmáis, duerman

7   **durmiera, durmieras, durmiera**
    durmiéramos, durmierais, durmieran

or: **durmiese, durmieses, durmiese**
    durmiésemos, durmieseis, durmiesen

Imperativo: **duerme (no duermas), duerma**
            durmamos, dormid (no durmáis), duerman
Note: The stem vowel **o** changes to **ue** because it is stressed. When the stem
       vowel **o** is not stressed, it changes to **u** if the syllable that follows contains
       stressed **a, ie,** or **ió.**

---

enviar to send   *gerundio* **enviando**   *past part.* **enviado**

1   **envío, envías, envía**
    enviamos, enviáis, **envían**

6   **envíe, envíes, envíe**
    enviemos, enviéis, **envíen**

Imperativo: **envía (no envíes), envíe**
            enviemos, enviad (no enviéis), envíen

---

errar to err, to wander, to roam   *gerundio* **errando**   *past part.* **errado**

1   **yerro, yerras, yerra**
    erramos, erráis, **yerran**

6   **yerre, yerres, yerre**
    erremos, erréis, **yerren**

Imperativo: **yerra (no yerres), yerre**
            erremos, errad (no erréis), yerren

estar to be   *gerundio* **estando**   *past part.* **estado**

1   **estoy, estás, está**
    estamos, estáis, **están**

3   **estuve, estuviste, estuvo
    estuvimos, estuvisteis, estuvieron**

6   **esté, estés, esté**
    estemos, estéis, **estén**

7   **estuviera, estuvieras, estuviera
    estuviéramos, estuvierais, estuvieran**

or: **estuviese, estuvieses, estuviese
    estuviésemos, estuvieseis, estuviesen**

Imperativo: **está (no estés), esté
        estemos, estad (no estéis), estén**

---

haber to have   *gerundio* **habiendo**   *past part.* **habido**
        (as an auxiliary verb to form the compound tenses)

1   **he, has, ha
    hemos,** habéis, **han**

3   **hube, hubiste, hubo
    hubimos, hubisteis, hubieron**

4   **habré, habrás, habrá
    habremos, habréis, habrán**

5   **habría, habrías, habría
    habríamos, habríais, habrían**

6   **haya, hayas, haya
    hayamos, hayáis, hayan**

7   **hubiera, hubieras, hubiera,
    hubiéramos, hubierais, hubieran**

or: **hubiese, hubieses, hubiese,
    hubiésemos, hubieseis, hubiesen**

Imperativo: **he (no hayas), haya
        hayamos, habed (no hayáis), hayan**

hacer to do, to make   *gerundio* **haciendo**   *past part.* **hecho**

1   **hago,** haces, hace
     hacemos, hacéis, hacen

3   **hice, hiciste, hizo**
     hicimos, hicisteis, hicieron

4   **haré, harás, hará**
     haremos, haréis, harán

5   **haría, harías, haría**
     haríamos, haríais, harían

6   **haga, hagas, haga**
     hagamos, hagáis, hagan

7   **hiciera, hicieras, hiciera**
     hiciéramos, hicierais, hicieran

or: **hiciese, hicieses, hiciese**
     hiciésemos, hicieseis, hicieran

Imperativo: **haz (no hagas), haga**
             hagamos, haced (no hagáis), hagan

---

huir to flee, to run away   *gerundio* **huyendo**   *past part.* **huido**

1   **huyo, huyes, huye**
     huimos, huís, **huyen**

3   huí, huiste, **huyó**
     huimos, huisteis, **huyeron**

6   **huya, huyas, huya**
     huyamos, huyáis, huyan

7   **huyera, huyeras, huyera**
     huyéramos, huyerais, huyeran

or: **huyese, huyeses, huyese**
     huyésemos, huyeseis, huyesen

Imperativo: **huye (no huyas), huya**
             huyamos, huid (no huyáis), huyan

Note: In Spanish novels, newspapers, and magazines the trend is to drop the
       accent mark on **í** in the past participle **huido** and others that end in **uido.**

ir to go   *gerundio* **yendo**   *past part.* **ido**

1   **voy, vas, va
vamos, vais, van**

2   **iba, ibas, iba
íbamos, ibais, iban**

3   **fui, fuiste, fue
fuimos, fuisteis, fueron**

6   **vaya, vayas, vaya
vayamos, vayáis, vayan**

7   **fuera, fueras, fuera
fuéramos, fuerais, fueran**

or: **fuese, fueses, fuese
fuésemos, fueseis, fuesen**

Imperativo: **ve (no vayas), vaya
vamos (no vayamos), id (no vayáis), vayan**

jugar to play   *gerundio* **jugando**   *past part.* **jugado**

1   **juego, juegas, juega**
jugamos, jugáis, **juegan**

3   **jugué,** jugaste, jugó
jugamos, jugasteis, jugaron

6   **juegue, juegues, juegue**
juguemos, juguéis, **jueguen**

Imperativo: **juega (no juegues), juegue
juguemos, jugad (no juguéis), jueguen**
Note: Compare the irregular forms of this verb with those of **contar** above and
llegar below.

llegar to arrive   *gerundio* **llegando**   *past part.* **llegado**

3   **llegué,** llegaste, llegó
llegamos, llegasteis, llegaron

6   **llegue, llegues, llegue
lleguemos, lleguéis, lleguen**

Imperativo: **llega (no llegues), llegue
lleguemos, llegad (no lleguéis), lleguen**
Note: **gar** verbs change **g** to **gu** before **e.**

---

mostrar to show   *gerundio* **mostrando**   *past part.* **mostrado**

1 **muestro, muestras, muestra**
       mostramos, mostráis, **muestran**

6 **muestre, muestres, muestre**
       mostremos, mostréis, **muestren**

Imperativo: **muestra (no muestres), muestre**
             mostremos, mostrad (no mostréis), muestren
Note: The stem vowel **o** changes to **ue** because it is stressed.

---

oír to hear   *gerundio* **oyendo**   *past part.* **oído**

1 **oigo, oyes, oye**
       oímos, oís, **oyen**

3 oí, oíste, **oyó**
       oímos, oísteis, **oyeron**

6 **oiga, oigas, oiga**
       oigamos, oigáis, oigan

7 **oyera, oyeras, oyera**
       oyéramos, oyerais, oyeran

or: **oyese, oyeses, oyese**
     oyésemos, oyeseis, oyesen

Imperativo: **oye (no oigas), oiga**
             oigamos, oíd (no oigáis), oigan

---

oler to smell, to scent   *gerundio* **oliendo**   *past part.* **olido**

1 **huelo, hueles, huele**
       olemos, oléis, **huelen**

6 **huela, huelas, huela**
       olamos, oláis, **huelan**

Imperativo: **huele (no huelas), huela**
             olamos, oled (no oláis), huelan

---

pedir to ask for, to request   *gerundio* **pidiendo**   *past part.* **pedido**

1 **pido, pides, pide**
   pedimos, pedís, **piden**

3 pedí, pediste, **pidió**
   pedimos, pedisteis, **pidieron**

6 **pida, pidas, pida**
   pidamos, pidáis, pidan

7 **pidiera, pidieras, pidiera**
   pidiéramos, pidierais, pidieran

or: **pidiese, pidieses, pidiese**
     pidiésemos, pidieseis, pidiesen

Imperativo: **pide (no pidas), pida**
             pidamos, pedid (no pidáis), pidan
Note: The stem vowel **e** changes to **i** because it is stressed. When the stem vowel
       e is not stressed, it changes to **i** if the syllable that follows contains stressed
       a, ie, or **ió.**

pensar to think   *gerundio* **pensando**   *past part.* **pensado**

1 **pienso, piensas, piensa**
   pensamos, pensáis, **piensan**

6 **piense, pienses, piense**
   pensemos, penséis, **piensen**

Imperativo: **piensa (no pienses), piense**
             pensemos, pensad (no penséis), piensen
Note: The stem vowel **e** changes to **ie** because it is stressed.

---

poder to be able, can *gerundio* **pudiendo** *past part.* **podido**

1 **puedo, puedes, puede**
podemos, podéis, **pueden**

3 **pude, pudiste, pudo**
pudimos, pudisteis, pudieron

4 **podré, podrás, podrá**
podremos, podréis, podrán

5 **podría, podrías, podría**
podríamos, podríais, podrían

6 **pueda, puedas, pueda**
podamos, podáis, **puedan**

7 **pudiera, pudieras, pudiera**
pudiéramos, pudierais, pudieran

or: **pudiese, pudieses, pudiese**
pudiésemos, pudieseis, pudiesen

Imperativo: **puede (no puedas), pueda**
podamos, poded (no podáis), puedan

---

poner to put, to place *gerundio* **poniendo** *past part.* **puesto**

1 **pongo,** pones, pone
ponemos, ponéis, ponen

3 **puse, pusiste, puso**
pusimos, pusisteis, pusieron

4 **pondré, pondrás, pondrá**
pondremos, pondréis, pondrán

5 **pondría, pondrías, pondría**
pondríamos, pondríais, pondrían

6 **ponga, pongas, ponga**
pongamos, pongáis, pongan

7 **pusiera, pusieras, pusiera**
pusiéramos, pusierais, pusieran

or: **pusiese, pusieses, pusiese**
pusiésemos, pusieseis, pusiesen

Imperativo: **pon (no pongas), ponga**
pongamos, poned (no pongáis), pongan

---

preferir to prefer   *gerundio* **prefiriendo**   *past part.* **preferido**

1   **prefiero, prefieres, prefiere**
     preferimos, preferís, **prefieren**

3   preferí, preferiste, **prefirió**
     preferimos, preferisteis, **prefirieron**

6   **prefiera, prefieras, prefiera**
     prefiramos, prefiráis, prefieran

7   **prefiriera, prefirieras, prefiriera**
     prefiriéramos, prefirierais, prefirieran

or: **prefiriese, prefirieses, prefiriese**
     prefiriésemos, prefirieseis, prefiriesen

Imperativo: **prefiere (no prefieras), prefiera**
             prefiramos, preferid (no prefiráis), prefieran
Note: The stem vowel **e** changes to **ie** because it is stressed. When the stem vowel
       e is not stressed, it changes to **i** if the syllable that follows contains stressed
       a, ie, or **ió.**

---

querer to want, to wish, to like   *gerundio* **queriendo**   *past part.* **querido**

1   **quiero, quieres, quiere**
     queremos, queréis, **quieren**

3   **quise, quisiste, quiso**
     quisimos, quisisteis, quisieron

4   **querré, querrás, querrá**
     querremos, querréis, querrán

5   **querría, querrías, querría**
     querríamos, querríais, querrían

6   **quiera, quieras, quiera**
     queramos, queráis, **quieran**

7   **quisiera, quisieras, quisiera**
     quisiéramos, quisierais, quisieran

or: **quisiese, quisieses, quisiese**
     quisiésemos, quisieseis, quisiesen

Imperativo: **quiere (no quieras), quiera**
             queramos, quered (no queráis), quieran

reír to laugh	*gerundio* **riendo**	*past part.* **reído**

1   **río, ríes, ríe**
   reímos, reís, **ríen**

3   reí, reíste, **rió**
   reímos, reísteis, **rieron**

6   **ría, rías, ría**
   riamos, riáis, rían

7   **riera, rieras, riera**
   riéramos, rierais, rieran

or: **riese, rieses, riese**
   riésemos, rieseis, riesen

Imperativo: **ríe (no rías), ría**
          riamos, reíd (no riáis), rían

saber to know, to know how	*gerundio* **sabiendo**	*past part.* **sabido**

1   **sé,** sabes, sabe
   sabemos, sabéis, saben

3   **supe, supiste, supo**
   supimos, supisteis, supieron

4   **sabré, sabrás, sabrá**
   sabremos, sabréis, sabrán

5   **sabría, sabrías, sabría**
   sabríamos, sabríais, sabrían

6   **sepa, sepas, sepa**
   sepamos, sepáis, sepan

7   **supiera, supieras, supiera**
   supiéramos, supierais, supieran

or: **supiese, supieses, supiese**
   supiésemos, supieseis, supiesen

Imperativo: **sabe (no sepas), sepa**
          sepamos, sabed (no sepáis), sepan

> Note: The form **(yo) sé** (I know), 1st pers., s., pres. ind. (tense no. 1), is the same as the 2d pers., s., imperative of the verb **ser**, which is given below. There can be no doubt as to the meaning of **sé** when used in a sentence. Note also that the accent mark on **sé** is used to distinguish it from the Spanish reflexive pronoun **se** (himself, herself, yourself, oneself, itself, yourselves, themselves). The pronunciation of **sé** and **se** is the same. Review §6.1—6 and §6.1—5, box 7, where **le** or **les** changes to **se**.

---

salir to go out, to leave   *gerundio* **saliendo**   *past part.* **salido**

1   **salgo,** sales, sale
     salimos, salís, salen

4   **saldré, saldrás, saldrá
     saldremos, saldréis, saldrán**

5   **saldría, saldrías, saldría
     saldríamos, saldríais, saldrían**

6   **salga, salgas, salga
     salgamos, salgáis, salgan**

Imperativo: **sal (no salgas), salga
             salgamos, salid (no salgáis), salgan**

---

sentarse to sit down   *gerundio* **sentándose**   *past part.* **sentado**

1   **me siento, te sientas, se sienta**
     nos sentamos, os sentáis, **se sientan**

6   **me siente, te sientes, se siente**
     nos sentemos, os sentéis, **se sienten**

Imperativo: **siéntate (no te sientes), siéntese (no se siente)
             sentémonos (no nos sentemos), sentaos (no os sentéis),
             siéntense (no se sienten)**
Note: The stem vowel **e** changes to **ie** because it is stressed.

---

sentir to feel sorry, to feel   *gerundio* **sintiendo**   *past part.* **sentido**

1   **siento, sientes, siente**
     sentimos, sentís, **sienten**

3   sentí, sentiste, **sintió**
     sentimos, sentisteis, **sintieron**

6   **sienta, sientas, sienta
     sintamos, sintáis, sientan**

7   **sintiera, sintieras, sintiera
     sintiéramos, sintierais, sintieran**

or: **sintiese, sintieses, sintiese
     sintiésemos, sintieseis, sintiesen**

Imperativo: **siente (no sientas), sienta
             sintamos, sentid (no sintáis), sientan**
Note: The stem vowel **e** changes to **ie** because it is stressed. When the stem vowel
       e is not stressed, it changes to **i** if the syllable that follows contains stressed
       a, ie, or **ió.**

---

sentirse to feel (well, ill)   *gerundio* **sintiéndose**   *past part.* **sentido**

1   **me siento, te sientes, se siente**
      nos sentimos, os sentís, **se sienten**

3   me sentí, te sentiste, **se sintió**
      nos sentimos, os sentisteis, **se sintieron**

6   **me sienta, te sientas, se sienta**
      nos sintamos, os sintáis, se sientan

7   **me sintiera, te sintieras, se sintiera**
      nos sintiéramos, os sintierais, se sintieran

or: **me sintiese, te sintieses, se sintiese**
      nos sintiésemos, os sintieseis, se sintiesen

Imperativo: **siéntete (no te sientas), siéntase**
             sintámonos, sentíos (no os sintáis), siéntanse

Note: The stem vowel **e** changes to **ie** because it is stressed. When the stem vowel
       e is not stressed, it changes to **i** if the syllable that follows contains stressed
       a, ie, or **ió.**

---

ser to be   *gerundio* **siendo**   *past part.* **sido**

1   **soy, eres, es**
      somos, sois, son

2   **era, eras, era**
      éramos, erais, eran

3   **fui, fuiste, fue**
      fuimos, fuisteis, fueron

6   **sea, seas, sea**
      seamos, seáis, sean

7   **fuera, fueras, fuera**
      fuéramos, fuerais, fueran

or: **fuese, fueses, fuese**
      fuésemos, fueseis, fuesen

Imperativo: **sé (no seas), sea**
             seamos, sed (no seáis), sean

Note: The form **sé** (be), 2d pers., s., imperative is the same as the 1st pers., s. **(yo)**
       sé (I know), pres. ind. (tense no. 1) of the verb **saber,** which is given above.
       See the note under **saber.**

---

servir to serve   *gerundio* **sirviendo**   *past part.* **servido**

1   **sirvo, sirves, sirve**
     servimos, servís, **sirven**

3   serví, serviste, **sirvió**
     servimos, servisteis, **sirvieron**

6   **sirva, sirvas, sirva**
     sirvamos, sirváis, sirvan

7   **sirviera, sirvieras, sirviera**
     sirviéramos, sirvierais, sirvieran

or: **sirviese, sirvieses, sirviese**
     sirviésemos, sirvieseis, sirviesen

Imperativo: **sirve (no sirvas), sirva**
             sirvamos, servid (no sirváis), sirvan
Note: The stem vowel **e** changes to **i** because it is stressed. When the stem vowel
       e is not stressed, it changes to **i** if the syllable that follows contains stressed
       a, ie, or **ió.**

---

tener to have, to hold   *gerundio* **teniendo**   *past part.* **tenido**

1   **tengo, tienes, tiene**
     tenemos, tenéis, **tienen**

3   **tuve, tuviste, tuvo**
     tuvimos, tuvisteis, tuvieron

4   **tendré, tendrás, tendrá**
     tendremos, tendréis, tendrán

5   **tendría, tendrías, tendría**
     tendríamos, tendríais, tendrían

6   **tenga, tengas, tenga**
     tengamos, tengáis, tengan

7   **tuviera, tuvieras, tuviera**
     tuviéramos, tuvierais, tuvieran

or: **tuviese, tuvieses, tuviese**
     tuviésemos, tuvieseis, tuviesen

Imperativo: **ten (no tengas), tenga**
             tengamos, tened (no tengáis), tengan

traer to bring	*gerundio* **trayendo**	*past part.* **traído**

1   **traigo,** traes, trae
    traemos, traéis, traen

3   **traje, trajiste, trajo
    trajimos, trajisteis, trajeron**

6   **traiga, traigas, traiga
    traigamos, traigáis, traigan**

7   **trajera, trajeras, trajera
    trajéramos, trajerais, trajeran**

or: **trajese, trajeses, trajese
    trajésemos, trajeseis, trajesen**

Imperativo: **trae (no traigas), traiga
    traigamos, traed (no traigáis), traigan**

valer to be worth	*gerundio* **valiendo**	*past part.* **valido**

1   **valgo,** vales, vale
    valemos, valéis, vale

4   **valdré, valdrás, valdrá
    valdremos, valdréis, valdrán**

5   **valdría, valdrías, valdría
    valdríamos, valdríais, valdrían**

6   **valga, valgas, valga
    valgamos, valgáis, valgan**

Imperativo: **val** *or* **vale (no valgas), valga
    valgamos, valed (no valgáis), valgan**

venir to come   *gerundio* **viniendo**   *past part.* **venido**

1 **vengo, vienes, viene**
   venimos, venís, **vienen**

3 **vine, viniste, vino**
   vinimos, vinisteis, vinieron

4 **vendré, vendrás, vendrá**
   vendremos, vendréis, vendrán

5 **vendría, vendrías, vendría**
   vendríamos, vendríais, vendrían

6 **venga, vengas, venga**
   vengamos, vengáis, vengan

7 **viniera, vinieras, viniera**
   viniéramos, vinierais, vinieran

or: **viniese, vinieses, viniese**
   viniésemos, vinieseis, viniesen

Imperativo: **ven (no vengas), venga**
   vengamos, venid (no vengáis), vengan

ver to see   *gerundio* **viendo**   *past part.* **visto**

1 **veo,** ves, ve
   vemos, veis, ven

2 **veía, veías, veía**
   veíamos, veíais, veían

6 **vea, veas, vea**
   veamos, veáis, vean

Imperativo: **ve (no veas), vea**
   veamos, ved (no veáis), vean

§26.

Definitions of Basic Grammatical Terms with Examples

active voice

When we speak or write in the active voice, the subject of the verb performs the action. The action falls on the direct object.

Example:
The robber opened the window / **El ladrón abrió la ventana.**
The subject is *the robber.* The verb is *opened.* The direct object is *the window.*

Review **§7.5—16.** *See also passive voice.* Compare the above sentence with the example in the passive voice.

adjective

An adjective is a word that modifies a noun or a pronoun. In grammar, to modify a word means to describe, limit, expand, or make the meaning particular.

Examples:
a beautiful garden / **un jardín hermoso**; she is pretty / **ella es bonita.**
The adjective *beautiful/hermoso* modifies the noun *garden/jardín.* The adjective *pretty/bonita* modifies the pronoun *she/ella.*

In Spanish there are different kinds of adjectives. *See also* comparative adjective, demonstrative adjective, descriptive adjective, interrogative adjective, limiting adjective, possessive adjective, superlative adjective.

Review **§5.**

adverb

An adverb is a word that modifies a verb, an adjective, or another adverb. An adverb says something about how, when, where, to what extent, or in what way.

Examples:
Mary runs swiftly / **María corre rápidamente.** The adverb *swiftly/rápidamente* modifies the verb *runs/corre.* The adverb shows *how* she runs.

John is very handsome / **Juan es muy guapo.** The adverb *very/muy* modifies the adjective *handsome/guapo.* The adverb shows *how handsome* he is.

The boy is talking very fast now / **El muchacho habla muy rápidamente ahora.** The adverb *very/muy* modifies the adverb *fast/rápidamente.* The adverb shows *to what extent* he is talking *fast.* The adverb *now/ahora* tells us *when.*

The post office is there / **La oficina de correos está allá.** The adverb *there/allá* modifies the verb *is/está.* It tells us *where* the post office is.

Mary writes meticulously / **María escribe meticulosamente.** The adverb *meticulously/meticulosamente* modifies the verb *writes/escribe.* It tells us *in what way* she writes.

Review **§8.**

affirmative statement, negative statement

A statement in the affirmative is the opposite of a statement in the negative. To negate an affirmative statement is to make it negative.

Examples:
In the affirmative: I like ice cream / **Me gusta el helado.**

In the negative: I do not like ice cream / **No me gusta el helado.**

Review **§7.6—9.**

agreement of adjective with noun

Agreement is made on the adjective with the noun it modifies in gender (masculine or feminine) and number (singular or plural).

Examples:
a white house / **una casa blanca**. The adjective **blanca** is feminine singular because the noun **una casa** is feminine singular.
many white houses / **muchas casas blancas**. The adjective **blancas** is feminine plural because the noun **casas** is feminine plural.

Review **§5.1, §5.2, §5.3.**

agreement of verb with its subject

A verb agrees in person (1st, 2d, or 3d) and in number (singular or plural) with its subject.

Examples:
Paul tells the truth / **Pablo dice la verdad.** The verb **dice** (of **decir**) is 3d person singular because the subject *Pablo/Paul* is 3d person singular.

Where are the tourists going? / **¿Adónde van los turistas?** The verb **van** (of **ir**) is 3d person plural because the subject *los turistas/the tourists* is 3d person plural.

Review **§7.1—1.** *See also* **§6.1—1** for subject pronouns. Use the verb tables in the back pages of this book in **§24.** and **§25.**

antecedent

An antecedent is a word to which a relative pronoun refers. It comes *before* the pronoun.

Examples:
The girl who is laughing loudly is my sister / **La muchacha que está riendo a carcajadas es mi hermana.** The antecedent is *girl/la muchacha*. The relative pronoun *who/que* refers to the girl.

The car that I bought is very expensive / **El carro que yo compré es muy costoso.**
The antecedent is *car/el carro*. The relative pronoun *that/que* refers to the car.

Review **§6.5.** *See also* relative pronoun.

auxiliary verb

An auxiliary verb is a helping verb. In English grammar it is *to have.* In Spanish grammar it is haber/*to have.* An auxiliary verb is used to help form the compound tenses.

Example:
I *have* eaten / (Yo) *he* comido.

Review the forms of **haber** in the seven simple tenses in the irregular verbs table on page 303. You need to know them to form the seven compound tenses.

cardinal number

A cardinal number is a number that expresses an amount, such as *one, two, three,* and so on.

Review **§16.1.** *See also* ordinal number.

clause

A clause is a group of words that contains a subject and a predicate. A predicate may contain more than one word. A conjugated verb form is revealed in the predicate.

Example:
Mrs. Gómez lives in a large apartment / La señora Gómez vive en un gran apartamento.
The subject is *Mrs. Gómez/la señora Gómez.* The predicate is *lives in a large apartment/ vive en un gran apartamento.* The verb is *lives/ vive.*

See also dependent clause, independent clause, predicate. Use the verb tables in the back pages of this book in **§24.** and **§25.**

comparative adjective

When making a comparison between two persons or things, an adjective is used to express the degree of comparison in the following ways.

Examples:
Of the same degree of comparison: Helen is *as tall as* Mary / Elena es *tan alta como* María.

Of a lesser degree of comparison: Jane is *less intelligent than* Eva / Juana es *menos inteligente que* Eva.

Of a higher degree of comparison: This apple is *more delicious than* that one / Esta manzana es *más deliciosa que* ésa.

Review **§5.6—1.** *See also* superlative adjective.

comparative adverb

An adverb is compared in the same way as an adjective is compared. *See* comparative adjective above.

Examples:
Of the same degree of comparison: Mr. Robles speaks *as well as* Mr. Vega / **El señor Robles habla** *tan bien como* **el señor Vega.**

Of a lesser degree of comparison: Alice studies *less diligently than* her sister / **Alicia estudia** *menos diligentemente que* **su hermana.**

Of a higher degree of comparison: Albert works *more slowly than* his brother / **Alberto trabaja** *más lentamente que* **su hermano.**

Review **§8.2.** *See also* superlative adverb.

complex sentence

A complex sentence contains one independent clause and one or more dependent clauses.

Examples:
One independent clause and one dependent clause: Joseph works but his brother doesn't / **José trabaja pero su hermano no trabaja.**

The independent clause is *Joseph works.* It makes sense when it stands alone because it expresses a complete thought. The dependent clause is *but his brother doesn't.* The dependent clause, which is introduced by the conjunction *but/pero,* does not make complete sense when it stands alone because it *depends* on the thought expressed in the independent clause.

One independent clause and two dependent clauses: Anna is a good student because she studies but her sister never studies / **Ana es una buena alumna porque estudia pero su hermana nunca estudia.**

The independent clause is *Anna is a good student.* It makes sense when it stands alone because it expresses a complete thought. The first dependent clause is *because she studies.* This dependent clause, which is introduced by the conjunction *because/porque,* does not make complete sense when it stands alone because it *depends* on the thought expressed in the independent clause. The second dependent clause is *but her sister never studies.* That dependent clause, which is introduced by the conjunction *but/pero*, does not make complete sense either when it stands alone because it *depends* on the thought expressed in the independent clause.

Use the verb tables in **§24.** and **§25.**
See also dependent clause, independent clause.

compound sentence

A compound sentence contains two or more independent clauses.

Example:
Mrs. Fuentes went to the supermarket, she bought a few things, and then she went home / La señora Fuentes fue al supermercado, compró algunas cosas, y entonces fue a casa.
This compound sentence contains three independent clauses. They are independent because they make sense when they stand alone.

See also independent clause. Review **ir** in **§7.7—8** and the preterit tense in **§7.5—3.** Use the verb tables in **§24.** and **§25.**

conditional perfect tense

In Spanish grammar, the conditional **(el potencial)** is considered a mood. This tense is defined with examples in **§7.5—12.**

conditional present tense

In Spanish grammar, the conditional **(el potencial)** is considered a mood. This tense is defined with examples in **§7.5—5.**

conjugation

The conjugation of a verb is the fixed order of all its forms showing their inflections (changes) in the three persons of the singular and plural in a particular tense.

For examples, review **§7.7—8** for the complete conjugation of **estar**/*to be*, **hacer**/*to do, to make,* **ir**/*to go,* and **ser**/*to be* in all their forms in the fourteen tenses and the imperative.

See also number and person (1st, 2d, 3d).

conjunction

A conjunction is a word that connects words or groups of words.

Examples:
and/y, or/o   but/pero   because/porque
Charles and Charlotte / Carlos y Carlota
You can stay home or you can come with me / (Tú) puedes quedarte en casa o venir conmigo.

Review **§10.** first, then **§7.5—18.**

contrary to fact

This term refers to an "if" clause. *See* if **(si)** clause.

declarative sentence

A declarative sentence makes a statement.

Example:
I have finished the work / (Yo) he terminado el trabajo.

definite article

The definite article in Spanish has four forms and they all mean *the*: **el, la, los, las.**

Review **§4.1** where they are used with examples.

demonstrative adjective

A demonstrative adjective is an adjective that points out. It is placed in front of a noun.

Examples:
this book/este libro; these flowers/estas flores

To see them all in Spanish and English, with examples using them, review **§5.4—3.**

demonstrative pronoun

A demonstrative pronoun is a pronoun that points out. It takes the place of a noun. It agrees in gender and number with the noun it replaces.

Examples:
I have two oranges; do you prefer *this one* or *that one?* /
Tengo dos naranjas; ¿prefiere usted *ésta* o ésa?
I prefer *those* [over there] / Prefiero *aquéllas*.

Review **§6.3.** For demonstrative pronouns that are neuter, *see* neuter.

dependent clause

A dependent clause is a group of words that contains a subject and a predicate. It does not express a complete thought when it stands alone. It is called *dependent* because it depends on the independent clause for a complete meaning. Subordinate clause is another term for dependent clause.

Example:
Edward is absent today because he is sick / Eduardo está ausente hoy porque está enfermo.
The independent clause is *Edward is absent today.* The dependent clause is *because he is sick.*

See also clause, independent clause.

descriptive adjective

A descriptive adjective is an adjective that describes a person, place, or thing.

Examples:
a pretty girl/una muchacha bonita; a big house/una casa grande; an expensive car/un carro costoso.

Review **§5.4—1.** *See also* adjective.

direct object noun

A direct object noun receives the action of the verb *directly.* That is why it is called a direct object, as opposed to an indirect object. A direct object noun is normally placed *after* the verb.

Example:
I am writing a letter / **Escribo una carta.**
The direct object is the noun *letter*/**una carta.**

See also direct object pronoun.

direct object pronoun

A direct object pronoun receives the action of the verb *directly.* It takes the place of a direct object noun. In Spanish a pronoun that is direct object of a verb is ordinarily placed *in front of* the verb.

Example:
I am writing it [the letter] / **La escribo.**
In the *affirmative imperative*, a direct object pronoun is placed *after* the verb and is joined to it, resulting in one word.

Example:
Write it [the letter] now! / **¡Escríbala ahora!**
An accent mark is added on the vowel **i** [**í**] in order to keep the emphasis on that vowel as it was in **escriba** before the direct object pronoun **la** was added to the verb form.
Review the simple rule about syllable emphasis and accent marks in **§2.**

Review **§6.1—2** for all the direct object pronouns and examples in sentences. *See also* imperative.

disjunctive pronoun

A disjunctive pronoun is a pronoun that is stressed; in other words, emphasis is placed on it. It is usually the object of a preposition. Prepositional pronoun is another term for disjunctive pronoun.

Examples:
for me/**para mí**; for you *(fam.)*/**para ti**

Review **§6.2.**

ending of a verb

In Spanish grammar the ending of a verb form changes according to the person and number of the subject and the tense of the verb.

Example:
To form the present indicative tense of a regular **-ar** type verb like **hablar**, drop **ar** of the infinitive and add the following endings: **-o, -as, -a** for the 1st, 2d, and 3d persons of the singular; **-amos, -áis, -an** for the 1st, 2d, and 3d persons of the plural.
You then get: **hablo, hablas, habla; hablamos, habláis, hablan**

Review **§7.5.** *See also* stem of a verb. Use the verb tables in **§24.** and **§25.**

feminine

In Spanish grammar the gender of a noun, pronoun, or adjective is feminine or masculine, not male or female.

See also gender.

future perfect tense

This tense is defined with examples in **§7.5—11.** It is also called the future anterior.

future tense

This tense is defined with examples in **§7.5—4.**

gender

Gender means masculine or feminine.

Examples:
Masculine: the boy/el muchacho   the book/el libro
Feminine: the girl/la muchacha   the house/la casa

Review **§3.**

gerund

In English grammar, a gerund is a word formed from a verb. It ends in *ing*. Actually, it is the present participle of a verb. However, it is not used as a verb. It is used as a noun.

Example:
Seeing is believing / **Ver y creer** *[to see and to believe]*. However, in Spanish grammar, the infinitive form of the verb is used, as in the above example, when the verb is used as a noun.
The Spanish gerund is also a word formed from a verb. It is the present participle of a verb. The Spanish gerund **[el gerundio]** regularly ends in **ando** for **ar** type verbs (of the 1st conjugation)**,** in **iendo** for **er** type verbs (of the 2d conjugation), and **iendo** for **ir** type verbs (of the 3d conjugation). There are also irregular present participles that end in **yendo**. *See also* present participle.

Examples of a Spanish gerund:
hablando/talking   **comiendo**/eating   **viviendo**/living

Review **§7.3—2.**

if (si) clause

An "if" clause is defined with examples in verb tenses in **§7.6—1.** *See also* clause.

imperative

The imperative is a mood, not a tense. It is used to express a command. In Spanish it is used in the 2d person of the singular **(tú)**, the 3d person of the singular **(usted)**, the 1st person of the plural **(nosotros, nosotras)**, the 2d person of the plural **(vosotros, vosotras)**, and in the 3d person of the plural **(ustedes)**.

Review **§7.5—17** for examples. *See also* person (1st, 2d, 3d).

imperfect indicative tense

This tense is defined with examples in **§7.5—2.**

imperfect subjunctive tense

This tense is defined with examples in **§7.5—7.**

indefinite article

In English the indefinite articles are *a*, *an*, as in *a book, an apple.* They are indefinite because they do not refer to any definite or particular noun.

In Spanish there are two indefinite articles in the singular: one in the masculine form **(un)** and one in the feminine form **(una)**.

Examples:
Masculine singular: un libro/*a book*
Feminine singular: una manzana/*an apple*
In the plural they change to **unos** and **unas**.

Examples:
unos libros/some books   unas manzanas/some apples

Review **§4.2.** *See also* definite article.

indefinite pronoun

An indefinite pronoun is a pronoun that does not refer to any definite or particular noun.

Examples:
something/algo someone, somebody/alguien

Review **§6.7.**

independent clause

An independent clause is a group of words that contains a subject and a predicate. It expresses a complete thought when it stands alone.

Example:
The cat is sleeping on the bed / El gato está durmiendo sobre la cama.

See also clause, dependent clause, predicate.

indicative mood

The indicative mood is used in sentences that make a statement or ask a question. The indicative mood is used most of the time when we speak or write in English or Spanish.

Examples:
I am going to the movies now/Voy al cine ahora.
Where are you going?/¿Adónde vas?

indirect object noun

An indirect object noun receives the action of the verb *indirectly.*

Example:
I am writing a letter to Christine *or* I am writing Christine a letter / **Estoy escribiendo una carta a Cristina.**

The verb is *am writing/**estoy escribiendo**.* The direct object noun is *a letter/**una carta**.* The indirect object noun is *Christine/**Cristina**.*

Review **§6.1—3** and the examples in sentences. *See also* indirect object pronoun.

indirect object pronoun

An indirect object pronoun takes the place of an indirect object noun. It receives the action of the verb *indirectly.*

Example:
I am writing a letter to her *or* I am writing her a letter / **Le escribo una carta.**
The indirect object pronoun is *(to) her/**le**.*

Review **§6.1—3** and **§6.1—4** for all the indirect object pronouns and their position in sentences.

For the position of double object pronouns (direct and indirect), review **§6.1—5.** *See also* indirect object noun.

infinitive

An infinitive is a verb form. In English, it is normally stated with the preposition *to,* as in *to talk, to drink, to receive.* In Spanish, the infinitive form of a verb consists of three major types: those of the 1st conjugation that end in **-ar,** the 2d conjugation that end in **-er,** and the 3d conjugation that end in **-ir.**

In Spanish grammar, the infinitive **(el infinitivo)** is considered a mood.

Examples:
hablar/*to talk, to speak*;   **beber**/*to drink*;
recibir/*to receive*

Review **§7.8.** Use the verb tables in **§24.** and **§25.**

interjection

An interjection is a word that expresses emotion, a feeling of joy, of sadness, an exclamation of surprise, and other exclamations consisting of one or two words.

Examples:
Ah! / ¡Ah!   Ouch! / ¡Ay!   Darn it! / ¡Caramba!
My God! / ¡Dios mío!

interrogative adjective

In Spanish, an interrogative adjective is an adjective that is used in a question. As an adjective, it is placed in front of a noun.

Examples:
What book do you want? / ¿Qué libro desea usted?
What time is it? / ¿Qué hora es?

Review **§5.4—5.**

interrogative adverb

In Spanish, an interrogative adverb is an adverb that introduces a question. As an adverb, it modifies the verb.

Examples:
How are you? / ¿Cómo está usted?
How much does this book cost? / ¿Cuánto cuesta este libro?
When will you arrive? / ¿Cuándo llegará usted?

Review **§8.3.**

interrogative pronoun

An interrogative pronoun is a pronoun that asks a question. There are interrogative pronouns that refer to persons and those that refer to things.

Examples:
Who is it? / ¿Quién es?
What are you saying? / ¿Qué dice usted?

Review **§6.6.**

interrogative sentence

An interrogative sentence asks a question.

Example:
What are you doing? / ¿Qué hace usted?

intransitive verb

An intransitive verb is a verb that does not take a direct object.

Example:
The professor is talking / El profesor habla.
An intransitive verb takes an indirect object.

Example:
The professor is talking to us / El profesor nos habla.

Review **§7.2—3.**

irregular verb

An irregular verb is a verb that does not follow a fixed pattern in its conjugation in the various verb tenses.

Examples of basic irregular verbs in Spanish:
estar/to be   hacer/to do, to make   ir/to go   ser/to be

Use the tables of irregular verbs in **§24.** and **§25.**
See also conjugation, regular verb.

limiting adjective

A limiting adjective is an adjective that limits a quantity.

Example:
three lemons/tres limones a few candies/algunos dulces

main clause

Main clause is another term for independent clause.
See independent clause.

masculine

In Spanish grammar the gender of a noun, pronoun, or adjective is masculine or feminine, not male or female.

See also gender.

mood of verbs

Some grammarians use the term *the mode* instead of *the mood* of a verb. Either term means *the manner or way* a verb is expressed. In English and Spanish grammar a verb expresses an action or state of being in a particular mood.

In Spanish grammar, there are five moods **(modos)**: the infinitive **(el infinitivo)**, the indicative **(el indicativo)**, the imperative **(el imperativo)**, the conditional **(el potencial)**, and the subjunctive **(el subjuntivo)**.

In English grammar, there are three moods: the indicative mood, the imperative mood, and the subjunctive mood.

Most of the time, in English and Spanish, we speak and write in the indicative mood.

Review **§7.5.**

negative statement, affirmative statement

(*see* affirmative statement, negative statement)

neuter

A word that is neuter is neither masculine nor feminine. Common neuter demonstrative pronouns in Spanish are esto/*this*, eso/*that*, aquello/*that* [farther away].

Examples:
What's this? / ¿Qué es esto?
What's that? / ¿Qué es eso?

Review **§6.3** and **§6.3—1.** For demonstrative pronouns that are not neuter, *see* demonstrative pronoun.

There is also the neuter direct object pronoun **lo**. It usually refers to an idea or statement. It is not normally translated into English but often the translation is *so*.

Examples:
¿Estás enferma, María? / Are you sick, Mary? Sí, lo estoy / Yes, I am.
No lo creo / I don't think so.
Lo parece / It seems so.

Review **§6.1—2.**

noun

A noun is a word that names a person, animal, place, thing, condition or state, or quality.

Examples:
the man/el hombre   the woman/la mujer
the horse/el caballo   the house/la casa
the pencil/el lápiz   happiness/la felicidad
excellence/la excelencia

In Spanish the noun **el nombre** is the word for name and noun. Another word for noun in Spanish is el sustantivo/*substantive*.

Review **§3.** and **§4.**

number

In English and Spanish grammar, number means singular or plural.

Examples:
Masc. sing.: the boy/el muchacho
the pencil/el lápiz   the eye/el ojo

Masc. pl.: the boys/los muchachos
the pencils/los lápices   the eyes/los ojos

Fem. sing.: the girl/la muchacha   the house/la casa
the cow/la vaca

Fem. pl.: the girls/las muchachas
the houses/las casas   the cows/las vacas

Review **§3.1, §3.2.**

ordinal number

An ordinal number is a number that expresses position in a series, such as *first, second, third*, and so on. In English and Spanish grammar we talk about 1st person, 2d person, 3d person singular or plural regarding subjects and verbs.

Review **§16.** *See also* cardinal number.

orthographical changes in verb forms

An orthographical change in a verb form is a change in spelling.

Example:
The verb conocer/*to know, to be acquainted with* changes in spelling in the 1st person singular of the present indicative. The letter **z** is inserted in front of the second **c**. When formed regularly, the ending **er** of the infinitive drops and **o** is added for the 1st person singular form of the present indicative. That would result in *conoco*, a peculiar sound to the Spanish ear for a verb form of **conocer**. The letter **z** is added to keep the sound of **s** as it is in the infinitive **conocer**. Therefore, the spelling changes and the form is **yo conozco**. In the other forms of **conocer** in the present indicative **z** is not inserted because they retain the sound of **s.**

There are many verb forms in Spanish that contain orthographical changes.

Review the verb **conocer** in the present indicative tense in **§7.7—1.** Use the verb tables in **§24.** and **§25.**

passive voice

When we speak or write in the active voice and change to the passive voice, the direct object becomes the subject, the subject becomes the object of a preposition, and the verb becomes *to be* plus the past participle of the active verb. The past participle functions as an adjective.

Example:
The window was opened by the robber / La ventana fue abierta por el ladrón.
The subject is **la ventana**. The verb is *fue*. The word **abierta** is a feminine adjective agreeing with **la ventana**.

Actually, it is the past participle of abrir/*to open* but here it serves as an adjective. The object of the preposition *by*/*por* is *the robber*/el ladrón.

Review **§7.5—16.** *See also* active voice. Compare the above sentence with the example in the active voice.

past anterior tense

This tense is defined with examples in **§7.5—10.** It is also called the preterit perfect.

past participle

A past participle is derived from a verb. It is used to form the compound tenses. Its auxiliary verb is haber/*to have.* It is part of the verb tense.

Examples:
hablar/to speak, to talk   I have *spoken*/he *hablado*
comer/to eat   I have *eaten*/he *comido*
recibir/to receive   I have *received*/he *recibido*

Review **§7.3—1** for the regular formation of a past participle and a list of common irregular past partciples.

past perfect tense

This tense is also called the pluperfect indicative tense. *See* **§7.5—9** for a definition with examples.

past subjunctive tense

This tense is defined with examples in **§7.5—13.** It is also known as the present perfect subjunctive.

person (1st, 2d, 3d)

Verb forms in a particular tense are learned systematically according to person (1st, 2d, 3d) and number (singular, plural).

Example, showing the present indicative tense of the verb ir/to go:

Singular	Plural
1st person: **(yo) voy**	1st person: **(nosotros, nosotras) vamos**
2d person: **(tú) vas**	2d person: **(vosotros, vosotras) vais**
3d person: **(Ud., él, ella) va**	3d person: **(Uds., ellos, ellas) van**

Review **§6.1—1** and **§7.7—8.** Use the verb tables in **§24.** and **§25.**

personal pronoun

A personal pronoun is a pronoun that refers to a person. For examples review **§6.**

pluperfect indicative tense

This tense is defined with examples in **§7.5—9.** It is also called the past perfect indicative tense.

pluperfect subjunctive tense

This tense is defined with examples in **§7.5—14.** It is also called the past perfect subjunctive tense.

plural

Plural means more than one. *See also* person (1st, 2d, 3d) and singular.

possessive adjective

A possessive adjective is an adjective that is placed in front of a noun to show possession.

Examples:
my book/mi libro   my friends/mis amigos
our school/nuestra escuela

Review **§5.4—4** for all the forms of possessive adjectives with examples.

possessive pronoun

A possessive pronoun is a pronoun that shows possession. It takes the place of a possessive adjective with the noun. Its form agrees in gender (masculine or feminine) and number (singular or plural) with what it is replacing.

Examples in English: mine, yours, his, hers, its, ours, theirs
Examples in Spanish:

Possessive Adjective	Possessive Pronoun
my book/mi libro	*mine*/el mío
my house/mi casa	*mine*/la mía
my shoes/mis zapatos	*mine*/los míos

Review **§6.4** for all the forms of possessive pronouns with examples.

predicate

The predicate is that part of the sentence that tells us something about the subject. The main word of the predicate is the verb.

Example:
Today the tourists are going to the Prado Museum / **Hoy los turistas van al Museo del Prado.**
The subject is *the tourists/los turistas.* The predicate is *are going to the Prado Museum/van al Museo del Prado.* The verb is *are going/van.*

preposition

A preposition is a word that establishes a rapport between words.

Examples: with, without, to, at, between
with her/**con ella**   *without* money/*sin* **dinero**
to Spain/*a* **España**
at six o'clock/*a* **las seis**
between you and me/*entre* **tú y yo**

Review **§7.4** and **§9.** *See* **§6.2** for **entre tú y yo**.

prepositional pronoun

A prepositional pronoun is a pronoun that is the object of a preposition. The term disjunctive pronoun is also used.
See **§6.2** and disjunctive pronoun.

present indicative tense

This tense is defined with examples in **§7.5—1.**

present participle

A present participle is derived from a verb form. In English a present participle ends in *ing.* In Spanish a present participle is called **un gerundio.**

Examples:
cantando/singing   **comiendo**/eating   **yendo**/going

Review **§7.3—2** for regular and irregular present participles and their uses.
See also gerund.

present subjunctive tense

This tense is defined with examples in **§7.5—6.**

preterit tense

This tense is defined with examples in **§7.5—3.** In Spanish it is called **el pretérito.**

preterit perfect tense

This tense is defined with examples in **§7.5—10.** It is also called the past anterior.

pronoun

A pronoun is a word that takes the place of a noun.

Examples:
el hombre/*él*   **la mujer/***ella*
the man/*he*   the woman/*she*

Review **§6.** for the different kinds of pronouns and their uses.

reflexive pronoun and reflexive verb

In English a reflexive pronoun is a personal pronoun that contains *self* or *selves*. In Spanish and English a reflexive pronoun is used with a verb that is called reflexive because the action of the verb falls on the reflexive pronoun.

In Spanish there is a required set of reflexive pronouns for a reflexive verb.

Examples:
lavarse   (Yo) me lavo.
to wash oneself   I wash myself.
afeitarse   Pablo se ha afeitado.
to shave oneself   Paul has shaved himself.

Review **§6.1—6.**

regular verb

A regular verb is a verb that is conjugated in the various tenses according to a fixed pattern.

Review **§7.** for examples and uses, in particular **§7.5.** Use the verb tables beginning on page 270. *See also* conjugation, irregular verb.

relative pronoun

A relative pronoun is a pronoun that refers to its antecedent.

Example:
The girl who is talking with John is my sister / La muchacha que está hablando con Juan es mi hermana. The antecedent is *girl/la muchacha.* The relative pronoun *who/que* refers to the girl.

Review **§6.5.** *See also* antecedent.

sentence

A sentence is a group of words that contains a subject and a predicate. The verb is contained in the predicate. A sentence expresses a complete thought.

Example:
The train leaves at two o'clock in the afternoon / El tren sale a las dos de la tarde.
The subject is *train/el tren.* The predicate is *leaves at two o'clock in the afternoon.* The verb is *leaves/sale.*

See also complex sentence, compound sentence, simple sentence.

simple sentence

A simple sentence is a sentence that contains one subject and one predicate. The verb is the core of the predicate. The verb is the most important word in a sentence because it tells us what the subject is doing.

Example:
Mary is eating an apple from her garden / María está comiendo una manzana de su jardín.
The subject is *Mary/María.* The predicate is *is eating an apple from her garden/está comiendo una manzana de su jardín.* The verb is *is eating/está comiendo.* The direct object is *an apple/una manzana. From her garden/de su jardín* is an adverbial phrase. It tells you from where the apple came.

See also complex sentence, compound sentence.

singular

Singular means one. *See also* plural.

stem of a verb

The stem of a verb is what is left after we drop the ending of its infinitive form. It is needed to add to it the required endings of a regular verb in a particular verb tense.

Examples:

Infinitive	Ending of infinitive	Stem
hablar/to talk	**ar**	**habl**
comer/to eat	**er**	**com**
escribir/to write	**ir**	**escrib**

See also ending of a verb. Use the verb tables in **§24.** and **§25.**

stem-changing verb

In Spanish there are many verb forms that change in the stem.

Example:
The verb dormir/*to sleep* changes the vowel **o** in the stem to **ue** when the stress (emphasis, accent) falls on that **o**; for example, **(yo) duermo.**

When the stress does not fall on that **o**, it does not change; for example, **(nosotros) dormimos.** Here, the stress is on the vowel **i.**

Review the verb **dormir** in the present indicative tense in **§7.7—1.** Use the verb tables in **§24.** and **§25.**

subject

A subject is that part of a sentence that is related to its verb. The verb says something about the subject.

Example:
Clara and Isabel are beautiful / Clara e Isabel son hermosas.

Review **§5.1.** To know when to use **e** instead of **y** for *and*, review **§10.2—4.**

subjunctive mood

The subjunctive mood is the mood of a verb that is used in specific cases, *e.g.,* after certain verbs expressing a wish, doubt, emotion, fear, joy, uncertainty, an indefinite expression, an indefinite antecedent, certain conjunctions, and others. The subjunctive mood is used more frequently in Spanish than in English.

Review the uses of the subjunctive mood with examples in **§7.5—18.**

subordinate clause

Subordinate clause is another term for dependent clause. *See* dependent clause.

superlative adjective

A superlative adjective is an adjective that expresses the highest degree when making a comparison of more than two persons or things.

Examples:

Adjective	Comparative	Superlative
bueno/good	**mejor**/better	**el mejor**/best
alto/tall	**más alto**/taller	**el más alto**/tallest

Review **§5.6—1, §5.6—2, §5.6—3.** *See also* comparative adjective.

superlative adverb

A superlative adverb is an adverb that expresses the highest degree when making a comparison of more than two persons or things.

Example:

Adverb	Comparative	Superlative
lentamente	**más lentamente**	**lo más lentamente**
slowly	more slowly	most slowly

Review **§8.** *See also* comparative adverb.

tense of verb

In English and Spanish grammar, tense means time. The tense of the verb indicates the time of the action or state of being. The three major segments of time are past, present, and future. In Spanish there are fourteen major verb tenses, of which seven are simple tenses and seven are compound.

Review **§7.5—19** for the names of the fourteen major tenses and **§7.7—8** where you can see four commonly used verbs conjugated fully in all the tenses as well as in the imperative mood.

Use the verb tables in **§24.** and **§25.**

transitive verb

A transitive verb is a verb that takes a direct object.

Example:
I am closing the window / **Cierro la ventana.**

The subject is *I* / *(Yo).* The verb is *am closing* / *cierro.* The direct object is *the window* / *la ventana.*

Review **§7.2—2.**

verb

A verb is a word that expresses action or a state of being.

Examples:
Action: **Los pájaros están volando** / The birds are flying.
The verb is *están volando* / *are flying.*

State of being: **La señora López está contenta** / Mrs. López is happy.
The verb is *está* / *is.*

§27.

The Spanish Alphabet and the New System of Alphabetizing

The Association of Spanish Language Academies met in Madrid for its 10th Annual Congress on April 27, 1994 and voted to eliminate **CH** and **LL** as separate letters of the Spanish alphabet.

Words beginning with **CH** will be listed alphabetically under the letter **C.** Words beginning with **LL** will be listed alphabetically under the letter **L.** The two separate letters historically have had separate headings in dictionaries and alphabetized word lists. Spanish words that contain the letter **ñ** are now alphabetized accordingly with words that do not contain the tilde over the **n.** For example, the Spanish system of alphabetizing used to place the word **andar** before **añadir** because the **ñ** would fall in after all words containing **n.** According to the new system, **añadir** is placed before **andar** because alphabetizing is now done letter by letter. The same applies to words containing **rr.**

The move was taken to simplify dictionaries, to make Spanish more compatible with English, and to aid computer standardization and translation. The vote was 17 in favor, 1 opposed, and 3 abstentions. Ecuador voted "no" and Panama, Nicaragua, and Uruguay abstained (printed in *The New York Times*, International Section, May 1, 1994, page 16).

§28.

New Frequently Used Basic Spanish Words and Phrases in Technical Communication in Today's World

This special vocabulary contains new basic Spanish words and phrases used frequently in telecommunication on the Web, Internet, keyboard, computer, laptop, cell phones, and other media in today's world of the 21st century. It also includes a selection of Spanish words and phrases popular in sports, physical activities, and fitness.

> **TIP** Do your best to work on a schedule. Study this compilation of special vocabulary each day for about 15 or 20 minutes. You are studying and reviewing Spanish, so get acquainted with the entries in Spanish first and look at the English translations. Do this daily and you will be surprised to see how many of the Spanish words and phrases you will begin to recognize and remember their meanings. This will help you increase your Spanish word power.

adelantar *v.* to go forward
aficionado deportivo *n.m.* sports fan
alpinismo *n.m.* mountain climbing
apagado *adj.* power off
apagar *v.* to turn off
arrancar *v.* to boot up (a computer)
arrastrar *v.* to drag
auriculares *n.m.* headphones
balón *n.m.* **de baloncesto** ball (of basketball)
baloncesto *n.m.* basketball (the game)
base *n.f.* **de texto** data base
básquetbol *n.m.* basketball
béisbol *n.m.* baseball
byte *n.m.* byte

cable *n.m.* cable
cargar *v.* to load
cartucho *n.m.* **de tinta** print cartridge
casete *n.m.* cassette
charla *n.f.* chat; **charlar** *v.* to chat
cinta *n.f.* tape; **la cinta magnética de video** videotape
computadora *n.f.* computer
computadora *n.f.* **personal** personal computer
computadora *n.f.* **portátil** laptop
conexión *n.f.* **de redes** networking
contestador *n.m.* **automático** telephone answering
  machine
contraseña *n.f.* password
correo electrónico *n.m.* e-mail
correr *v.* **a trote corto** to jog
cursor *n.m.* cursor
desarrollar *v.* **la musculatura** to body build
descargar *v.* to download, unload
disco *n.m.* disk; **disco flexible** floppy disk; **disco duro**
  hard disk
disco compacto *n.m.* compact disc
disco interno *n.m.* internal drive
encendido *adj.* power on
encuentro deportivo *n.m.* sports event
enlace *n.m.* link
escáner *n.m.* scanner
escucho un disco compacto I'm listening to a CD.
fácil de manejar user-friendly
gimnasia *n.f.* gymnastics
gimnasio *n.m.* gymnasium
grabadora *n.f.* tape recorder
grabadora *n.f.* **de CD** CD burner
grabadora *n.f.* **de DVD** DVD player
grabar *v.* to record
guardar *v.* to save
hacer *v.* **gimnasia** to work out
hacer *v.* **clic** to click (on an Internet link)
icono *n.m.* icon
impresora *n.f.* printer; **impresora láser** laser printer
imprimir *v.* to print
informática *n.f.* information technology
Internet *n.m.* Internet
lenguaje *n.m.* **de computadora** computer language
levantar *v.* **pesas** to weightlift
megabyte *n.m.* megabyte
memoria *n.f.* memory

memoria *n.f.* **de acceso aleatoria** random access memory (RAM)

mensaje *n.m.* message

microcomputadora *n.f.* microcomputer

mochila *n.f.* backpack

módem *n.m.* modem

monitor *n.m.* monitor

monopatín *n.m.* skateboard, scooter

multimedia *n.f.* multimedia

nadar *v.* to swim

natación *n.f.* swimming

navegar *v.* **en Internet** to surf (browse) the Internet

ordenador *n.m.* computer

ordenador *n.m.* **personal** personal computer

palabra *n.f.* **clave** keyword

pantalla *n.f.* screen, television or cinema screen

patín *n.m.* skate, ice skate, roller skate

patinaje *n.m.* skating

patinaje *n.m.* **sobre ruedas** roller skating

patinar *v.* to skate

pelota *n.f.* ball

poner *v.* to turn on

procesador *n.m.* **de texto** word processor

procesamiento *n.m.* **de texto** word processing

programa *n.m.* program

programador *n.m.*, **programadora** *n.f.* programmer

ratón *n.m.* mouse

red *n.f.* net, network

regresar *v.* to go back

reproductor *n.m.* **portátil de CD** portable CD player

salvapantallas *n.m.* screensaver

sistema *n.m.* **operativo** operating system

software *n.m.* software

submarinismo *n.m.* scuba diving

teclado *n.m.* keyboard

teléfono *n.m.* **celular, el teléfono móvil** portable cell phone

teléfono remoto *n.m.* cordless phone

televisión *n.f.* television

televisor *n.m.* television set

tocacintas *n.m.* cassette player

tocar *v.* to play a recording

videocasete *n.m.* videocassette

videojuego *n.m.* video game

zapatilla *n.f.* **deportiva** running shoe

APPENDIX

Spanish-English Vocabulary

After you look up a verb form in this vocabulary, remember to consult also the Spanish Verb Conjugation Tables and the Irregular Verb Tables in **§24.** and **§25.** as well as **§7.** in this book. A list of abbreviations is also provided on page xvii.

A

a *prep.* at, to; *see* §9.

a eso de *adv.* at around; **a eso de las nueve** at around nine o'clock; *see* **a** in §12.2

aba *1st & 3d pers., s., impf. ind. ending of* regular **ar** verbs; *see* Verb Tables in §24. and §25.

abandonar *v.* to abandon

abrir *v.* to open

aburrida *adj.* bored

acababa *1st & 3d pers., s., impf. ind. of* **acabar**

acabar *v.* to finish, to end, to complete; *see* **acabar de** in §7.6—2

aceptar *v.* to accept

acomodarse *r v.* to make oneself comfortable

acompañar *v.* to accompany

acuerdo *n.m.* agreement; **de acuerdo** in agreement, in favor

adelante *adv.* forward; **en adelante** henceforth, from now on

además *adv.* morever, besides

adiós *int.* good-bye

admiración *n.f.* admiration

adonde *adv.* to where, where to; **¿Adónde va Ud.?** Where are you going (to)?

adorarse *r v.* to adore each other

aeropuerto *n.m.* airport

afición *n.f.* fondness, liking

agradable *adj.* pleasant

agradecido, -da *adj.. m.f.* grateful, thankful

aguas *n.f., pl.* waters; **el agua** water

ahí *adv.* there

ahora *adv.* now

al at the, to the; **a + el** changes to **al**; *see* §4.1 and **al** in §12.2

al llegar upon arriving

aldea *n.f.* village

alegría *n.f.* joy

algo *pron.* something; *see* §18.

algunas, algunos *adj.* some

alimento *n.m.* food

allí *adv.* there

almorzar *v.* to lunch; *see* **almorzar** in Verb Tables

almuerzo *n.m.* lunch

alojamiento *n.m.* lodging, accommodations

alojar *v.* to lodge

alojó *3d pers., s., pret. of* **alojar**

alrededor (de) *adv.* around, about; **alrededor de las dos** around two o'clock

amable *adj.* kind, amiable

amigo *n.m.* friend; **la amiga**

amistad *n.f.* friendship

amor *n.m.* love

anchos *adj.* wide

animal, animales *n.m., s.pl.* animal, animals

aniversario *n.m.* anniversary

año *n.m.* year; **tener quince años** to be fifteen years old; see **tener** in §12.2

anoche *adv.* last night, yesterday evening

anterior *adj.* previous

antes (de) *adv.* before

antibiótico *n.m.* antibiotic

antiguas *adj.,f.pl.* ancient, old

anual *adj.* annual

anunciar *v.* to announce

anunciará *3d pers., s., fut. of* **anunciar**

anuncio *n.m.* announcement

anunció *3d pers., s., pret. of* **anunciar**

aparte *adj.* separate

aperitivo *n.m.* appetizer

apreciado *adj. & past part. of* **apreciar**; appreciated

apreciar *v.* to appreciate

aquella *dem. adj.* that; **aquella ciudad** that city; *see* §5.4—3

aquí *adv.* here

Aquí tiene usted mi pasaporte. Here is my passport.

argentino *adj.* Argentine

arriba *adv.* above, up

arte *n.m.* art

asegura *3d pers., s., pr. ind. of* **asegurar**

asegurar *v.* to assure

así *adv.* so, thus

aspirador *n.m.* vacuum cleaner

atlética *adj.* athletic

atún *n.m.* tuna

aumentar *v.* to augment, to increase

aumente *1st & 3d pers., s., pr. sbj. of* **aumentar**

aumentó *3d pers., s., pret. of* **aumentar**

aunque *conj.* although; *see* §7.5—18, §10.1

ausente *adj.* absent

auténtica *adj.* authentic

autor *n.m.* author

¡Ay! Oh!

ayer *adv.* yesterday

ayuda *n.f.* aid, help

ayudado *adj., past part. of* **ayudar**; aided, helped

ayudar *v.* to aid, to help

B

bailando *gerundio* (pr. part.) of **bailar**; **están bailando** they are dancing

bailar *v.* to dance

bailarín *n.m.* dancer

bailé *1st pers., s., pret. of* **bailar**; I danced

bajados *adj.* lowered

bajo *adj., prep.* low; down; under

banana *n.f.* banana

banano *n.m.* banana tree

banqueta *n.f.* footstool

banquete *n.m.* banquet

bar *n.m.* bar; **los bares** bars; **de bar en bar** from bar to bar

barato *adj.* inexpensive

barco *n.m.* boat

bares *n.m.* bars

baronesa *n.f.* baroness

beber *v.* to drink

bebida *n.f.* drink, beverage

bebiendo *gerundio* (pr. part.) of **beber**; **están bebiendo** they are drinking

bien *adv.* well; *see* §18.

billete *n.m.* **de ida y vuelta** round-trip ticket

blanco *adj.* white

boca *n.f.* mouth

bola *n.f.* ball; **una bola de nieve** snowball

bolsa *n.f.* purse; bag

bonita *adj.* pretty

brazo *n.m.* arm

buen, bueno *adj.* good; **un buen día** one fine day; **un buen libro** a good book; *see* §5.5

bufanda *n.f.* scarf

C

caballo *n.m.* horse

cabello *n.m.* hair (on head)

cabeza *n.f.* head

cabra *n.f.* goat

cada *adj.* each; **cada vez** each time

caer *v.* to fall

café *n.m.* coffee; coffee shop

calle *n.f.* street; **por la calle** down (along) the street

callos *n.m.* tripe

calmarse *rv.* to calm oneself; **Me calmo los nervios.** I calm my nerves.

cama *n.f.* bed

cámara *n.f.* camera

cambiado *adj. & past part. of* **cambiar**

cambiar *v.* to change

caminar *v.* to walk

cancelada *adj.* canceled

canción *n.f.* song; **las canciones** songs

candidato *n.m.* candidate

cantante *n.m.f.* singer

cantar *v.* to sing

canté *1st pers., s., pret. of* **cantar**; I sang

capitán *n.m.* captain

cápsula *n.f.* capsule

cara *n.f.* face

carne *n.f.* meat

caro *adj.* expensive

carro *n.m.* car

casa *n.f.* house

casamiento *n.m.* marriage

casarse *rv.* to get married

casera *adj., f.* housekeeper; **la medicina casera** home medicine (home remedies)

celebración *n.f.* celebration

celebrar *v.* to celebrate; **se celebró** was celebrated

célebre *adj.* famous

cena *n.f.* dinner

cenando *gerundio* (pr. part.) of **cenar**; **están cenando** they are dining; *see* §7.5—15

cenar *v.* to dine, to have dinner

cereza *n.f.* cherry

cerveza *n.f.* beer

chal *n.m.* shawl

chica *n.f.* little girl

chico *n.m.* little boy

Cien años de soledad *One hundred years of solitude*

cien, ciento one hundred; *see* §5.5

cierto, cierta *adj., m.f., s.* certain; a certain

cigarrillo *n.m.* cigarette; *see* §3.3—2

cima *n.f.* top

cinco five; *see* §16.; **son las once y cincuenta y cinco de la noche** it's 11:55 pm

cincuenta fifty; *see* §14., §16.

cine *n.m.* cinema, movies; **al cine** to the movies

clara *adj., f.* clear

clase *n.f.* class; type, kind

clásica *adj., f.s.* classic, classical

clave *adj.* key; **seis países claves** six key countries

clientela *n.f.* customers, clientele

clima *n.m.* climate

cocinando *gerundio* (pr. part.) of **cocinar**; **están cocinando** they are cooking

cocinar *v.* to cook

col *n.f.* cabbage

cola *n.f.* tail

colapso *n.m.* collapse

coma *3d pers., s. (Usted), imp.* of **comer**; eat

combatir *v.* to combat, to fight

come *3d pers., s., pr. ind.* of **comer**; **se come** one eats

comedor *n.m.* dining room

comer *v.* to eat

comí *1st pers., s., pret.* of **comer**; I ate

cómico *n.m.* comedian

comida *n.f.* meal

comiendo *gerundio* (pr. part.) of **comer**; **está comiendo** is eating; *see* §7.5—15

comienzo *n.m.* beginning

como *conj.* as; *see* §10.1; **¿cómo?** *adv.* how?; *see* §8.3

compositor *n.m.* composer

comprar *v.* to buy; **se compra** is bought

común, comunes *adj.* common; **amigos comunes** mutual friends

comunicación, comunicaciones *n.f., s., pl.* communication, communications

con *prep.* with; **conmigo** with me; *see* §6.2

conejo *n.m.* rabbit

conocer *v.* to know, to be acquainted with; *see* **conocer** in Verb Tables and §7.6—3

conocí *1st pers., s., pret.* of **conocer**; I met; *see* §7.6—3 and Verb Tables in §24. and §25.

conocido *past part.* of **conocer**; known; **he conocido** I have known; *see* Verb Tables in §24. and §25.

conseguir *v.* to obtain

contaminadas *adj.* contaminated

contestar *v.* to answer

contestó *3d pers., s., pret.* of **contestar**

continuar *v.* to continue

convencer *v.* to convince

convenció *3d pers., s., pret.* of **convencer**; **se convenció** convinced himself

conversación *n.f.* conversation

conversar *v.* to converse

conviene *3d pers., s., pr. ind.* of **convenir** to be suitable, advisable

correr *v.* to run

corriendo *gerundio* (pr. part.) of **correr**; **está corriendo** is running; *see* §7.5—15

corriente *n.m.* current; *adj.* ordinary, regular

cortos *adj.* short

cosa *n.f.* thing

creencia *n.f.* belief

crema *n.f.* cream

crítica *n.f.* criticism

cruzar *v.* to cross

cuadro *n.m.* painting; **los cuadros de El Greco** the paintings of El Greco; *see* §4.1

¿cuál? ¿cuáles? *adj.* which (one, ones)?; *see* §5.4—5, §13.1

cuando *adv.* when

¿Cuánto cuesta? How much does it cost?

cuatro four; *see* §16.

cuello *n.m.* neck

D

dan *3d pers., pl., pr. ind. of* **dar**

dar *v.* to give; *see* Verb Tables in §24. and §25.

dar un paso to take a step; **dar un paseo** to take a walk

darse cuenta de to realize

datos *n.m., pl.* data

de *prep.* of, from; **de la mañana (la noche)** in the morning (evening); *see* **de** in §12.2

dé *1st & 3d pers., s., pr. sbj. & 3d pers., s., imp. of* **dar**; *see* Verb Tables in §24. and §25.

debajo *adv.* under, underneath

deben *3d pers., pl., pr. ind. of* **deber**

deber *v.* to owe, must, ought

decaer *v.* to decay

decir *v.* to say, to tell; *see* **decir** in Irregular Verb Tables in §24. and §25.

declarar *v.* to declare

declararon *3d pers., pl., pret. of* **declarar**

dedicar *v.* to dedicate

dedicará *3d pers., s., fut. of* **dedicar**

dejar *v.* to leave; to let go; **dejar de ser** to stop being; see §7.6—5, §7.6—6

dejará *3d pers., s., fut. of* **dejar**

del of the, from the; **de + el** changes to **del**; *see* §4.1

dependiente *n.m.f.* clerk, employee

derecha *n.f.* right; **a la derecha** on the right

desagradable *adj.* unpleasant

desagradecido *adj.* ungrateful

desayunar *v.* to have breakfast

desayuno *n.m.* breakfast

descansar *v.* to rest

descanse *3d pers., s. (Usted), imp. of* **descansar**; rest

deseamos *1st pers., pl., pres. ind. of* **desear**

desear *v.* to desire

deseo *1st pers., s., pr. ind. of* **desear**; I desire; *n.m.* desire

desfavorable *adj.* unfavorable

después (de) *adv.* after

detener *v.* to detain

determinar *v.* to determine

día *n.m.* day; **todo el día** all day; **todos los días** every day; *see* **todo** in §12.2

diariamente *adv.* daily

dice *3d pers., s., pr. ind. of* **decir**; **se dice** it is said, they say; *see* §7.5—16

diciembre *n.m.* December; *see* §13.3

diez ten; *see* §16.

diferencia *n.f.* difference

diferente *adj.* different

difícil *adj.* difficult

dinero *n.m.* money

Dios God

disco *n.m.* record, disk

discurso *n.m.* speech

disfrutar *v.* to enjoy

distinguido *adj.* distinguished

distinta *adj.* distinct

divertirse *rv.* to enjoy oneself

divierten *3d pers, pl., pr. ind. of* **divertir**

doce twelve; *see* §16.

dólar *n.m.* dollar; **dólares** *pl.* dollars

doler *v.* to ache, to pain

dolor *n.m.* pain, ache

dormir *v.* to sleep; *see* Irregular Verb Tables in §24. and §25.

dos two; *see* §16.

duda *n.f.* doubt

duele *3d pers., s., pr. ind. of* **doler**; **me duele el cuello** I have a pain in the neck.

dueño *n.m.* owner, proprietor

dulce *n.m.* candy

duplicado *adj. & past part. of* **duplicar**; **se había duplicado** had doubled (itself)

duplicar *v.* to duplicate, to double

durante *prep.* during

E

e *conj.* and; *see* §10.2—4

económico *adj.* economic

edad *n.f.* age

edificio *n.m.* building, edifice

editar *v.* to edit; **se editan** are edited

efecto *n.m.* effect

ejemplo *n.m.* example; **por ejemplo** for example

él *pron.* he, him; *see* §6.1—1; **para él** for him; *see* §6.2

el, los *def. art.* the; *see* §4.1

elegido *adj.* selected, by choice

elegir *v.* to select, to choose

ella *pron.* she; **ella es bonita** she is pretty; **con ella** with her; *see* §6.1, §6.2

embajada *n.f.* embassy

embajador *n.m.* ambassador

eminente *adj.* eminent, distinguished

empezar *v.* to begin

empezó *3d pers., s., pret. of* **empezar**

en *prep.* in; *see* §12.2 for idiomatic expressions with **en**

encontrar *v.* to find; **encontrarse** *rv.* to meet (each other)

encuentra *3d pers., s., pr. ind. of* **encontrar**

enfermera *n.f.* nurse

enfermo, enferma *adj.* sick

enfrente *adv.* opposite; in front

enojada *adj.* annoyed

ensalada *n.f.* salad

entonces *adv.* then

entrada *n.f.* entrance

entrante *adj.* entering, incoming

entrar *v.* to enter, to come in

entre *3d pers., s. (Usted), imp. of* **entrar**; come in; **entre** *prep.* between, among

entrevistar *v.* to interview; **entrevistarle** to interview him

entusiasmo *n.m.* enthusiasm

época *n.f.* epoch

equipo *n.m.* equipment; team

era *1st & 3d pers., s., impf. ind. of* **ser**; *see* **ser** in Irregular Verb Tables

es *3d pers., s., pr. ind. of* **ser**; *see* **ser** in §7.7—8

esa *dem. adj., f.s.* that; *see* §5.4—3

escapar *v.* to escape

escaparate *n.m.* (store) window display

escoba *n.f.* broom

escolar *adj.* school; **una reunión escolar** school meeting

escribir *v.* to write

escritor *n.m.* writer

escuchar *v.* to listen (to)

escuela *n.f.* school

esfuerzos *n.m., pl.* efforts

eso *dem. pron., neuter* that; **por eso** for that reason; *see* §6.3, §6.3—1

espacio *n.m.* space

España *n.f.* Spain

español *n.m.* Spanish (language)

española *adj.* Spanish

especial *adj.* special

especialidades *n.f., pl.* specialties

especialmene *adv.* especially

espectáculo *n.m.* show, performance

esperanza *n.f.* hope

espinacas *n.f.* spinach

esta *dem. adj., f.s.* this; *see* §5.4—3; **esta noche** this evening, tonight

está *3d pers., s., pr. ind. of* **estar**; *see* §7.7—8

estaba *1st & 3d pers., s., impf. ind. of* **estar**; *see* **estar** in §7.7—8

establecido *past part. of* **establecer**; **se ha establecido** has been established

Estados Unidos *n.m., pl.* United States

estallar *v.* to burst, to explode

están *3d pers., pl., pr. ind. of* **estar**; *see* §7.7—8

estar *v.* to be; *see* Irregular Verb Tables

estarán *3d pers., pl., fut. of* **estar**; *see* **estar** in §7.7—8

estas *dem. adj., f., pl.* these; *see* §5.4—3

estatal *adj.* state; **ayuda estatal** state aid

este *dem. adj., m.s.* this; *see* §5.4—3

estilo *n.m.* style

esto *dem. pron., neuter* this; *see* §6.3, §6.3—1

estómago *n.m.* stomach

estos *dem. adj., m., pl.* these; *see* §5.4—3

estoy *1st pers., s., pr. ind. of* **estar**; *see* **estar** in §7.7—8

estructura *n.f.* structure

estudiante *n.m.f.* student

estudiar *v.* to study

estudio *n.m.* study

Europa *n.f.* Europe

evento *n.m.* event, happening

excelente *adj.* excellent

exhibir *v.* to exhibit

exilio *n.m.* exile

existe *3d pers., s., pr. ind. of* **existir**

existir *v.* to exist

explicar *v.* to explain

exposición *n.f.* exhibit, exposition

extraordinario *adj.* extraordinary

F

falta *n.f.* lack

faltan *3d pers., pl., pr. ind. of* **faltar** to lack

familia *n.f.* family

famoso *adj.* famous

fanáticos *n.m.* fanatics, sports fans

favor *n.m.* favor; **por favor** please

fecha *n.f.* date; *see* §13.1; **en estas fechas** around these dates

feria *n.f.* fair

fiesta *n.f.* party; holiday

fin *n.m.* end

fino *adj.* thin, fine, slender

flor *n.f.* flower

flora *n.f.* **y fauna** *n.f.* flora and fauna

flotando *gerundio* (pr. part.) of **flotar**; **está flotando** is floating; *see* §7.5—15

flotar *v.* to float

forma *n.f.* form

forzado *adj.* forced

frecuentemente *adv.* frequently

frente *n.m.* front; *n.f.* forehead

fritos *adj.* fried

fruta *n.f.* fruit
fue *3d pers., s., pret. of* **ir** or **ser**; *see* **ir** and **ser** in §7.7—8
fueron *3d pers., pl., pret. of* **ir** or **ser**; *see* **ir** and **ser** in §7.7—8
fui *1st pers., s., pret. of* **ir** or **ser**; *see* **ir** and **ser** in §7.7—8
fumar *v.* to smoke

G

gana *n.f.* desire; **tener** or **sentir ganas de + inf.** to feel like (doing something)
ganar *v.* to gain, to earn, to win
gastar *v.* to spend (money); to waste
gente *n.f.* people
gerundio *n.m.* gerund (present participle)
gobierno *n.m.* government
gozaba *1st & 3d pers., s., impf. ind. of* **gozar; se gozaba** one enjoyed
gozar *v.* to enjoy
gracia a... thanks to...
gran *adj.* great; *see* §5.5
grande *adj.* big, great; **más grande** greater, greatest
grave *adj.* serious, grave
gripe *n.f.* grippe, flu, influenza
gritando *pres. part. (gerundio) of* **gritar**; shouting
gritándoles a mis chicos shouting (at them) at my children
gritar *v.* to shout
guante *n.m.* glove
guisantes *n.m.* peas
gustar *v.* to please, to be pleasing; *see* §7.6—9

H

ha *3d pers., s., pr. ind. of* **haber**; *see* **haber** in Irregular Verb Tables
haber *v.* to have; (helping verb used to form the compound tenses); *see* §7.5—19
había *1st & 3d pers., s., impf. ind. of* **haber**
habichuelas verdes *n.f.* green string beans
hablaba *1st & 3d pers., s., impf. ind. of* **hablar**
hablar *v.* to talk, to speak; **hablarnos** to speak to us
habrá *3d pers., s., fut. of* **haber**; **habrá una exposición** there will be an exhibit
habría *1st & 3d pers., s., cond. of* **haber**; *see* §7.5—19; *see* **haber de** in §7.6—10

hace *3d pers., s., pr. ind. of* **hacer**; *see* §7.7—8; **hace años** years ago; *see* §12.2
hacer *v.* to do, to make; *see* Irregular Verb Tables and §7.7—8
hacerse *rv.* to make oneself, to become
hacia *prep.* toward
hacía *1st & 3d pers., s., imp. ind. of* **hacer**
haciendo *gerundio* (pr. part.) of **hacer**; **está haciendo** is doing; *see* §7.5—15
hasta *prep.* until
hay there is..., there are...; *see* §12.1
he *1st pers., s., pr. ind. of* **haber**; *see* §7.5—19; **he conocido** I have known
hecho *adj.* made, done; *past part. of* **hacer**; *see* §7.7—8
helado *n.m.* ice cream
hermana *n.f.* sister
hermano *n.m.* brother
higiene *n.f.* hygiene
hija *n.f.* daughter
hijo *n.m.* son
hijos *n.m., pl.* children (sons and daughters)
himno *n.m.* hymn
historia *n.f.* history; story
histórico *adj.* historical
hombre *n.m.* man
hombro *n.m.* shoulder
homenaje *n.m.* homage
honrado *adj.* honored
hora *n.f.* hour, time; **¿a qué hora?** at what time? *see* §14.
hoy *adv.* today
huéspedes *n.m., pl.* guests
huevo *n.m.* egg
humanitarios *adj., m., pl.* humanitarian
humano *adj.* human, humane

I

iba *1st & 3d pers., s., impf. ind. of* **ir**; *see* Irregular Verb Tables in §24. and §25.
idea *n.f.* idea
idioma *n.m.* language
ignorante *adj.* ignorant
ilusión *n.f.* illusion
ilustre *adj.* illustrious, famous
importado *adj.* imported
importancia *n.f.* importance
imposible *adj.* impossible
impresionar *v.* to impress
impresionó *3d pers., s., pret. of* **impresionar**
impuesto *n.m.* tax

independencia *n.f.* independence
información *n.f.* information
inglés *n.m.* English (language)
ingrato *adj.* ungrateful
inteligente *adj.* intelligent
intención *n.f.* intention
interés *n.m.* interest
interesante *adj.* interesting
internacional *adj.* international
interpretar *v.* to interpret; **interpretarlas** to interpret them
invitación, invitaciones *n.f., s.pl.* invitation, invitations
ió *3d pers., s., pret. ending of regular **er** and **ir** verbs; see Verb Tables in §24. and §25.
ir *v.* to go; see Irregular Verb Tables in §24. and §25.
izquierda *n.f.* left; **a la izquierda** on the left

J

jamón *n.m.* ham
jardín, jardines *n.m., s.pl.* garden, gardens
jarrón *n.m.* vase
joven *n.m.; adj.* young man; young
jóvenes *n.pl.* the young ones
juego *n.m.* game
jugador, jugadores *n.m., s., pl.* player, players
jugar *v.* to play
jugaron *3d pers., pl., pret. of **jugar***
jugo *n.m.* juice
juguete *n.m.* toy
junio *n.m.* June; see §13.3
junto a near, close to; **juntos** *adj.* together

L

la, las *def. art.* the; see §4.1; also *dir. obj. pron.* see §6.1—2
ladrón *n.m.* **los ladrones** thief, thieves
lámpara *n.f.* lamp
lanzado *past part. of **lanzar***
lanzar *v.* to fling, to throw
lavadora *n.f.* washer (clothes washing machine)
le, les *ind. obj. pron.* to you, to him, to her, to it, to them; see §6.1—3
lección *n.f.* **las lecciones** the lesson, the lessons
leche *n.f.* milk
leer *v.* to read; see Verb Tables
lenguado *n.m.* sole (fish)
letra *n.f.* letter (of the alphabet)

levantados *adj.* raised
levantar *v.* to raise, to lift
leyendo *gerundio* (pr. part.) of **leer**; **está leyendo** is reading; see §7.5—15
libertad *n.f.* liberty, freedom
libro *n.m.* book
ligera *adj.f.* light (in weight)
lista *n.f.* list
literario *adj.* literary
llamada *n.f.* call
llamado *adj. & past part. of **llamar**; called
llamar *v.* to call
llamarse *rv.* to be named; **La chica se llamaba María.** The girl's name was Mary.
llamé *1st pers., s., pret. of **llamar***
llega *3d pers., s., pr. ind. of **llegar***
llegada *n.f.* arrival
llegado *past part. of **llegar***
llegar *v.* to arrive; see Irregular Verb Tables
llego *1st pers., s, pr. ind. of **llegar***
llenos *adj.* full
llorando *gerundio* (pr. part.) of **llorar**; **está llorando** is crying; see §7.5—15
llorar *v.* to cry, to weep
lo *dir. obj. pron.* him, it; see §6.1—2
lo que *pron.* that which; see §6.5—4
los *dir. obj. pron.* them; see §6.1—2; **los, el** *def. art.* the; see §4.1
lugar *n.m.* place; **tener lugar** to take place; see idioms with **tener** in §12.2
lugares *n.m., pl.* places
luz *n.f.* light, **las luces** *pl.* lights

M

madre *n.f.* mother
madrileño *adj.* Madrilenian (from or pertaining to Madrid)
mal, mala *adj.* bad; **¡Qué mala suerte!** What bad luck!
manera *n.f.* manner, way
mano *n.f.* hand
manta *n.f.* blanket
mantequilla *n.f.* butter
mar *n.m.* sea; **por mar** by sea; **los mares** the seas
mariscos *n.m.* shellfish
más *adv.* more; see Antonyms in §18.; **más grande** greater, greatest
más de cien mil more than one hundred thousand; see §16.
máxima *adj.* maximum; top
mayo *n.m.* May; see §13.3

me *pron.* me, to me, myself; *see* §6.1—2, §6.1—3, §6.1—6
me gustó I liked; It pleased me.
media *n.f.* stocking
medianoche *n.f.* midnight
medicina *n.f.* medicine
médico *n.m.* doctor
mejor *adj., adv.* better; **mejor que** better than; **el mejor** the best
mejorado *adj.* improved
mejorar *v.* to improve
menos *adv.* less, fewer
mensaje *n.m.* message
menú *n.m.* menu
mes, meses *n.m., s.pl.* month, months; **al mes** monthly, by the month
mesa *n.f.* table
mexicano *adj.* Mexican
Mi nombre es... My name is...
mí *pron.* me; **por mí; para mí** for me; *see* §6.2, §9.5—3
mi, mis *poss. adj.* my; *see* §5.4—4
micrófono *n.m.* microphone
mil thousand; **miles** thousands; *see* §16.
militar *adj.* military
millón, millones million, millions; *see* §16.
minuto *n.m.* minute
mirar *v.* to watch, to look at
miré *1st pers., s., pret. of* **mirar**; I watched, I looked at
moderno *adj.* modern
montaña *n.f.* mountain
Moscú Moscow
mostrador *n.m.* counter
mostrar *v.* to show; *see* **mostrar** in Irregular Verb Tables in §24. and §25.
movimiento *n.m.* movement
muchacha *n.f.* girl
muchacho *n.m.* boy
muchísimo *adj.* very much, quite a lot; **muchísima alegría** very much joy
mucho *adj., adv.* much
muerte *n.f.* death
muestran *3d pers., pl., pr. ind. of* **mostrar**
mujer *n.f.* woman; wife
mundo *n.m.* world; **todo el mundo** everybody
museo *n.m.* museum
música *n.f.* music
músico *n.m.* musician
muy *adv.* very

N

nacer *v.* to be born
nació *3d pers., s., pret. of* **nacer**
nacional *adj.* national
nacionalidad *n.f.* nationality
nada *indef. pron.* nothing; *see* §6.8
nadar *v.* to swim
nadé *1st pers., s., pret. of* **nadar**
naranja *n.f.* orange
necesitan *3d pers., pl., pr. ind. of* **necesitar**
necesitar *v.* to need
necesitarse *rv.* to need each other
negaba *1st & 3d pers., s., impf. ind. of* **negar**
negar *v.* to deny; **negarse** *rv.* to refuse
nervios *n.m., pl.* nerves; **me calmo los nervios** I calm my nerves
ni *conj.* neither, nor; **ni... ni...** neither... nor...
nieve *n.f.* snow; **una bola de nieve** snowball
niña *n.f.* child (girl); **el niño** child (boy)
ningún *adj.* not any; *see* §5.5
ninguno *indef. pron.* none, not any
noche *n.f.* night; **son las once y cincuenta y cinco de la noche** it's 11:55 pm
nombre *n.m.* name
norte *n.m.* north
norteamericano, -na *adj., m.f.* North American (of the U.S.A.)
nos *pron.* us, to us, ourselves; *see* §6.1—2, §6.1—3, §6.1—6
notar *v.* to note
novela *n.f.* novel
nuestro, nuestra, nuestros, nuestras *poss. adj.* our; *see* §5.4—4
nueva, nuevo *adj., f.m.* new
nueve nine; *see* §16.
número *n.m.* number
nunca *adv.* never; *see* **nunca** in §17.

O

o *conj.* or
obra *n.f.* work
obtener *v.* to obtain
ocho eight; *see* §16.
octubre *n.m.* October; *see* §13.3
ocurrir *v.* to occur, to happen
ocurrirá *3d pers., s. fut. of* **ocurrir**
oído *past part. of* **oír**
oír *v.* to hear; *see* Irregular Verb Tables
once eleven; *see* §14., §16.

ordinario *adj.* ordinary
oreja *n.f.* ear
otro *adj., pron.* other, another; **por otra parte** on the other hand
oye *3d pers., s., pr. ind. of* **oír**; **se oye** is heard
oyó *3d pers., s., pret. of* **oír**; he (she) heard

P
padre *n.m.* father
padres *n.m.* parents
pagar *v.* to pay
país, países *n.m., s.pl.* country, countries; *see* §3.3—4
palabra *n.f.* word
pálida *adj.* pale
pan *n.m.* bread
papel *n.m.* paper
papelería *n.f.* stationery shop
para *prep.* for, in order (to); *see* §9.; **¿para qué?** for what purpose? *see* §9.5—5
para que *conj.* in order that; *see* §7.5—18.1
paraguayo *adj., m.s.* Paraguayan
parasol *n.m.* parasol (sun umbrella)
parece *3d pers., s., pr. ind. of* **parecer** to appear; **parece que...** it appears that...
pareja *n.f.* pair
parque *n.m.* park
parte *n.f.* part; **por una parte** on the one hand; **por otra** on the other
participar *v.* to participate
partir *v.* to leave; **a partir del aquel día** from that day on
pasaporte *n.m.* passport
pasar *v.* to pass, to spend (time)
pasar un buen rato to have a good time
pasaron *3d pers., pl., pret. of* **pasar**
paseaba *1st & 3d pers., s., impf. ind. of* **pasear**
pasear *v.* to pass by; **pasearse** to take a walk
pasillo *n.m.* hallway, corridor
pasó *3d pers., s., pret. of* **pasar**
patatas *n.f.* potatoes
paz *n.f.* peace
pecho *n.m.* chest (human body)
pedir *v.* to request, to ask for; *see* Irregular Verb Tables
película *n.f.* film
peligro *n.m.* danger
pelo *n.m.* hair (on head)
pelota *n.f.* ball

pensar (en) *v.* to think (about); *see* §7.6—15; *see* **pensar** in Verb Tables
pequeño *adj.* small, little
perder *v.* to lose
perdida *adj.* lost
perdió *3d pers., s., pret of* **perder**
perfume *n.m.* perfume
periódico *n.m.* newspaper
periodista *n.m.f.* journalist
pero *conj.* but; *see* §10.
perro *n.m.* dog
persona *n.f.* person
pesar *v.* to weigh; **a pesar de** in spite of; *see* idioms with **a** in §12.2
pescado *n.m.* fish
pescar *v.* to fish
peseta *n.f.* peseta (monetary unit of Spain)
petróleo *n.m.* petroleum
petrolero *adj.* oil, petroleum
pidió *3d pers., s., pret. of* **pedir**
pie *n.m.* foot
piensa *3d pers., s., pr. ind. of* **pensar**
pierden *3d pers., pl., pr. ind. of* **perder**; *see* **perder** in Verb Tables
pierna *n.f.* leg
pieza *n.f.* piece
pintor, pintora *n.m.f.* painter, artist
pintura *n.f.* painting
piscina *n.f.* swimming pool
plato *n.m.* dish, plate
playa *n.f.* beach
pluma *n.f.* pen
poco, poca, pocos, pocas *adj.* a few, a little; **pocas veces** seldom
poder *v.* to be able, can; *see* Irregular Verb Tables
podía *1st & 3d pers., s., impf. ind. of* **poder**; **se podía comer** one was able to eat
podrá *3d pers., s., fut. of* **poder**
poesía *n.f.* poetry
política *adj.* political
político *n.m.* political figure
pollo *n.m.* chicken
polución *n.f.* pollution
poner *v.* to put, to place; *see* Irregular Verb Tables
por *prep.* for, by; *see* §9.5—3; **por una parte** on the one hand; **por favor** please
¿por qué? *adv.* why?; *see* §8.3
porción, porciones *n.f., s.pl.* portion, portions
porque *conj.* because; *see* §10.1
practicar *v.* to practice

precio *n.m.* price
preferido *adj. & past part. of* **preferir**
preferir *v.* to prefer; *see* **preferir** in Irregular Verb Tables
prefiero *1st pers., s., pr. ind. of* **preferir**
prensa *n.f.* press; printing press
presentaba *3d pers., s., impf. ind. of* **presentar**
presentador *n.m.* presenter
presentados *adj.* presented
presentarse *rv.* to present oneself, to make an appearance
primero, primera *adj.* first; *see* §5.5; **la primera vez** the first time
probar *v.* to try
problema *n.m.* problem
programa *n.m.* program
prohibe *3d pers., s., pr. ind. of* **prohibir**
prohibía *1st & 3d pers., s., impf. ind. of* **prohibir**
prohibir *v.* to prohibit
próximo *adj.* next
publicado *past part. of* **publicar**; published
publicar *v.* to publish; **se publica** is published
público *adj.* public
pudieron *3d pers., pl., pret. of* **poder**
puede *3d pers., s., pr. ind. of* **poder**
puedo *1st pers., s., pr. ind. of* **poder**
puerta *n.f.* door
puertorriqueños *n.m., pl.* **Puerto Ricans**
punto *n.m.* point, period; **estaba a punto de salir** was about to leave; *see* **a** in §12.2
puré *n.m.* purée; **puré de patatas** mashed potatoes
puso *3d pers., s., pret. of* **poner**; *see* **poner** in Irregular Verb Tables

Q

que *conj.* that; *see* §10.; **que** *pron.* who, that, whom, which; *see* §6.5
¡Qué mala suerte! What bad luck! *see* §11.
¡Qué ricas! How rich! *see* §11.
¿Qué tiempo hace hoy? What's the weather like today? *see* §15.
¿Qué...? *adj.* What...?; *see* §5.4—5; **¿A qué hora?** At what time? *see* §14.
quedarse *rv.* to remain, to stay; **(yo) tuve que quedarme** I had to stay
querer *v.* to want, to like; *see* Irregular Verb Tables in §25.

querían *3d pers., pl., impf. of* **querer**
queso *n.m.* cheese; **queso suizo** *n.m.* Swiss cheese
quien *pron.* who, whom; *see* §6.5—1, §6.5—2
quiere *3d pers., s., pr. ind. of* **querer**
quieren *3d pers., pl., pr. ind. of* **querer**
quieres *2d pers., s., pr. ind. of* **querer**
quiero *1st pers, s., pr. ind. of* **querer**
quince fifteen; *see* §16.
quisiera *1st & 3d pers., s., impf. sbj. of* **querer**; would like
quiso *3d pers., s., pret. of* **querer**; *see* Irregular Verb Tables in §25.
quizá, quizás *adv.* perhaps, maybe

R

rapidez *n.f.* rapidity, swiftness, speed
razón, razones *n.f., s., pl.* reason, reasons
realizado *adj.* carried out
rebajado *adj. & past part. of* **rebajar**; **habían rebajado** had lowered
rebajar *v.* to lower (prices)
rebelión *n.f.* rebellion
reciben *3d pers., pl., pr. ind. of* **recibir**; *see* Verb Tables
recibí *1st pers., s., pret. of* **recibir**
recibido *past part. of* **recibir**; **ha recibido** has received
recibió *3d pers., s., pret. of* **recibir**
recibir *v.* to receive
recientemente *adv.* recently; **recién llegado** recently arrived
recreo *n.m.* recreation
reducir *v.* to reduce
refrigerador *n.m.* refrigerator
regalo *n.m.* gift
regresar *v.* to return
regresó *3d pers., s., pret. of* **regresar**
relativamente *adv.* relatively
religiosa *adj.* religious
reparación *n.f.* repair
representar *v.* to represent
República *n.f.* Republic; **la República española** Spanish Republic
resfriado *n.m.*; **resfrío** *n.m.* head cold
residencia *n.f.* residence
resolver *v.* to resolve
restaurante *n.m.* restaurant
resuelve *3d pers., s., pr. ind. of* **resolver**
resultaba *3d pers., s., impf. ind. of* **resultar**
resultado *n.m.* result
resultar *v.* to result

reunidas *adj.* gathered
reunión *n.f.* reunion, meeting, assemblage
revista *n.f.* magazine
rey *n.m.* king
rigor *n.m.* rigor; **los rigores de** the rigors of
risa *n.f.* laughter
ritmo *n.m.* rhythm
robar *v.* to rob
rodilla *n.f.* knee
romántica *adj.* romantic
romper *v.* to break; **romperse el brazo** to break one's arm
rompió *3d pers., s., pret. of* **romper**
roquefort *n.m.* roquefort (cheese)
rubia *adj.* blond
Rusia *n.f.* Russia
ruso *n.m.* Russian (language)
rusos *adj.* Russian; **los rusos**, *n.m., pl.* the Russians

S

sabe *3d pers., s., pr. ind. of* **saber**
saber *v.* to know; *see* **saber** in §7.6—3 and Irregular Verb Tables in §25.
salir *v.* to leave
salmón *n.m.* salmon
santo *n.m.* saint
se *reflexive pron.* yourself, himself, herself, itself; *see* §6.1—6, §7.1—2
se va a cambiar is going to change
se van a exhibir sus pinturas his paintings are going to be exhibited
sé *1st pers., s., pr. ind. of* **saber**; *see* Verb Tables in §25.
sea *1st & 3d pers., s., pr. sbj. of* **ser**; *see* **ser** in §7.7—8
sección *n.f.* section
seductor, seductora *adj., m.f.* tempting
según *prep.* according to; *see* §9.1
seis six; *see* §16.
selección *n.f.* selection
semana *n.f.* week
señor *n.m.* gentleman; sir; Mr.
sentado *adj.* seated, sitting
sentir *v.* to feel; *see* Irregular Verb Tables in §25.
septiembre *n.m.* September; *see* §13.3
ser *v.* to be; *see* **ser** in Irregular Verb Tables
será *3d pers., s, fut. of* **ser**; *see* **ser** in §7.7—8
servicio *n.m.* service

servir *v.* to serve; *see* **servir** in Irregular Verb Tables
si *conj.* if
sí *adv.* yes
siento *1st pers., s., pr. ind. of* **sentir**
siete seven; *see* §16.
sino, sino que *conj.* but, but rather; *see* §10.2—1
sirve *3d pers., s., pr. ind. of* **servir**; *see* **servir** in Irregular Verb Tables
sistema *n.m.* system
sobre *prep.* on
sobrehumano *adj.* superhuman
sobretodo *n.m.* overcoat
sol *n.m.* sun; **hace sol** it's sunny
sola *adj.* single
solamente *adv.* only
soledad *n.f.* solitude, loneliness
sólo *adv.* only
sombrero *n.m.* hat
son *3d pers., pl., pr. ind. of* **ser**; *see* **ser** in §7.7—8
sopa *n.f.* soup
su, sus *poss. adj.* his, her, its, your, their; *see* §5.4—4
subir *v.* to go up; to raise (prices)
suerte *n.f.* luck; **¡Qué mala suerte!** What bad luck!
sufrir *v.* to suffer
suizo *adj.* Swiss
suyo, suya *poss. pron.* yours, his, hers, its; *see* **el suyo, la suya** in §6.4

T

taberna *n.f.* tavern
tan *adv.* so; **tan grande** so big
tapas *n.f.* appetizers
tapicería *n.f.* tapestry; upholstery shop
tarde *n.f.* afternoon; *adv.* late
taza *n.f.* cup
teatro *n.m.* theater
tejidos *n.m., pl.* fabrics, textiles
telas *n.f.* cloth, fabric
telefonema *n.m.* telephone message
teléfono *n.m.* telephone; **por teléfono** on the telephone
teletas *n.f.* blotters
televisión *n.f.* television
televisor *n.m.* television set; **televisores** *n.m.* television sets
tener *v.* to have, to hold; *see* Irregular Verb Tables
tener lugar to take place; *see* **tener** in §12.2

tengo *1st pers., s., pr. ind. of* **tener**; *see* Irregular Verb Tables

Tengo una reservación. I have a reservation.

tenía *1st & 3d pers., s., impf. ind. of* **tener**

terminarse *v.* to terminate, to complete, to end

tiempo *n.m.* time; weather; *see* §3.3—5, §15.

tienda *n.f.* store

tiene *3d pers., s., pr. ind. of* **tener**

tienen *3d pers., pl., pr. ind. of* **tener**

tocadiscos *n.m., s.* record player

tocar *v.* to play (a musical instrument); *see* §7.6—11

todas horas all hours

todavía *adv.* still, yet

todo, toda, todos, todas *adj.* all; **todo el día** all day; *see* **todo** in §12.2

todos los días every day

tomar *v.* to take; to take food or drink

tonelada *n.f.* ton

tostado *adj.* toasted

trabajando *gerundio (pr. part.) of* **trabajar**; working

trabajar *v.* to work

trabajo *n.m.* work

tradicional *adj.* traditional

traer *v.* to bring

Tráigame... Bring me...; *see* **traer** in Irregular Verb Tables

tranquilidad *n.f.* tranquillity

tranquilizante *n.m.* tranquilizer

tranquilos *adj.* tranquil, calm, peaceful

transporte *n.m.* transportation

tratado *past part. of* **tratar**; **por haber tratado** for having tried

tratamiento *n.m.* treatment

tratando *pr. part. (gerundio)* trying; **está tratando** is trying; *see* §7.5—15

tratar *v.* to try

tres three; *see* §16.

trucha *n.f.* trout

tú *pron., 2d pers., s., fam.* you; *see* §6.1—1

tu, tus *poss. adj., fam., 2d pers., s.* your; *see* §5.4—4

turismo *n.m.* tourism

turistas *n.m.* tourists

tuve *1st pers., s., pret. of* **tener; (yo) tuve que...** I had to...; *see* §7.6—4

tuvieron *3d pers., pl., pret. of* **tener**; *see* **tener que** (to have to) in §12.2

tuvo *3d pers., s., pret. of* **tener**; *see* idioms with **tener** in §12.2

U

u *conj.* or; *see* §10.2—3

un, una *indef. art.* a, an; **unos, unas** some, a few; *see* §4.2

único *adj., m., s.* only; **el único festival** the only festival

únicos *adj., m., pl.* only; **los únicos animales** the only animals

unida *adj.* united

uso *n.m.* use

V

va *3d pers., s., pr. ind. of* **ir**; *see* **ir** in §7.7—8

vaca *n.f.* cow

van *3d pers., pl., pr. ind. of* **ir**; *see* **ir** in §7.7—8

varias *adj., f.pl.* various

variedad *n.f.* variety

ve *3d pers., s., pr. ind. of* **ver**

veces *n.f., pl.* times; *pl. of* **vez**; *see* §3.2

velero *n.m.* sailboat; **un velero de juguete** toy sailboat

velita *n.f.* little candle

vende *3d pers., s., pr. ind. of* **vender; se vende** is sold; **se venden** are sold

vender *v.* to sell

vendidos *adj.* sold

vendió *3d pers., s., pret. of* **vender**

vengo *1st pers., s., pr. ind. of* **venir**; *see* Irregular Verb Tables

venir *v.* to come; *see* Verb Tables

ver *v.* to see; *see* **ver** in Irregular Verb Tables

verano *n.m.* summer; *see* §13.4

versión *n.f.* version

vez *n.f.* time; **una vez más** one more time; *see* §3.3—5; **la primera vez** the first time

vi *1st pers., s., pret. of* **ver**

viaja *3d pers., s., pr. ind. of* **viajar**

viajar *v.* to travel

viaje *n.m.* trip, travel

viajeros *n.m., pl.* travelers

vida *n.f.* life

viejo *adj.* old

viene *3d pers., s., pr. ind. of* **venir**; *see* Irregular Verb Tables

vino *3d pers., s., pret. of* **venir**; *see* Irregular Verb Tables; **vino** *n.m.* wine

vio *3d pers., s., pret. of* **ver**

visita *n.f.* visit

visitante *n.m.f.* visitor
visto *past part. of* **ver**
volumen *n.m.* volume
volver *v.* to return; **estaba a punto de volver** was about to return; *see* **a** in §12.2
votar *v.* to vote
voy *1st pers., s., pr. ind. of* **ir**
voz *n.f.* voice
vuestro, vuestra, vuestros, vuestras *poss. adj., 2d pers., pl.* your; *see* §5.4—4

Y

y *conj.* and; *see* §12.2 for idiomatic expressions with **y**
ya *adv.* already; *see* idioms with **ya** in §12.2

Z

zanahoria *n.f.* carrot
zapatería *n.f.* shoe store
zapatero *n.m.* shoemaker
zapato *n.m.* shoe

English-Spanish Vocabulary

Regarding verb forms, remember to consult the Spanish Verb Conjugation Tables and the Irregular Verb Tables in **§25.**, as well as **§7.** in this book. A list of abbreviations is also provided on page xvii.

References to **§** numbers in this vocabulary list will help you master points in Spanish grammar and vocabulary if you refer to them for study.

If you do not find the desired English-Spanish word in the following vocabulary list, consult a standard English-Spanish dictionary.

A

a, an *indef. art.* **un, una**; *pl.* **unos, unas** some, a few; *see* §4.2

able, to be *v.* **poder**; *see* §7.6—16 and Verb Tables

about (on) *prep.* **sobre**; about art **sobre el arte**

above *adv.* **arriba**

absent *adj.* **ausente**

accept *v.* **aceptar**

ache *n.* **el dolor**; headache **el dolor de cabeza**; *v.* to ache **doler**

affectionately *adv.* **cariñosamente**

after *adv.* **después**; *prep.* **después de**

again *adv.* **otra vez**; *see* **vez, veces** in §12.2; **de nuevo**; *see* **de** in §12.2

age *n.f.* **edad**

air *n.* **el aire**

airplane *n.* **el avión**

airport *n.* **el aeropuerto**

all *adj.* **todo, toda, todos, todas**; *see* these words with idioms in §12.2

already *adv.* **ya**; *see* **ya** in §12.2

and *conj.* **y, e**; *see* §10.2—4 and **y** in §12.2

arm *n.* **el brazo**

arrive *v.* **llegar**; *see* §7.6—12 and Verb Tables

art *n.* **el arte**

at *prep.* **a**; *see* §9.; at around nine o'clock **a eso de las nueve**; *see* **a** in §12.2

at what time? **¿a qué hora?** *see* §14.1

B

bad *adj.* **malo, mala**

baker *n.m.* **el panadero**

bakery *n.f.* **la panadería**

ball *n.* **la pelota**

banana *n.* **la banana**

banana tree *n.* **el banano**

banquet *n.* **el banquete**

be *v.* **ser, estar**; *see* §7.6—17, §12.2, and Verb Tables

be pleasing to **gustar**; *see* §7.6—9

beach *n.* **la playa**

because *conj.* **porque**; *see* §10.

bed *n.* **la cama**

bedroom *n.* **el dormitorio**

believe *v.* **creer**; *see* Verb Tables in §24. and §25.

big *adj.* **gran, grande**; *see* §5.5

birthday *n.* **el cumpleaños**

blanket *n.* **la manta de cama**

book *n.* **el libro**

bread *n.* **el pan**

break *v.* **romper**; to break one's arm **romperse el brazo**

bring *v.* **traer**; *see* Verb Tables in §24. and §25.

Bring me... **Tráigame...** *see* §7.5—17

broom *n.* **la escoba**

brother *n.* **el hermano**

but *conj.* **pero**; *see* §10.

butter *n.* **la mantequilla**

buy *v.* **comprar**; *see* Verb Tables in §24. and §25.

C

cabbage *n.* **la col**
can (be able) *v.* **poder**; *see* §7.6—16 and Verb Tables in §24. and §25.
car *n.* **el carro, el coche**
carrot *n.* **la zanahoria**
carry *v.* **llevar**; *see* §7.6—13
cat *n.* **el gato**
chair *n.* **la silla**
cheap *adj.* **barato**
cheese *n.* **el queso**
cherry *n.* **la cereza**
chest (body) *n.* **el pecho**
Christmas *n.* **la Navidad**
clothes washing machine *n.* **la lavadora**
coffee *n.* **el café**; coffee shop **el café**
come *v.* **venir**; *see* Verb Tables
country *n.* **el campo, el país, la patria, la nación**; *see* §3.3—4
cream *n.* **la crema**
cross *v.* **cruzar**
cup *n.* **la taza**; a cup of coffee **una taza de café**

D

dance *v.* **bailar**; *see* Verb Tables
date *n.* **la fecha**; *see* §13.l
day *n.* **el día**; *see* §13.2 and **día, días** in §12.2
decay *v.* **decaer**
dessert *n.* **el postre**
detain *v.* **detener**
difficult *adj.* **difícil**
dine *v.* **cenar**; *see* Verb Tables
do *v.* **hacer**; *see* Verb Tables and idioms with **hacer** in §12.1, §12.2
Do you want...? **¿Quieres (tú)... ? ¿Quiere (Ud.)... ?** *see* **querer** in Verb Tables
doctor *n.* **el doctor, el médico**
dog *n.* **el perro**
dollar *n.* **el dólar**; dollars **los dólares**; one hundred dollars **cien dólares**; *see* §5.5
done *past part.* **hecho**; *see* **hacer** in Verb Tables
drink *v.* **beber**; *see* Verb Tables

E

ear *n.* **la oreja**
early *adv.* **temprano**
easy *adj.* **fácil**; *see* §18.

eat *v.* **comer**; *see* Verb Tables
egg *n.* **el huevo**
eight **ocho**; *see* §16.
end *n.* **el fin**
enough *adv.* **bastante**
enter *v.* **entrar**
evening *n.* **la noche**; in the evening **de la noche, por la noche**; *see* §14.
expensive *adj.* **caro**
explain *v.* **explicar**
extraordinary *adj.* **extraordinario**
eye *n.* **el ojo**

F

face *n.* **la cara**
fall *v.* **caer**; *see* Verb Tables
family *n.* **la familia**; with my family **con mi familia**
father *n.* **el padre**
fear (be afraid) *v.* **tener miedo de**; *see* **tener** in §12.2
feel *v.* **sentir, sentirse**; *see* Verb Tables
fill *v.* **llenar**
film *n.* **la película**
finger *n.* **el dedo**
fish *n.* **el pescado**
flee *v.* **huir**; *see* Verb Tables in §24. and §25.
foot *n.* **el pie**
for *prep.* **para, por**; *see* §9.5—3, §12.2; for me **para mí**; *see* §6.2
fried *adj.* **frito, frita, fritos, fritas**; fried eggs **huevos fritos**
friend *n.* **el amigo, la amiga**; some friends **algunos amigos**
from *prep.* **de**; *see* idiomatic expressions with **de** in §12.2; from the **del**; *see* §4.1
fruit *n.* **la fruta**

G

garden *n.* **el jardín**; gardens **los jardines**
get on (bus, train) *v.* **subir a**
gift *n.* **el regalo**
give *v.* **dar**; *see* Verb Tables and idioms with **dar** in §12.2
gloves *n.* **los guantes**
go *v.* **ir**; *see* §7.6—7 and Verb Tables
go down *v.* **bajar**
go out *v.* **salir**; *see* Verb Tables
good *adj.* **buen, bueno, buena, buenos, buenas**; a good book **un buen libro**; *see* §5.5

good-bye *int.* **adiós**
grateful *adj.* **agradecido, agradecida**
green *n., adj.* **verde**
green string beans *n.* **las habichuelas verdes**
grocery store *n.* **la bodega**

H

hair (on head) *n.* **el pelo, el cabello**
hand *n.* **la mano**
handkerchief *n.* **el pañuelo**
hat *n.* **el sombrero**
have *v.* **tener; haber;** *see* §7.6—10, §12.2, and Verb Tables
have a good time **pasar un buen rato**
have dinner *v.* **cenar;** *see* Verb Tables
head *n.* **la cabeza**
headache *n.* **el dolor de cabeza**
hear *v.* **oír;** *see* Verb Tables
help *v.* **ayudar**
here *adv.* **aquí;** here is... **aquí tiene usted..., aquí está**
horse *n.* **el caballo**
hospital *n.* **el hospital**
hour *n.* **la hora;** *see* §14.
house *n.* **la casa**
how *adv.* **como;** how? **¿cómo?** How much does it cost? **¿Cuánto cuesta?**
how much **cuanto, cuanta, cuantos, cuantas;** *see* these words in §12.2
hunger *n.* **el hambre;** to be hungry **tener hambre;** *see* **tener** in §12.2

I

I am sick. **Estoy enfermo (enferma).** *See* **estar** in §7.6—17, §12.2, and Verb Tables
I ate **(yo) comí;** *see* **comer** in Verb Tables
I can **puedo;** *see* **poder** in §7.6—16 and Verb Tables
I danced **(yo) bailé;** *see* **bailar** Verb Tables
I desire **Deseo**
I don't want... **No quiero...;** *see* **querer** in Verb Tables
I have... **Tengo...** ; *see* **tener** in §7.6—10, §12.2
I know **yo sé;** *see* **saber** in §7.6—16 and Verb Tables
I liked it a lot **Me gustó mucho**
I prefer **(yo) prefiero;** *see* **preferir** in Verb Tables
I sang **(yo) canté;** *see* Verb Tables
I saw **(yo) vi;** *see* **ver** in Verb Tables

I swam **(yo) nadé**
I want... **Deseo...**
I watched **(yo) miré**
I went **(yo) fui;** *see* **ir** in §7.6—7 and Verb Tables
I would like... **Quisiera...**
ice cream *n.m.* **el helado**
I'm going to... **(Yo) voy a...;** *see* **ir** in §7.6—7 and Verb Tables
in *prep.* **en;** *see* **en** in §12.2
inexpensive *adj.* **barato**
interesting *adj.* **interesante**
invitation *n.* **la invitación**
It's a present for a friend. **Es un regalo para un amigo (una amiga).**
It's sunny. **Hace sol.**

J

jacket *n.* **la chaqueta**
January *n.* **el enero;** *see* §13.3
juice *n.* **el jugo**
July *n.* **el julio;** *see* §13.3

K

keep *v.* **guardar**
key *n.* **la llave**
kind *adj.* **amable**
knee *n.* **la rodilla**
know *v.* **saber, conocer;** *see* §7.6—3 and Verb Tables

L

lamp *n.* **la lámpara**
learn *v.* **aprender;** *see* Verb Tables
leave *v.* **partir, dejar, salir (de);** *see* §7.6—5 and Verb Tables
left *(side, direction) n.f.* **la izquierda;** on the left **a la izquierda**
leg *n.* **la pierna**
lesson *n.f.* **la lección, las lecciones**
light (in weight) *adj.* **ligero, ligera**
light *n.f.* **la luz, las luces**
like to + *inf.* **gustarle a uno + inf.** ; I like to travel **Me gusta viajar;** *see* §7.6—9
lips *n.* **los labios**
listen (to) *v.* **escuchar**
little (in quantity) *adj., adv.* **poco;** *see* §12.2; small (in size) **pequeño**
live *v.* **vivir;** *see* Verb Tables
look (at) *v.* **mirar**
love *n.* **el amor;** *v.* **amar;** *see* Verb Tables
lunch *v.* **almorzar;** *see* Verb Tables; *n.* **el almuerzo**

M

make *v.* **hacer**; *see* Verb Tables and idioms with **hacer** in §12.1, §12.2

man *n.* **el hombre**

many *adj.* **mucho, muchos, mucha, muchas**; many presents **muchos regalos**

mashed potatoes *n.* **el puré de patatas**

maybe *adv.* **quizá, quizás**

me *prep.* **me**; *see* §6.1—2, §6.1—3; for me **para mí**; *see* §6.2

mean (to signify) *v.* **querer decir**; *see* **decir** in §12.2

milk *n.* **la leche**

modern *adj.* **moderno**

moreover *adv.* **además**

morning *n.* **la mañana**; *see* §12.2

mother *n.* **la madre**

mountain *n.* **la montaña**; in the mountains **en las montañas**

mouth *n.* **la boca**

movies (theater) *n.* **el cine**; to the movies **al cine**

much *adj.* **mucho**; very much **muchísimo**

music *n.* **la música**

must, ought to *v.* **deber**; *see* Verb Tables

My name is... **Mi nombre es..** *or* **Me llamo** + (your name)

my *poss. adj.* **mi, mis**; *see* §5.4—4

N

name *n.* **el nombre**

nationality *n.f.* **la nacionalidad**

neck *n.* **el cuello**

newspaper *n.* **el periódico**

night *n.* **la noche**; last night **anoche**

no *adv.* **no**; *see* idiomatic expressions with **no** in §12.2

O

of *prep.* **de**; *see* idiomatic expressions with **de** in §12.2; of the **del**; *see* §4.1

on (about) *prep.* **sobre**; on (about) art **sobre el arte**

one hundred **cien, ciento**; *see* §5.5, §16.

open *v.* **abrir**; *see* Verb Tables

opposite *adv.* **enfrente**

orange *n.* **la naranja**; orange juice **el jugo de naranja**

overcoat *n.* **el sobretodo**

P

pain *n.* **el dolor**; in the neck **en el cuello**

parasol *n.* **el parasol**

park *n.* **el parque**; to the park **al parque**

party *n.* **la fiesta**

passport *n.* **el pasaporte**

pay *v.* **pagar**

peas *n.* **los guisantes**

pen *n.* **la pluma**

perhaps *adv.* **quizá, quizás**

person *n.* **la persona**

pleasant *adj.* **agradable**

please *v.* **gustar**; *see* §7.6—9; a cup of coffee, please **una taza de café, por favor**

potato *n.* **la patata**; mashed potatoes **el puré de patatas**

present (gift) *n.* **el regalo**

R

radio *n.* **la radio**

read *v.* **leer**

realize *v.* **darse cuenta de**

receive *v.* **recibir**; I received **(yo) recibí**; *see* **recibir** in Verb Tables

refrigerator *n.* **el refrigerador**

remain *v.* **quedarse**

reservation *n.* **la reservación**

restaurant *n.* **el restaurante**

right *(side, direction) n.f.* **la derecha**; on the right **a la derecha**

roquefort (cheese) *n.* **el roquefort**

S

salmon *n.* **el salmón**

same *adj.* **mismo**; *see* §12.2

say *v.* **decir**; *see* Verb Tables and §12.2

shave oneself *v.* **afeitarse**

shoulder *n.* **el hombro**

sick *adj.* **enfermo (enferma)**

since *adv.* **desde**; *see* §12.1

sing *v.* **cantar**

sister *n.* **la hermana**

small *adj.* **pequeño**

snowball *n.* **la bola de nieve**

sole (fish) *n.* **el lenguado**

some *adj.* **algunos, algunas**; some friends **algunos amigos**

soup *n.* **la sopa**

speak *v.* **hablar**; *see* Verb Tables

spend (time) *v.* **pasar**

spinach *n.* **las espinacas**

stay *v.* **quedarse**; I'm staying here **Me quedo aquí**

still, yet *adv.* **todavía**

stomach *n.* **el estómago**; stomachache **el dolor de estómago**

story *n.* **una historia**; a love story **una historia de amor**
string beans *n.* **las habichuelas verdes**
summer *n.* **el verano**
sun *n.* **el sol**
sun umbrella *n.* **el parasol**
superhuman *adj.* **sobrehumano**
swim *v.* **nadar**
swimming pool *n.* **la piscina**
Swiss *adj.* **suizo**; Swiss cheese **el queso suizo**

T

take *v.* **tomar; llevar**; *see* §7.6—13
take a step **dar un paso**
take a walk *v.* **pasearse**; I'm going to take a walk. **Voy a pasearme; dar un paseo**
talk *v.* **hablar**; *see* Verb Tables
television set *n.* **el televisor**
tell *v.* **decir**; *see* Verb Tables and §12.2
thankful *adj.* **agradecido, agradecida**
there *adv.* **ahí**; there is, there are **hay**
these *dem. adj.* **estos, estas**; *see* §5.4—3
thief *n.* **el ladrón, los ladrones**
thing *n.* **la cosa**
this *dem. adj.* **este, esta**; *see* §5.4—3
three **tres**; *see* §16.
throw *v.* **lanzar**
time *n.* **la hora, el tiempo, la vez**; *see* §3.3—5; *see* **vez, veces** in §12.2
to *prep.* **a**; *see* §9.
to the **al, a la, a los, a las**; *see* §4.1 and **a la** and **al** in §12.2
to the movies **al cine**
to the park **al parque**
toaster (machine) *n.* **el tostador**
today *adv.* **hoy**
tonight *adv.* **esta noche**
top *n.* **la cima**
towel *n.* **la toalla**
trout *n.* **la trucha**
tuna *n.* **el atún**
two **dos**; *see* §16.

U

umbrella *n.* **el paraguas**; sun umbrella (parasol) **el parasol**
underneath *adv.* **debajo (de)**
understand *v.* **comprender**
ungrateful *adj.* **desagradecido, ingrato**
United States *n.* **los Estados Unidos**
until *prep.* **hasta**; *conj.* **hasta que**; *see* §12.2

up *adv.* **arriba**
upon arriving **al llegar**
use *v.* **usar**; *n.* **el uso**

V

vacation *n.* **las vacaciones**
vacuum cleaner *n.* **el aspirador**
vase *n.* **el jarrón**
vegetables *n.* **las legumbres**
very *adv.* **muy**; very much **muchísimo**
visit *v.* **visitar**; *n.* **la visita**

W

walk *v.* **caminar**; *n.* **el paseo**; to take a walk **dar un paseo**; *see* **dar** in §12.2
washing machine (clothes) *n.* **la lavadora**
watch *v.* **mirar**; to watch television **mirar la televisión**
water *n.* **el agua** *n.f.*; *pl.* **las aguas**; a glass of water **un vaso de agua**
We will stay... **(Nosotros) nos quedaremos...**
wear *v.* **llevar**; *see* §7.6—13
weather *n.* **el tiempo**; *see* §15.
week *n.* **la semana**
What time is it? **¿Qué hora es?** *see* §14.
What's the weather like today? **¿Qué tiempo hace hoy?** *see* §15.
when *adv.* **cuando**; *see* §12.1
with *prep.* **con**; *see* **con** in §12.2; with me **conmigo**; *see* §6.2
with some friends **con algunos amigos**
without *prep.* **sin**; *see* expressions with **sin** in §12.2
woman *n.* **la mujer**
write *v.* **escribir**

Y

year *n.* **el año**
yes *adv.* **sí**
yesterday *adv.* **ayer**
yesterday evening *adv.* **anoche**
yet, still *adv.* **todavía**
you *pron.* **tú, vosotros (vosotras), usted, ustedes**; *see* §6.1
young *adj.* **joven, jóvenes**
your *poss. adj.* **tu, tus, vuestro, vuestros, su, sus**; *see* §5.4—4

Index

References are to § numbers in this book. Some references are to page numbers. As for verb tense forms, consult not only the § numbers given but also the Tables of Spanish Verb Conjugations and the Tables of Irregular Verbs in §24. and §25.

NOTES

NOTES

NOTES

NOTES

Helpful Guides for
Mastering a Foreign Language

2001 Idiom Series

Indispensable resources, these completely bilingual dictionaries in six major languages present the most frequently used idiomatic words and phrases to help students avoid stilted expression when writing in their newly acquired language. Each book includes illustrative sentences. Each feature is easy to locate and designed with clarity in mind.

2001 French and English Idioms, 3rd
0-7641-3750-6 $16.99, Can $19.99

2001 German and English Idioms
0-8120-9009-8 $18.99, Can $25.99

2001 Italian and English Idioms
0-8120-9030-6 $18.99, Can $27.50

2001 Japanese and English Idioms
0-8120-9433-6 $18.99, Can $27.50

2001 Russian and English Idioms
0-8120-9532-4 $21.95, Can $31.95

2001 Spanish and English Idioms, 3rd
0-7641-3744-1 $16.99, Can $19.99

201/301 Verb Series

The most commonly used verbs are presented alphabetically and in all their forms, one to a page, in each of the many foreign languages listed here. Features of this series include discussions of participles, punctuation guides, listings of compounds, the phrases and expressions often used with each verb, plus much more!

201 Dutch Verbs
0-8120-0738-7 $14.95, Can $21.95

201 Mandarin Chinese Verbs, 2nd
0-7641-3761-1 $16.99, Can $21.50

201 Modern Greek Verbs
0-8120-0475-2 $14.99, Can $21.99

301 Polish Verbs
0-7641-1020-9 $16.99, Can $24.50

201 Swedish Verbs
0-8120-0528-7 $18.99, Can $27.50

201 Turkish Verbs
0-8120-2034-0 $16.99, Can $23.99

501 Verb Series

Here is a series to help the foreign language student successfully approach verbs and all their details. Complete conjugations of the verbs are arranged one verb to a page in alphabetical order. Verb forms are printed in boldface type in two columns, and common idioms using the applicable verbs are listed at the bottom of the page in each volume. Some titles include a CD-ROM.

501 Arabic Verbs
0-7641-3622-4, $18.99, Can $23.75

501 English Verbs, 2nd, with CD-ROM
0-7641-7985-3 $16.99, Can $21.50

501 French Verbs, 6th, with CD-ROM
0-7641-7983-7 $16.99, Can $21.50

501 German Verbs, 4th, with CD-ROM
0-7641-9393-7, $16.99, Can $21.50

501 Hebrew Verbs, 2nd
0-7641-3748-4, $18.99, Can $22.50

501 Italian Verbs, 3rd, with CD-ROM
0-7641-7982-9 $16.99, Can $21.50

501 Japanese Verbs, 3rd
0-7641-3749-2, $18.99, Can $22.50

501 Latin Verbs, 2nd
0-7641-3742-5, $18.99, Can $22.50

501 Portuguese Verbs
0-7641-2916-3 $16.95, Can $24.50

501 Russian Verbs, 3rd
0-7641-3743-3, $18.99, Can $22.50

501 Spanish Verbs, 6th, with CD-ROM
0-7641-7984-5 $16.99, Can $21.50

Books may be purchased at your bookstore, or by mail from Barron's. Enclose check or money order for total amount plus sales tax where applicable and add 18% for postage and handling (minimum charge $5.95). All books are paperback editions. New York, New Jersey, Michigan, Tennessee, and California residents add sales tax. Prices subject to change without notice.

Visit our website at: www.barronseduc.com

Barron's Educational Series, Inc.
250 Wireless Boulevard, Hauppauge, NY 11788
Call toll-free: 1-800-645-3476
In Canada: Georgetown Book Warehouse,
34 Armstrong Avenue, Georgetown, Ont. L7G 4R9
Call toll-free: 1-800-247-7160

(#33) R 8/07

3 Foreign Language Series From Barron's!

The **VERB SERIES** offers more than 300 of the most frequently used verbs.
The **GRAMMAR SERIES** provides complete coverage of the elements of grammar.
The **VOCABULARY SERIES** offers more than 3500 words and phrases with their foreign language translations. Each book: paperback.

FRENCH
GRAMMAR
ISBN: 0-7641-1351-8
$6.99, Can. $9.99

GERMAN
GRAMMAR
ISBN: 0-8120-4296-4
$7.99, Can. $11.50

ITALIAN
GRAMMAR
ISBN: 0-7641-2060-3
$6.99, Can. $9.99

JAPANESE
GRAMMAR
ISBN: 0-7641-2061-1
$6.95, Can. $9.95

RUSSIAN
GRAMMAR
ISBN: 0-8120-4902-0
$7.99, Can. $9.99

SPANISH
GRAMMAR
ISBN: 0-7641-1615-0
$6.99, Can. $9.99

FRENCH
VERBS
ISBN: 0-7641-1356-9
$6.99, Can. $9.99

GERMAN
VERBS
ISBN: 0-8120-4310-3
$8.99, Can. $12.99

ITALIAN
VERBS
ISBN: 0-7641-2063-8
$6.99, Can. $8.75

SPANISH
VERBS
ISBN: 0-7641-1357-7
$6.99, Can. $8.50

FRENCH
VOCABULARY
ISBN: 0-7641-1999-0
$6.99, Can. $9.99

GERMAN
VOCABULARY
ISBN: 0-8120-4497-5
$8.99, Can. $11.99

ITALIAN
VOCABULARY
ISBN: 0-7641-2190-1
$6.95, Can. $9.95

JAPANESE
VOCABULARY
ISBN: 0-8120-4743-5
$8.99, Can. $11.99

RUSSIAN
VOCABULARY
ISBN: 0-8120-1554-1
$6.95, Can. $8.95

SPANISH
VOCABULARY
ISBN: 0-7641-1985-3
$6.95, Can. $9.95

Barron's Educational Series, Inc.
250 Wireless Blvd., Hauppauge, NY 11788 •
Call toll-free: 1-800-645-3476
In Canada: Georgetown Book Warehouse
34 Armstrong Ave., Georgetown, Ontario L7G 4R9 •
Call toll-free: 1-800-247-7160
www.barronseduc.com
Can. $ = Canadian dollars

Books may be purchased at your bookstore or by mail from Barron's. Enclose check or money order for total amount plus sales tax where applicable and 18% for postage and handling (minimum charge $ 5.95 U.S. and Canada). Prices subject to change without notice. New York, New Jersey, Michigan, Tennessee, and California residents, please add sales tax to total after postage and handling.

(#26) R 8/07

NOW YOU'RE TALKING SERIES
Will Have You Talking In No Time!

Barron's presents easy, convenient, and inexpensive language kits designed for busy travelers, tourists, and students. Each package contains: a 90-minute cassette, or one or two CDs, on which a native narrator helps listeners master colloquial phrases and business-related terms; an audioscript that guarantees proper pronunciation through phonetics; and a pocket-sized dictionary that includes over 1,500 popular expressions and 2,000 key words. Color maps, travel tips, plus food and shopping guides make these lightweight packages terrific companions!

ARABIC IN NO TIME
ISBN: 0-7641-7359-6, $16.95, Can.$23.95

FRENCH IN NO TIME
With one CD, ISBN: 0-7641-7668-4, $16.95, Can.$24.50

GERMAN IN NO TIME
With two CDs, ISBN: 0-7641-7671-4, $16.99, Can.$24.50

ITALIAN IN NO TIME
ISBN: 0-7641-7664-1, $14.95, Can.$21.95
With two CDs, ISBN: 0-7641-7669-2, $18.99, Can.$27.50

JAPANESE IN NO TIME
ISBN: 0-7641-7165-8, $16.95, Can.$23.95
With one CD, ISBN: 0-7641-7955-1, $18.99, Can.$23.75

MANDARIN CHINESE IN NO TIME
ISBN: 0-7641-7361-8, $16.95, Can.$23.95
With one CD, ISBN: 0-7641-7954-3, $18.99, Can.$23.75

RUSSIAN IN NO TIME
ISBN: 0-7641-7362-6, $16.95, Can.$23.95

SPANISH IN NO TIME
ISBN: 0-7641-7666-8, $14.95, Can.$21.95
With two CDs, ISBN: 0-7641-7670-6, $16.99, Can.$24.50

Books may be purchased at your bookstore, or by mail from Barron's. Enclose check or money order for total amount plus sales tax where applicable and 18% for postage and handling (minimum charge $5.95).
New York, New Jersey, Michigan, Tennessee, and California residents add sales tax. Prices subject to change.

Barron's Educational Series, Inc.
250 Wireless Blvd.
Hauppauge, NY 11788
Call toll-free: 1-800-645-3476

In Canada:
Georgetown Book Warehouse
34 Armstrong Avenue
Georgetown, Ontario L7G 4R9
Call toll-free: 1-800-247-7160

Visit our website at:
www.barronseduc.com

(#36) R8/07